THE NINTH OF TWELVE
FROM THE USTA PLACE

THE NINTH OF TWELVE FROM THE USTA PLACE

BY

Helen Beatrice Sexton

A division of Squire Publishers, Inc.
4500 College Blvd.
Leawood, KS 66211
1/888/888-7696

A division of Squire Publishers, Inc.
4500 College Blvd.
Leawood, KS 66211
1/888/888-7696

DEDICATION

This book of memories is dedicated to my parents, Edward D. and Dora Anna (Whiteside) Clark, with a special dedication to my precious children, Gary Rhodes and Sherri (Rhodes) Stenseng, and to my four loving grandchildren, Rusty and Kristi Stenseng and Marcus and Trenton Rhodes.

I also want to make an additional dedication to another very special person who came into my life after this book was written. Logan Cole Stenseng, my great-grandson, these memories are also dedicated to you. When you grow up and can read this book, I hope you will treasure the memories I have written for you. God bless you always.

Love,
Granny Helen

CONTENTS

Author's Preface

Dedication

Chapter 1   Papa and Mama and How It Began .... Page   1

Chapter 2   The Lean Years .... Page   21

Chapter 3   Christmas at the Usta Place .... Page   52

Chapter 4   The Depression (1930s) .... Page   59

Chapter 5   Papa and Mama and All of Us Kids .... Page   85

Chapter 6   I Learn To Roller Skate .... Page   97

Chapter 7   How We Met .... Page 105

Chapter 8   Mother and Father-In-Laws .... Page 123

Chapter 9   Kansas, Here We Come .... Page 131

Chapter 10   Course in Cosmetology .... Page 141

Chapter 11   Busy in the Sixties .... Page 155

Chapter 12   Years at the Ammunition Plant .... Page 175

Chapter 13   Meeting More In-laws .... Page 185

Chapter 14   Lost Rings, Found Rings .... Page 197

Chapter 15   Name in A Bottle .... Page 203

Chapter 16   The Flood of 1993 .... Page 209

Chapter 17   He Touched Me .... Page 215

Chapter 18   Fun Time at the Theater .... Page 221

Chapter 19   More Precious Memories .... Page 229

Chapter 20   The Wedding of the Year .... Page 261

Chapter 21   The Grand Finale .... Page 267

AUTHOR'S PREFACE

I WANT ALL OF YOU to know the good, hard, and worst times of a family the size of ours trying to survive. I know other families suffered lean years back in the "olden" days, too. The big difference is I came from a much larger family than most.

Perhaps after reading my story, all of you will be more thankful and appreciate everything you have that we did not have then. I know it will at least make you stop and think about what your parents and grandparents went through and appreciate them even more than you do now.

My sisters, nieces, and a lot my friends have been so helpful when they were told I had decided to write my story. They have given me some information that I could honestly remember happening and some that was before my time. Some were also able to confirm parts of what I had already written.

Now, I've had a good life. I've had lots of happy times and some sad times, too. The good times certainly out weigh the others. For the sad and bad times, you have to ask for a little more assistance. All you have to do is ask.

I've had reasonably good health and keep busy. Sometimes I would rather be doing something than to go to bed. I realize that it sounds a little far out, but if you aren't sleepy, why go to bed?

My children both say to me, "Mom, you sure don't look your age!" Sherri told me she hopes when she gets to be my age, she looks and feels as good as I do. She will.

I think to a certain extent, I have wanted someone, maybe one of my older siblings, to write this story, but they just did not get it done. We had talked about it for some time and it just seemed like there was not room in the fire for that last iron. I want my children and grandchildren to learn more about their heritage.

Before Dana, sister number one, passed away, she and I had talked about and planned on working together to combine our childhood memories and years of growing up at the Usta Place and perhaps putting it into a book. Just think, with all of her memories and mine too, what great stories could be told. Wow!

Well, we lost Dana before we got this project started. Dana told me she had started to write some of her memories, but when the children had to sort through her things, it was not found. With what she had told me about wanting to do this, it inspired me to put these precious memories on paper, so that they would not be lost forever.

CHAPTER 1

HELLO. MY NAME IS HELEN. If you have some time to spend fruitfully, I would love all of you to read my story. I decided to write my memories for you so you would know what it was like for me when I was growing up and in later years after your mamas and daddies were born. Now you will be able to read my story any time you want, as will your children and grandchildren in years to come. If you have trouble reading, please find someone to help you. I do not want you to miss one thing that I have to tell you.

The difference between my story and some of the stories you may have read and heard is that mine is real and very true. I know this to be a fact, because I have lived it. I've lived several years of it, seventy-three to be exact! I consider my memories to be treasures, growing more precious every year. I don't want them to be lost forever when I'm gone. By putting them on paper, my great-grandchildren will be able to read what it was like to have lived the years their ancestors lived.

Can you imagine living in a time like the twenties and thirties, with eleven children and both parents in a house with only four rooms? Yes, I said four rooms. We had a kitchen, living room, and two bedrooms. Can you imagine not having electricity for lights, washer, dryer, cooking, ironing, and all the other chores you do with electricity? Can you imagine not having running water in the house and having to carry it from the well? It is hard to believe we have come as far as we have since all twelve of us were born. There were nine girls and three boys. I was ninth from the oldest, fourth from the youngest. One baby boy was stillborn after Mama had the flu while pregnant. She had taken too much of one kind of medication and she said the doctor had told her that it most likely caused the stillbirth.

We were all born in the same house, later called the "Usta Place." It was when we moved from this home in 1936, that sister number nine, Meryl Darlene, referred to it as the "Usta Place." She was only five years old at the time and you can expect cute things from little ones. After all these years, our old house is still known to all of us, even our grandchildren, as the "Usta Place." The house was located on an eighty-acre farm southwest of Moundville, Missouri, in Vernon County. The house is gone now, but we still have lots of precious memories. You can bet your bottom dollar that we will as long as we live.

About two years ago, I advertised some items for sale on our local radio station. I was kidding with the announcer about I don't know what. After I hung up, the phone rang and I thought I was going to make a sale. What I was about to get was much better! When I answered the phone, this lovely voice on the other end said, "Hello, who is this?" I told her. She told me she thought I sounded like one of the Clark girls. I said, "I am. Who are you?" We started a conversation and talked a little bit. What a beautiful surprise!

She told me her name was Mildred Willey and that in 1908 she attended English School. Mildred said her teacher's name was Miss Anna Whiteside, my Mama. (Now this is the first I knew of that our Mama taught anywhere other than Lone Star). I told Mildred I wanted to meet her and asked if I could take her to lunch. It was fine with her, so I called Dana, my sister, and told her about visiting with Mildred. I invited her to have lunch with Mildred and me. We picked her up and had a big time.

About a week later, Mildred called and wanted me to come to her house because she had some pictures she thought I might like to have. One picture was of Mama and all of her students at English School. Little Mildred, all dressed up in her little white dress and black shoes, was standing in the front row. Believe me, I treasure this one! Mama was wearing a long black dress with a short white apron. You can bet your bottom dollar she had made it herself. Mildred told me that while Mama was teaching there at English School, she had room and board at the Sid Quigley home, who are relatives of Mildred.

Mildred also told me she remembered her father bought cut wood for cooking and heating from our Papa. Mildred is certainly a sweet person and I consider myself fortunate to have met her.

I feel I must write this note right here. Sometime back in the fifties Mama asked me if I knew what my mother-in-law's maiden name was. I told her it was Stella Young. She told me back in about 1896, when she went to school at Lone Star, she was friends with a girl who looked a lot like her. She asked if she had two brothers, Dee and Leland. I told her yes. Mama and Stella, my mother-in-law, were good friends when they were little girls, but we hadn't realized it for many years. Mama only knew Stella by her maiden name.

When Mama was in grade school, the students were graded like 85, 90,100. (If you were smart.) Mama never made below an 85 and most of her grades were 100. How do I know? I have some of her grade cards, and her teaching certificates. Her first certificate was in 1908, at the age of twenty.

Mama used to talk about the children and play time when she was a young child going to school at Lone Star. She grew up and later was the teacher there. She told me years ago there was a family by the name of Butts who had a boy and a girl she played with at that school. They named the boy Harry and the girl Rosy. I've wondered so often if the parents had taken a little more time searching for names, they could have come up with names that were more appropriate. Don't you?

I'm not sure how Papa and Mama met. I understand Papa was batching pretty close to where Mama grew up. I understand he had baked four or five pies the day they found each other. Do you suppose Mama learned to bake from this handsome baker? (Mama was a good cook, but seldom used a cookbook.) The word probably got around about this good looking pistol-totin' young fellow, and Mama did all she was allowed to do to meet him. Knowing how pretty and smart Mama was, this pistol packin' papa (not just yet) just happened to run into each other at Ashbaugh's Grocery in Moundville and fell deeply in love at first sight. After they met, they did their courtin' in a buggy. Can you imagine? In a buggy! Darlin' things like this really did happen back then.

Please let me say this right here. Our darlin' Papa had been engaged to another lady before this great meeting at Ashbaugh's Grocery. From what I hear, he had dated my Aunt Leona, Mama's sister. I'm beginning to think this tall good looking pistol-totin' young man got around some.

Now I understand there was plenty of air conditioning in those buggies, but no heating, so they would heat big rocks on the stove to haul in the buggy to keep their feet warm. Mama told me this. I suppose if they forgot to heat rocks, they got cold feet and stayed home. They also had big lap robes made like a quilt in the buggy. Hey, those would sure come in handy, wouldn't they?

I guess he finally got wise, and realized he was wasting all this valuable time, so he asked Mama for a date September 8, 1910. There was a big dance at the Rollie Zilliox home and he asked her to go with him. I'm sure glad he did. Earl and Berl Davis played the music for the dance. I know Berl played his accordion. I'm not sure about Earl. I never was to sure about him, if you know what I mean.

Since I mentioned Berl Davis, here is another story about him. He was a student when Mama taught at Lone Star School. According to a letter we found in Mama's treasures, Berl wasn't always making music. In school, he was making trouble with my Mama, Miss Anna.

The letter dated November 9, 1910, to Miss Anna, didn't say what kind of trouble he caused, but the school board didn't think Berl was responsible for his behavior and therefore no punishment was required. Although Miss Anna didn't agree with them, all three board members thought he should be allowed to come back to school. The board mailed the signed letter to the Superintendent of Schools, W.Y. Foster.

Mama received a letter from Mr. Foster dated November 21, 1910. It read: "Dear Miss Anna, I have your letter and regret very much that you are not receiving the cooperation of all of your patrons, which is so necessary for a successful school. I think that a mistake was made when the boy was allowed to come back to school without punishment. A boy that treated a teacher as he treated you, should be punished and if he is too big to receive punishment, then he should take his books and leave school, and be given an opportunity to obey his parents at home."

Maybe the fault started at home. None of the letters that were exchanged on this matter stated what Berl had done, but it sounded to me like something that didn't belong in Miss Anna's classroom, so

This photo of Edward & Dora Anna (Whiteside) Clark, my Mama and Papa, was taken on their wedding day, May 14, 1911.

she dismissed him and sent him home. After he "outgrew" this kid stuff, he turned out to be a nice person. I loved to listen to Berl play his accordion, don't you know?

Our parents were married May 14, 1911, after a short courtship. She made her wedding dress. From the pictures, you can tell it was absolutely gorgeous. I'm not really sure where they were married or by whom. Mama never talked too much about dating Papa or where they went. I don't suppose they had a honeymoon, because Mama was teaching school and couldn't go far away. I'm so glad my parents met and got married. Just think, had they not met, I wouldn't have this story to tell you, nor you the pleasure of reading it.

Mama was expecting a baby right away and like most mothers back in the olden days, she stayed home and did everything and more than was expected of her. Our precious Mama did just that. Bless her in every way. Looking back now, she must have been expecting about all the time. I don't know if the doctor was there before each of her babies were born or a mid-wife came instead. These types of things were not discussed back then and Mama didn't ever say after we were grown.

Mama was a teacher at Lone Star School, when she and my Papa met. She was teaching at the same school where she had gone as a child. The old Lone Star School still stands as I write this.

Mama was teaching at Lone Star School when she and Papa were married, too. Her top wages were $31.00 a month and she had thirty-one students in one room. Mama told me once that some of the boy students were so big she was afraid of them. (Maybe Berl, the boy I mentioned before, was one she was talking about.) With thirty-one kids in one room, what a noise it must have been! Maybe not though, with Miss Anna as the teacher.

Please let me jot down some family history here. Keep in mind, I did not live this section of my story, but it is true. It came from our family tree that was brought up to date not long ago. Dana had this history copied in our new "Five Generation Cookbook From the Usta Place."

In 1855, my great-grandfather, Andrew Clark, laid out a town in northern Missouri and gave it the name of Cainsville, after a dear friend, Mr. Cain. He built buildings and furnished accommodations for those who brought grain to be ground for flour and cornmeal. He also built a hotel. He should have called the hotel Clark's Castle. That has sort of a ring to it, doesn't it? He had stables, a post office, and even got a doctor, Dr. T. M. Fullerton, to come to his town. The doctor's office was still there when my sisters, Dana and Ruby and her husband, John Base, visited back there recently.

Our grandfather, Phillip O'Dell Clark, was born in Cainsville in 1841. The only picture I have of him proves he was a handsome dude. Of course, my Papa was born in Cainsville, too. Some very handsome young "fellows" came of that town. Do you suppose it was something in the water? We certainly had exceptionally good-looking parents, but we are descendants from Cainsville, so how could we miss?

Phillip O'Dell Clark, my grandfather, was born in 1841 at Cainsville, Missouri.

My great-great grandfather owned slaves, but that did not make him a bad person. There were, during that time, many people who owned slaves. Many of these landowners were good to their slaves, providing more than the expected food, housing, and clothing. Even though we may not approve of what went on back then, it is a part of our history and I didn't want to leave it out.

My grandfather, Joshua Whiteside, came from Preston, England, when he was nine years old with his parents, entering by way of New Orleans, up the Mississippi River to Pike County, Illinois. The family settled there and he later married Miss Fannie Taylor, my granny. When they came by covered wagon to Vernon County, they settled on a farm four miles west of Moundville, home of Ashbaugh's Grocery. I'll tell you more about Ashbaugh's later in my story. (It was truly a fun place to go, because they had penny candy just for the Clark kids. I believe to this day, the owners would see us kids coming and make a "special" for a penny. We would tell the clerk we

My Grandpa Joshua (born 1846) and Grandma Fannie (Taylor) Whiteside (born 1853) settled on a farm near Moundville, Missouri.

wanted a penny's worth of all kinds. We got just that!)

When they came to the farm, there was nothing but tall prairie grass and prairie chickens. Granny Fanny said she got so tired of eating Prairie Chicken. I believe a piece of that would taste pretty good right now.

Grandpa told us that when people came west in their covered wagons, they would travel across his land. If a death occurred along the trail, they would be buried right there on his land. There was a grave on our grandparent's farm in a pasture across the fence in the backyard. Grandpa Joshua took care of the grave and put flowers on the grave.

Grandpa Joshua was a self-educated man. He was in the picture of the first Vernon County Court held in Nevada, Missouri. This was in his obituary: "As he was eighty-two years old, he had been in failing health for several years. Probably no man in the southwest part of the county was better or more favorably known. Both physically and mentally, he was a giant."

"While Grandpa Joshua was not a man of finished education, the writer who met him does not think there was ever a more naturally brilliant mind. He was a great reader and once anything was stored away in that gruff and kindly head, it never escaped. He could recite sayings and writings of great men by the hour. He was honest and dependable, a gentleman of the old school. In fact, as few men we have known, he was entitled to be called a diamond in the rough. We could be so lucky to have someone like grandpa in the big office and all of the smaller ones."

I was three years old when Grandpa Joshua died, but I remember him. He called me his little blue-eyed Sally. It would have been just as easy for him to say blue-eyed Helen, don't you know? When one of my sisters, Margie, and I were really young, I would try to pick her up to carry her. Grandma Fannie would say, "Let her be, honey, let her be."

In later years, I remember Papa making beer. He would get his brown bottles washed up and ready to fill. These bottles would be capped for storage. He also had some stored in a big stone jar behind the kitchen stove. When it was time, if there was any left, Papa would cap it to enjoy later. You could bet your bottom dollar, it was enjoyed. It was fun to help Papa with this kind of work. Any of us who were big enough to push the handle down got to help finish the job.

My brother, Herschel, and I sneaked a bottle of that delicious beverage one time and drank it all. Children will drink anything, if they are thirsty. Looking back now, I sure did not need half of that bottle, but our parents taught us to share.

Speaking of drinking makes me think of water. We had a neighbor at the Usta Place who loved to "witch" for water. For all of you who don't know what I'm talking about, I'll just try to explain it to you. Grover Franks would take a limb of a tree with a "fork" shape. Holding it tightly in his hands, with the tip upward, he would walk along. If the tip started to go downward, he knew he was getting close to a water vein. He held tightly, his hands shaking with grip and pressure of the vein would be so strong, the bark of the limb would be twisted off. He would most always find a vein of water. This sounds really wild, but it's true. I'm from Missouri. He showed me.

I never found the recipe for Papa's beer in Mama's recipe book. Papa had a good memory, like me. Mama had recipes dated back in 1908, but she seldom used recipes. She would take a scant cup of this, a pinch of this, and a pinch of that and ended up with delicious dishes. You should see this old book. Because it is so old, I have to lay it down to turn the pages.

For a special gift at Christmas, in 1963, Mama made each of us nine girls a cookbook. When I lived in Idaho Falls, Idaho, I had sent Mama a recipe for Angel Pie and Peanut Butter cookies. She had copied these in her "old" book. In this special gift cookbook, she had recipes for Horse Colic, Liniment, and Coconut Cake, a recipe I had created myself. I guess she figured I might have a horse sometime. I don't remember ever having a horse or child with colic.

My brother, Herschel, and I drove the cattle to the creek to drink almost every day. I would always ask Herschel if he thought the creek would be up or if they would be bank full, because I was afraid of flooding, don't you know? How funny! I have always been afraid of water. Herschel and Herman, another one of my brothers, threw me in water over my head one time when I was very young. It scared me something fierce and I have never gotten over the fear of water over my head.

When we would drive the cattle to the creek, I could hear a train whistle. For years, I had the silly idea the train traveled up and down the creek where Herschel and I herded the cattle to drink. The railroad track was about a mile and a half from the Usta Place and being the back-woodsy little kid I was, I had never seen the tracks. Since we spent so much time herding cows, filling water barrels, and swimming, I often wondered why we never saw the train. I had never seen the tracks so I didn't know there were rails to run on. After all, there weren't any trains between the Usta Place, Ashbaugh's, and school. Where else did I get to go where I would see the tracks?

Mama was very talented and clever in so many ways, but cutting hair was not one of them. She could not cut my hair like I wanted. She had one bowl and used it for all of our haircuts. She very often got scissor happy and if she thought you needed a trim, an old towel was spread over the shoulders and away she would go with those scissors. I was twelve years old when I started cutting my own hair. Now mind you, I appreciated her trying, but that bowl cut just was not me.

At one time Mama had very long hair and wore it rolled in a bun in the back. I can't honestly remember her wearing it this way, but she told me about it. Since there were so many little Clarks and

Papa to give haircuts to, I suppose Mama didn't have time to take care of her long hair. It was much cooler for her, too.

Mama told me this story once. She told me she had made up her mind she was going to have her hair cut, so Ed (my Papa) took the scissors and gave her a blunt cut. She said they laid the hair down flat, tied both ends with twine, and wrapped it in a cloth. She kept it for years. The cut hair was about fifteen inches long and was a medium brown. She had never had a permanent before the big cut. Believe me, there were a lot of women that had never had a permanent back then. I've talked to three of my sisters about Papa cutting Mama's hair. None of them can actually remember when she got it cut, but can remember seeing the hair wrapped in cloth.

In the olden days, women would sell their hair to big companies that made dolls. I understand these doll makers bought the hair and would either glue or sew the hair to the doll heads. I don't know why Mama saved her hair, unless she planned to sell it someday. I really don't know what year it was, but dear Mama decided to sell her beautiful hair. Do you suppose she got paid enough or do you think someone came by and she, needing the money, took whatever they would give her for it?

Mama, I love you and Papa for providing shelter, food and clothes for us, for caring for all of our aches and pains, for everything you had to sacrifice to provide for all of us.

When it came to picking blackberries, Mama did not want to leave any out there. She wanted us to get them all. Mama would have all of us kids, at least the ones that were big enough, out in the patch picking. If we got thirsty and wanted to get a drink, she would tell us to eat a berry. Mama would not let us leave the patch. We had to keep on picking. Of course, the blackberry vines were full of chiggers and once in awhile, a snake. I want to tell you right now, I did not care for snakes, and I did not get along with the chiggers at all. I still don't.

In the spring at garden planting time, Papa would spread barnyard manure all over the garden ground, then plow and harrow it down nicely, so Mama could plant the seeds and set out plants for her vegetable garden. We all learned how to plant and harvest everything we grew. What we grew is what we ate, so it was important to make sure we learned how to plant and grow lots of fruits and vegetables.

Mama also taught all of us how to can and preserve the fruits and vegetables we grew. When she canned, she used the cold pack method, hot water bath, or open kettle. Besides teaching us all of the gardening and canning, Mama taught me how to sew and to do Swedish embroidery. I've made lots of embroidered tea towels and occasionally, I've made a scarf for a table. (Friends love a homemade gift.)

We always had pigs to butcher and that was our main meat, unless you mention the wild rabbits and squirrels that were dressed and fried in lard. Now they claim lard is not good for you. You can bet your bottom dollar we had plenty of wild game. When you are a child and hungry, it all tastes good, don't you know?

When we were little kids at the "Usta Place," Papa would be milking the cow out in the barn and would squirt milk straight from the cow faucet to our little mouths. It tasted as good warm as it does out of the icebox. Herman would be helping with the milking and would squirt milk all over us. I didn't like that at all. I would rather drink it than wear it.

Later, when my brother, Herschel, was old enough to hunt, he and I would hunt and kill jackrabbits, then dress and sell them for ten cents each. If we had four or five inches of snow, they would be easier to catch. Our family dog, Buss, would run them until they would be run down and they would be easier to club. It sure was a good thing we had Buss. He made the hunt fun and without him, most of the rabbits would have gotten away from us. We did not get rich, but back yonder, ten cents went a lot further than now.

Mama's brother, Uncle Stub, gave us this puppy and someone came up with the name Buss. He was like one of the family and went to school with all of us every day. The kids at school liked Old Buss and fed him when it was time for lunch. Old Buss liked the kids too, but then who wouldn't if someone fed you?

Herschel would sometimes take his slingshot hunting and was a pretty good shot with it. This slingshot was made from an old inner tube off of Papa's old Model T Ford. Herschel cut two strips about twelve inches long and three-fourths of an inch wide. These rubber strips were attached to each end of a piece of leather to hold the rock he used for ammunition. He would then tie the other ends to a Y-shaped twig.

It was easy to shoot a rabbit! Herschel always got one on his first or second try. Because I was afraid I would hit a poor defenseless bunny, I didn't want to try using it. You could bet your bottom dollar I enjoyed a "piece of the hunt" later though.

Papa liked a certain kind of candy. I think it was called mounds. They were shaped like a haystack, white on the inside, and covered with chocolate. Back then, you could buy this candy for ten cents a pound. Even at that price, he seldom got to buy his favorite treat.

When Herschel and I were the youngest of the Clark kids at home, Mama would let us go through cabinet drawers or junk drawers, just to keep us busy. We did not have toys, so the drawers were fun to play in. Since Herschel was about two and a half years older than I was, I had to find another playmate when he started going to school. I looked forward to him coming home every day. When it was about time for him to get home from school, I would start watching for him.

While I was waiting to start going to school, Mama would let me cut quilt blocks from fabric scraps while she sewed them on her treadle sewing machine. It was a fun time for me because I loved to work with fabric. I still love to sew.

If walls could talk and floors could hear, just think of the minutes and hours of the precious memories I could cram into my story from the Usta Place. I can remember, as a small child, we would all be ready for bed. I can still hear Papa and Mama, lying there talking very low, I suppose of all the happenings of the day or maybe what they would have to do to start out the next day. I've wondered so many times, since I got older and grown up, where they found the energy, strength, and faith to face a new day, seven days a week.

Being a busy little kid like me, I was tired enough that while they were still talking, I would fall asleep. Now you can bet your bottom dollar, I would be up and ready to go in the morning by the time everyone else rolled out of bed.

It really puzzles me now as to how any of us got any rest at night. On all of our beds where we slept, the mattresses were made of straw stuffed into ticking, cut and shaped to fit each bed. The mattress was about five inches thick. The straw would either be changed or the old straw would be shook-up and fluffed a little every two or three years. This ticking, as most of you know, is a heavy fabric used only on mattresses and bed pillows.

Mama always had a lot of chickens, so we had plenty of feather pillows. Back in the olden days, we didn't have any trouble sleeping on feathers and never knew anything about allergies. You can bet your bottom dollar I don't sleep on feathers now. I don't care for the smell of them.

After Papa and Mama moved to the farm east of Nevada, Missouri, the hard times started to get a little "softer." There was a program set up in Nevada for people in need to sign up and get bed mattresses made. The company would furnish all of the material and machines and we did the labor.

Mama and I went to check out the program. I was about thirteen years old by now. It really was a hard job. These mattresses were covered with a satin fabric and had a cotton filling. Mama felt so proud that she finally had something new. By the way, I still have one of the mattresses Mama and I helped make that day.

We were surely blessed by the good Lord above, don't you know? In the olden days, we didn't realize what and how much we had. Of course, we younger ones didn't know how to give thanks for it all at the time. Just thriving to keep their heads above water and doing without certain items she wanted to buy, items all of us little Clarks needed, must have been a trial for Mama and Papa.

In September 1931, I started school at the age of six. We were still going to Totten School where ten of us started our formal education. My youngest sister, Meryl Darlene, started first grade at Stanton School, after our parents moved to east of Nevada from the "Usta Place."

My first grade teacher was Mr. Perle Whitworth. Now remember, I was only six years old, but to this day, I believe I was the teacher's pet. I did not have to bribe him with the famous apple. Just think what might have been had I brought him an apple. Maybe he would have advanced me to the third grade. He let me dust erasers, wash blackboards, and empty wastebaskets. You see, while I was doing these tasks, I was not having to study and I was getting to do the chores little kids like to do. Of course, he was also getting his work done.

I learned a lot in the first grade. I don't actually remember knowing my ABC's or how to count before I went to school. (Now most children have been introduced to computers and know how to use them when they start first grade.) Mr. Whitworth made it easy to learn and I wanted to study and get my lessons.

I loved English, spelling, and history. I remember having spelling tests a few times and won a pocket dictionary and an ink pen. I liked some arithmetic, but not fractions. I remember the multiplication tables were really easy for me to learn, except six times nine. I just could not get that one. Miss Hazel Ames, who was my teacher that year, said she would help me to remember it by naming Mr. George Washington number 54. She told me to just look at George and it would help me remember six times nine. You see, there was a large picture of George hanging on the west wall of the schoolhouse. To this day, if I need to multiply six times nine, I think of George.

Miss Hazel loved to wave my hair, sometimes at noon or recess. I had naturally curly hair. She thought it was pretty, I guess. My hair is still curly and you would never guess it, but turning a tad gray! (Only my operator knows for sure. My operator is me!)

When we were little youngins', you must remember there were several heads to be shampooed, so when it rained, Mama would catch the water to shampoo our hair. The soft water and homemade lye soap made our hair silky smooth and smell really nice. It also saved lots of water in the cistern for drinking.

Please let me write a line or two here about Totten School. Since I started writing my story, I have contacted some of my family, and it is amazing how much we learned while we were students at Totten School. We had chores to do at home and other responsibilities, besides walking two miles each way to school. It would seem we did not have much time left for homework. We all knew we had responsibilities and learned at an early age that work came first and play came second.

My sister, Pansy, wrote an article entitled *"The Oregon Trail."* As I said before, I am a pack rat and when I see articles or items in magazines or newspapers, I clip and save them. Pansy was in high school when she wrote her article and won. I have had this newspaper clipping in my scrapbook since 1936. I gave her the clipping and she was happy to have it. She could not believe I had kept it all these years.

My sister, Wilma, won the district spelling contest when she was in the seventh grade. She also gave a recitation on rally day in Moundville. She won some money, and her teacher gave her a sack of candy besides. Just think, she didn't have to spend her penny at Ashbaugh's.

Now I must admit, I had trouble memorizing poems. I was just not interested in poetry. When we had Christmas programs, pie suppers, or last day school programs, I did not have trouble learning my lines, because I was enjoying all of it. I especially enjoyed the programs we had on the last day of school, since it meant no more school for awhile.

We really had good teachers at Totten School and Stanton School, too. My oldest sister, Dana, was good to help me with my homework. She knew all of us little youngins' needed her help, because Mama was so busy doing lots of other work.

Speaking of Dana, I was looking for a special clipping I wanted to put in my story, but could not find it. I ran onto this one. I decided this precious note would add a lot of flavor and spice and a lot of things nice. Dana sent this in a letter to me a long time ago. It said: Sister Helen,

> *Nice to chat with, good to know,*
> *Glad to have her, where I go.*
> *Kind in trouble, bright in joy,*
> *Suits exactly, can't say why.*
> *Sweet and wholesome, always true,*
> *That's my sister. Yes, that's you.*

Dana said when Herschel was a little boy a plane flew over our house when they were outside playing. He was so young he thought it was a big bird. He said, "I'd sure like to find that thing's nest!" I guess he thought that "bird" would have some pretty big eggs in it.

Ten of the Clark Clan sang *"Hobo Bill's Last Ride"* at a pie supper one time at Totten School. Since I was so young, it's strange I can remember the words to that old song for so many years. We made our own music! Do any of you remember that old song?

Papa used to let me go with him to haul water for drinking, laundry, and our other needs. We got water from the creek for laundry and outside use, but hauled from Claude Springer's for drinking and house use. Papa had two wells and a cistern, but in dry weather, they had a bad habit of going dry.

When we hauled water from the creek, Papa drove his team of horses, Dick and Dock, hitched to a grain wagon that held four barrels. He would drive the team out into deep water, because it made it easier to dip up the water, don't you know? The water was so high in the wagon the barrels would float until we got water in them to weigh them down.

Do you suppose he knew how scared I was? I pretended to be a big girl, but I was not very courageous then, especially out in the middle of the creek. I was not over six or seven years old. I'm surprised I didn't float out of the wagon.

My brother, Herman, used to work out shucking corn for the neighbors. He had to take a sack lunch, walk about three miles, and got paid fifty cents a day. It was better than donating, I guess. It almost was. He was around fifteen years old and probably gave Papa some of his wages.

In 1938, when Herman was around twenty years old, he went to Iowa to shuck corn. His wages included room and board. Papa told him not to flash his money around when he started home. The bus stopped in Kansas City at a cafe for the passengers to eat. An old couple told Herman to be careful and not let anyone know he was carrying money and to hide part of it. His ticket was already paid for. After they ate and headed for the bus, two "punks" stuck a gun in his back and demanded money. I guess he flashed his money in front of the wrong people. He was just sick, but it taught him a lesson.

One time, not long after that, we were still living east of Nevada and Herman had Papa's single barrel shotgun outside. He had probably been hunting and when he came in, he started to put it away in our storage room. When he set it down, it discharged and shot a hole through the roof. When Mama heard the shot, she was terrified and she called out to him. The expression on her face, I'll never forget. It was such a blessing to know he was all right.

A little while after this happened, Herschel and I were outside playing. We heard a flock of geese flying rather low over the house from the north. He ran in and got the same single barrel and shot a goose right out of the sky. Mama dressed the goose and we had a feast. There was some homemade dressing with it. I bet I got a tablespoon of it raw. (I always did.) I still love raw dressing.

Here is another sweet story about corn-shucking time. Papa would take me along to the field to drive the horses while he did the hard part. I hadn't had much experience driving horses, so naturally they would get off the row and it looked like I was going to be in big trouble. Know what? Papa would take hold of the reins and get the horses straight on the rows again and again and again. He should have sent me to the house, but I guess he realized I hadn't had as much experience as my older brothers and sisters with this big people work. Anyway, he was very patient with me. It was hard work, but someone had to do it, don't you know? Mama said many times that if she needed to find Helen, all she had to do was find Ed, because I was usually out helping him. (Ed was my Papa and Anna was my Mama.)

When Margie was about two or three years old, she stuck a bead up her nose. (We never knew why). Papa and Mama had to take her to the doctor to get it out. On the way home, Mama got Margie an ice cream cone. I was just along for the ride, I guess, because I didn't get one. I never could understand why she was rewarded and I didn't get anything.

Now I have no idea when this business started, but I remember as a very young girl, a man and his wife came around through the neighborhood driving a truck of some sort, with a walk-in bed built up in the back. This grocery store on wheels had shelves for canned goods, bins for storing flour, cornmeal, sugar, etc. It was fun to see them drive in and know there was some excitement going on. I don't remember any candy department, but if there had been, we little ones couldn't support it because we spent our pennies at Ashbaugh's. You could bet your bottom dollar if Papa had an extra penny or two, he would have looked for candy or peanuts for us kids in that grocery store on wheels, don't you know?

The old Ashbaugh's store closed in later years. I recently heard that they were talking about reopening it. I wonder if it will also be called Ashbaugh's. I'm sure the original owners are not living anymore, but the same family may own it. If you blink once going through Moundville, Missouri, you will miss the important sights.

You know when you purchase a bag of apples for pie or applesauce you always have to peel one for a sample to make sure they are just right? The ones I found last week were just that. I suppose I ate three or four before I could make up my mind. I'm hard to please when choosing an apple. They have to be really red. These were Mississippi apples and so good fried. While I was peeling them, it brought back a precious memory of when I was a child. My Papa would peel the apples for us "wee ones." He would always start at the bottom of the apple, (don't ask me why), and peel toward the top or stem. He could peel the whole apple and not break the peeling. This was still at the Usta Place and I don't suppose the apples had to be washed. He would pull an apple from the tree, take out his knife and start peeling. If you were lucky to be the closest one to him, you could start eating at the end and eat until he got the top of the apple. Oh my, they were good eating. We would snack under the trees on a Jonathan or Delicious.

Herschel and I climbed those trees lots of times. He thought the biggest and the brightest red one was at the top, don't you know? You can bet your bottom dollar I was right behind him. Mama would peel and slice about five gallons of them and lay them up on the kitchen roof in the sun to dry. I imagine the ants had a field day.

Now days, we have machines to do the job.

Mama not only dried apples, but she always stored some for winter to eat fresh, sometimes with our popcorn in the evening. Papa and Mama would store these apples in a large bin that was usually used for storing flour and cornmeal. One day, being a hungry little kid, I was trying to find the apples. I was too short to reach them, so I pulled myself up on the side of the bin to peek in. Somehow I pulled the bin over on top of me. I wasn't very big, but the bin wasn't too full at the time and not too heavy, don't you know? I screamed and since there were plenty of little Clark kids around, help came right away. I was scared I would get a whippin', but Papa and Mama were just thankful I was all right, I guess, because I didn't get into trouble for trying to get into the apples. I never reached the apples for a snack, but you can bet your bottom dollar when it was time for supper, I had plenty to eat. We always did.

When I was a little girl, I remember hearing Mama sing a little love song. I believe it may have been called *"Little Black Mustache."* It may have been while she was peeling those apples. I don't suppose she wrote it, but she always did have a way of putting words together. I just loved the lyrics and when she sang, it had more meaning. Anyway, I still remember the lyrics to that old song and can still remember Mama singing it while doing her chores. It's a shame all of you reading this can't hear me sing it.

CHAPTER 2

I WAS RESPONSIBLE for making my own lunch when I started to school. Sometimes I would mash up beans, maybe chop a little onion in them, and put them on a biscuit left from breakfast and make a sandwich for my dinner bucket for school. More often, I took fried potatoes on the biscuit for a sandwich. Believe it not, they were really good! I had one for breakfast just today and do quite often.

I just imagine this is why cornbread and gravy was our breakfast lots of times at the Usta Place when I was growing up. This was a filling meal and helped hold us over until we ate our potato sandwich for lunch.

One day, my little friend, Doris, wanted to trade lunches. She had a fried chicken leg and thigh cooked together. We traded. Know what? It tasted almost as good as my tator sandwich.

We had one big day a year, maybe two. The Fourth of July Picnic at Moundville was a big time, with a prize for the largest family there. The prize was always twelve loaves of baker's bread or a fifty-pound sack of flour. You can bet your last bottom dollar that whoever thought up the contest was thinking how far that bread or flour would go in the Ed Clark family. We always won! It sure helped Papa and Mama. Now you remember there were eleven youngins', plus Papa and Mama. You would have had to have gotten up and started sooner to beat that, don't you know?

There came a time when some of the older siblings would hide out in the crowd. Because of our large family, some of them were embarrassed to go up for the prize. After all, we won year after year. I was still very young, but I do remember how good the bakery bread was and how much I liked it. It saved Mama the work of making it also.

While I was sitting here writing yesterday, my sister, Meryl Darlene, called to chat. The "Clark Clan" is widely known for their chatting. I mentioned to her I was writing my story plus happenings with the rest of the family at the Usta Place, Totten School, the years after, and up to now. She told me that one time Dana made her a new dress and Mama entered her in the baby contest at Moundville. She was just eight months old and I didn't remember it. I asked her if she won. You could bet your last dollar she won, because she was the only Clark running.

Occasionally, each of us little Clarks had five cents to spend on either a bottle of pop or an ice cream cone. I always got strawberry pop. It wasn't so much because I liked the taste of the pop, but because it made my lips red. I really liked that. I still like the color red in coats, pants, blouses, cars and lips!

Going back to the memories of the bakery bread, I used to go stay all night with my cousin, Norma Whiteside. Uncle Jimmy always bought their bread from the bakery. He kept it in a round wooden breadbox in his pantry. Now I was hungry when I went there and it was a big treat to get some of it. Now I would fight for a slice or loaf of the good home-baked bread.

A long-time school friend of mine, Martha Hupens, told me once that one of her fondest memories of the olden days was coming home, staying all night with me, getting to eat potato soup and, after supper, singing and playing the old pump organ. It was also a fun time for all of us. All of us Clarks were so musically talented and could all sing and play by ear the organ, piano, violin and guitar. There was not money for lessons. We were all windy enough for the harmonica, and some of us also learned to play it.

I have often wondered what happened to Papa's Jews Harp. I can almost still hear him playing it. Mama did her thing playing the harmonica. I learned to play *"Old Susanna,"* and by the time I was finished playing it I was out of air.

Musical talent seemed to swarm all around us Clarks. It started with Papa and Mama, was passed on down to the little Clarks, then floated on down to the grandchildren. There is no doubt in my mind, it will continue long after I have left this world. I can't imagine not playing a tune, if I know it, on the piano. I'm so thankful for all of the blessings and talents God has given me.

When I went to stay all night with my friend from school, Martha Hupens, we had pancakes for breakfast. I guess her mama put pieces of raw bacon in the batter and it didn't get browned in there. I like my bacon crisp. I say it was bacon, but I don't actually know for sure. Anyway, I told them I wasn't hungry. I lied! I can't remember what we took in our bucket for lunch that day. You could bet your second last dollar if I would have had a fried potato sandwich, I would have been happy.

I must add this postscript here. At one time, Martha's parents talked about returning to Germany. One of the daughters said she would kill herself before she would go back. I don't know if she would really have done it or not because they stayed in the old U.S.A.

Once in a while Papa would take us to school in the Model T. We all lived on mud roads, and the tracks would eventually get very deep. I guess it was because everyone who traveled those roads would try to stay in the deep tracks for traction. If you slipped out of the tracks, you were liable to slip in a ditch or out of sight. We were always lucky everyone was going the same direction. Once you got in those canyons, you drove until you reached the end of them, which was about two miles. You couldn't meet anyone because you were in too deep. Sometimes we would get stuck, so we all got out and pushed our way out of a bad situation.

My brother, Herschel, was two and one-half years old when I was born. Mama said the day I was born, Herschel swung around on the foot of the bed post and said, "Let's don't get any more kids. We've got plenty. Yes, sir, we've got plenty." He really said a mouth full. He was talking too much too soon, like all the rest of us. However, he came by it naturally, don't you know? He wasn't old enough to realize that until he started school, he and I would be playmates.

Mama told me years ago that when I was born, Dr. Carter stood me up in the wash pan and bathed me. If someone tried that now, I'd be a pan full. Sister number one, Dana, told me when I was born, Mama had a really hard time in her labor and that it took two to help Mama have me. I don't know why it took so long. I didn't know much about it and almost wish I hadn't heard of it, don't you know? Mama, I know it was hard for you and I'm sorry I was such a pain.

After I got a little bigger, I loved to go to the barnyard and lick the old cow's block salt. Sometimes I would have to wait for the cows to finish and move on. I like salt, pepper, chili powder, cumin and hot spices. I really like spicy food, and I guess I could probably eat it two times a day. You can bet your anti-acid I would probably be sorry though, but then maybe not. I can and do eat almost all of the foods I like.

My sister, Ruby, mentioned to me that when we were all little ones at home, we would be eating supper and all of us would eat really fast, trying to beat the other ones to the old pump organ. I'm sure I beat the rest of them my share of the time. Not one of the children had a lesson to learn to play the organ or piano. It sounds like that beautiful piece of furniture was a number one piece of joy to every last one living at the Usta Place.

I hadn't talked at any length to my sisters about the Usta Place days until I started writing my story. We all have memories of our own, and there are some memories we share. It's really amazing we can remember so many stories from the Usta Place.

We had so much down there at the Usta Place, but we didn't realize it then. We had a huge lilac bush near our front porch that bloomed every year. Ruby and the children in her age group, the first six or seven, would pretend they were graduating. They would go to the lilac bush and break off a piece to carry.

There was a step on the east side of the porch and a huge rock on the south side of the front porch. You could smell the flowers from that beautiful old lilac bush a long way. They would pretend they were marching up the steps and across the porch, like they were graduating. Later you will see a picture of me taken on a big flat rock there at the front porch. I looked so sad. Maybe because I wasn't graduating. I had on a white dress, black shoes (yes, I said shoes), and a pair of beads as big as me. Just a dashing darlin' standing there. I don't know where my hat was, but I looked like I owned a piece of that rock. Anyway, I guess I did. We all thought we grew up without a lot, but I guess that would depend on what you mean by without. There wasn't much money, but we had food, clothes, and a place to live. I see people going barefooted now sometimes. Are they poor?

Ruby and Pansy were in the 4-H Club years ago, and at the time Dana was the leader. Ruby had to make a shoe pocket as a 4-H project for the county fair. She didn't have quite enough material, but Dana showed her how to piece it together so there would be enough to make it. Ruby took top blue ribbon on her shoe pocket at the fair.

There at the Usta Place each little one enjoyed his or her own little space, not expecting much, and getting just that, don't you know? They say you don't miss what you've never had. Well, it doesn't make it any easier to wonder now what Papa and Mama did without to raise us all. I'm so thankful for all God has done for me and how He helped our parents provide for us during those tough years.

The first group of siblings learned hard work, responsibility, sharing, and accepting as well. It was a little harder when the second group came into the picture. It meant more of everything. As I said before though, the older girls got out and went to work and helped quite a bit. Our dear parents taught us all so much. I didn't take time to thank them. I will someday.

I can remember as a child, probably between two and three years old, we would go to my Grandma Whiteside's house for Sunday dinner. (Now days, it's called lunch.) Grandma would fix fried chicken. I'll bet you I ate the skin then. I don't now, but you see in the olden days scraps were not thrown away.

Grandma would catch, with a hook, two or three chickens and take them by the head and wring their necks, let them stop moving, scald them and start picking feathers. Please remember this is the same granny that lived on prairie chicken, so she knew just how to do this. I thought it looked like a big job. I'm not sure why she had to do the wringing part, but she sat down on the south steps, took them one by one and did the wringing. I can see her yet, sitting there in her long dress and apron, her white hair rolled up in a bun.

I have lots of memories of my Mama's old home place, but I never got to meet my grandparents on Papa's side. They lived far away and we never had the opportunity to meet most of them. However, I did get to meet three of his brothers and one sister.

When you come from a family the size of ours, you find yourselves pairing off with the one that is close in age to you. When Ruby and Pansy were home, I would be a buddy to each of them. After they grew up, up and away, I found new ones. By this time, there weren't many left. This is what we get for having so many siblings. Papa and Mama knew we would all need someone after the older ones left, so they kept busy providing us with just that. Poor little Meryl Darlene, being sister number nine, was the last one. All good things come to an end sometime. As I refer to my sisters by a certain number, I am counting only the sisters. Although Meryl was sibling number twelve, she was sister number nine. I hope this doesn't confuse you too much.

I almost forgot this. Several years ago, Dana, Ruby, and her husband, John, went to the cemetery where our grandparents are buried. They found there was not a headstone on the graves after all these years. Ruby and Dana pooled their money and shared the cost to have one made and set at their graves. Papa and Mama taught us to share, don't you know?

We used a lot of potatoes at the Usta Place and they were, of course, grown in Mama's garden. They were filling, and our parents needed all they could get to fill all of those little tummies. After boiling potatoes, Mama would save the broth for Meryl Darlene and Gayle. They would eat crackers and the broth like soup. I guess it tasted pretty good, if you are a hungry kid. I can also remember Mama using the water in which the potatoes were boiled in place of some of the milk when making gravy. I still use potato water for gravy, as does my daughter, Sherri.

We thought we were really poor, as we were growing up. But we had plenty of love to share and, of course, our parents had taught us to share what we had, right from wrong, and the difference between no and yes. Most of the time at home it was no! (Just teasing.)

Most, if not all the time, our parents had five children in school at the same time. Can you imagine fixing five dinner buckets? Mama saved the two-pound tin containers that lard came in and let us use them for our lunch pails. We each had our own pail with our name written on it. They were not at all like the lunch buckets today, but they served the purpose.

We didn't have fancy clothes, but our clothing was always clean. Mama had us change out of our school clothes when we got home and we would wear them again. Our "under lovelies" were made out of the flour sacks. After the flour was used up, Mama would wash the sacks and make our undergarments. Now we wore these every day, but for Sunday, we had store bought pink silk ones. Let me tell you right now, we thought we were really dressed up when we wore those. If we had Sunday visitors, we got to change into our Sunday dress-up clothes. Our Sunday outfits lasted quite awhile, because we didn't have much company or get to go very often.

Sometimes we would go to Moundville with Papa and Mama for

groceries. That meant an exciting trip to Ashbaugh's Grocery! Now Papa might have a penny or two for each of us. We would march up to the candy counter and tell the lady we wanted a penny's worth of all kinds. She knew our situation at home, and gave us just that.

It was really a pleasure to get to go to Ashbaugh's with Papa and Mama once in awhile. They would buy what they needed, and we little ones would go stand under the ceiling fan to get cool for just a little while.

I think I was about three when Papa told me he would give me five cents when I learned to tell time. He explained there were five minutes between all the numbers, the short hand was the hour hand, and the long hand was the half-hour hand. He said, "Like something thirty." Can any of you understand how I learned it this way? Me either, but it didn't take me very long. Five cents would buy quite a bit in the late twenties at Ashbaugh's.

We all went barefooted in the summer to save our shoes for winter and school. We wore hand-me-down shoes from the sibling just older when they grew out of them. The one next in line that had the right size foot fell heir to a new pair of shoes. If the soles of the shoes were thin, that meant a new pair of soles from Ashbaugh's or the mail order catalog. Mama would put the shoes on her "shoe last" and tack the soles on. She sometimes had to trim a little off to make them fit, then apply a coat of polish, and we would be steppin' high in our new shoes and were so proud of them. Now children think they have to have eighty-five to ninety-dollar tennis shoes (at least), and I can't see any of them steppin' any taller or straighter.

Our parents and neighbors took turns having dances, sometimes in their homes or maybe in a barn. They would sweep the barn clean and shave a little paraffin all around. This would make the floor nice and slick. In the house, if you were lucky enough to have a rug, it would be rolled back, some paraffin shaved onto the floor, and after a square dance or two the floor was ready for a good time.

Papa would tune his old fiddle and help make music for some of these dances. He taught me to waltz by putting my little feet on his big feet. He would keep time with the music. Now this "big coming out occasion" came about at this particular dance at one of our close neighbors. I guess you could say Helen learned to waltz at the Harry Beisley home. Those were the days when there was so much clean fun. It didn't cost much either. I know you think this sounds boring, but it really was a lot of fun. Some of you young folks should try some of this old-time entertainment.

One time after a dance at our house, I found a dollar bill. That was so much money, I didn't know the value of it. I showed it to Mama. She added some money to it and bought me some overshoes. For all of you that don't know what an overshoe is, it's a rubber high-topped shoe or boot that buckles up the front. You can wade through deep snow and water with them and your feet stay dry. We all needed these since we had to walk two miles each way to school.

My older sisters would see that I was wrapped up in my cap, mittens and scarf before leaving the house for the long walk to school. My cousin, Doris Taylor, told me one of her memories at Totten School was when it was bitter cold and snowing, Pansy would always see to it that she was all bundled up to go home through the cold. Pansy or Ruby made sure I was bundled up, too. Lucky me! I had sisters everywhere. That's what big sister and brothers are supposed to do, I guess.

At recess, Maurice Ripley would grab my stocking cap and I'd have to chase him to get it back. Where were my brothers when I needed them? Beats me! I didn't realize it then, but I guess he was flirting with me. All it did was make me mad at him.

I remember walking to school, and my shoes and socks would sometimes be wet when I got there. (I always liked to wade in water, but not above my knees). My teacher, Miss Hazel Ames, would take me back to the big stove and set me there until I got dried out. What a darlin' she was. I got word recently she had passed away in 1996.

As I am writing, one teacher, Miss Hester (Holman) Boone, is still living. She now lives in El Dorado Springs, Missouri. My sister number five, Pansy, lives in Nevada and says she sees Miss Hester now and then and says she is still very pretty.

I really don't know what kept our "top drawer" parents going with all the hard times and hardship day after day. They had crop failures due to hail, too much or not enough rain, and other bad luck. I guess they decided to keep pulling together. They would rather swim than sink. They did just that.

In all my years in school, I never got into trouble. I had good teachers, and they were so good to me. One day I was whispering and had to stand in the corner for awhile. I shouldn't have been in that corner. I came by that talking naturally. The whole family talks all the time. It used to be when we all got together, you couldn't hear yourself think, much less get a word in edgewise.

My sister, Dana, organized a Totten School reunion in the late eighties. I think around sixty students are still living. The school had closed in 1938, and this would be the first time we had gotten together. Several of us told her we would help her get it organized, and all sixty-five students came to reminisce with their old friends. I was sixty-five and I got the prize for the youngest student at the reunion. Bud Griffiths argued with me that he was younger, just as he did when were kids. He didn't win then, and he didn't win at the reunion either. He was older than me by one year.

A lady who had gone to school with my sisters, Dana, Wilma and Vena, was at our school reunion. She told me when she was a little girl, she wished she could have been one of the Clark girls. Isn't that absolutely fantastic? Just think, we would have had ten girls and three boys. This statement is really quite a compliment. If she had told us this when we were youngsters, we would not have understood why. Now we see she was looking at something we had that she didn't, and it definitely wasn't materials things.

My older sisters worked out and helped Papa and Mama with extra money to buy seed for planting and materials for sewing. Mama made all of our clothes, but taught each of us the art of sewing when we were old enough to help make our own. Can you imagine making dresses for all us girls? She, of course, made clothes for my brothers and Papa, too.

Now days people on low income, and in some cases no income, turn to welfare for help. In the olden days the county had an assistance program called Relief. Now my Mama and Papa never asked for help. They got what they had by the "sweat of their brow." I can remember the people on Relief didn't want it known and would try to hide the fact they were drawing assistance. Papa never applied for any kind of help. If he had a crop failure, he picked up and started over, if there was time to replant.

In some cases, it was too late in the season. With all the flooding, wind, hail and drought, it truly was discouraging. This time came in 1936. There was a crop failure and left our parents with no means of income and no money. Papa couldn't pay the taxes on the farm. Dana was working and earning three dollars a week. She gave Papa money to move to a farm east of Nevada, Missouri. There was some left to buy seed for planting.

This farm, of course, is the one sister Meryl referred to as the Usta Place. I remember we were kind of excited when we moved from the Usta Place, but we were scared and sad also. Mama and Papa had lived there twenty-four years. We kids didn't think we would ever leave the Usta Place and break in a new home. We thought and hoped we would be there until we all grew up and moved to our own place. I still have beautiful memories of that first home where all of us were born, but also have wonderful memories of the other six places where we lived. Yes, Mama had to pack up and move six times from 1936 to 1955. She made that last move alone in 1955, as Papa was gone. She lived at that home until 1970, when our Heavenly Father decided it was time for her to come home and take a rest.

Papa always had pigs for butchering and cows for milk and butter. When we butchered, Mama always saved and used as much of the pig as possible. She made headcheese and pickled the feet. She took the lean pieces of the pork, plus the tenderloin and made sausage. I guess she saved all of it but the squeal, but you wouldn't have heard the squeal around the Usta Place anyway, with all the music and singing going on.

You sure don't buy sausage today that tastes like the recipe Mama used. I haven't a clue how she seasoned it. Her recipe for the sausage wasn't in her recipe book when I got it. I know she ground all this pork and seasoned it to our taste. You could always expect some fresh ham or sausage with gravy after butchering. They saved the fat for rendering for lard. After cleaning the entrails thoroughly, they would be stuffed with her homemade sausage and hung in the smokehouse. Mama would also make cloth casings to pack the sausage in. After filling the casing, they would hang in the smokehouse with the ham and bacon. It was so good! Can't you just imagine having a patty or two of that forbidden food with biscuits and gravy? That's what you call "eating high on the hog," don't you know? Sometimes Mama would fry a bunch of ham and sausages and layer them in separate jars and seal them with hot fat. This would keep all winter. But let's face it, once that jar was opened, the contents didn't last too long.

You could bet your boots it was good while it lasted. Now these jars were placed in our cellar, the same one we used during a cyclone storm. The food was safe there and we were, too. Believe me, I've been down in there a time or two. When they would see that big old dark cloud coming, Papa and Mama would herd all of us kids, Old Buss, and the shoebox of valuables straight to the shelter. We were taught to take cover. At the first flash of lightning and thunder, we were gone.

If I have written this news flash somewhere else, just remember we experienced a lot of events down there. There was always excitement at the Clark house. Sister Margie said she remembers being in the cellar and one or two taller siblings would hand a bottle of Papa's bubbly out of the cellar vent, and there was always a sibling to help out. The bottle would come out the vent, and off to the other side of the barn they would go to sample this beverage. Now I wouldn't have done that, would I? While they were busy on that side of the barn, Herschel and I were probably on the other side rolling a cigarette out of just any kind of weed that was handy. It's true! I don't know where we learned to roll a cigarette, but we must have seen someone do it, don't you know? I was telling my husband, Harley, about the cellar vent with Margie and the other kids. I told him Margie was a sneaky little kid. He said, "She still is." I reminded him that his grandfather had told him that if he couldn't say something good about someone, not to say anything at all. He didn't remember it. I guess you remember what you want to remember. It was so funny, but I guess you would have had to be here to appreciate the conversation.

We stored our milk and butter in the cellar and sometimes hung it in a bucket down in the cistern. Once I accidentally dropped a container of butter in the cistern. Papa got the hook and fished it out. Another time, when Mama let Ruby get the butter up from the well, she accidentally dropped it to the bottom. I guess Ruby lived a thousand deaths, thinking she would be switched. Not! Our Papa got the rope with the four-prong hook on the end and fished around for the jar of butter. Oh, my goodness! That butter was good. When Mama would make fried mush, I would put some of that butter on it. You can't buy that taste anywhere.

The fried mush I mentioned is easy to make and so good to eat. You just mix cornmeal, milk, salt and maybe a little flour together and let it sit overnight. It will set up nicely and can be sliced and fried like a pancake. You serve it with butter and sugar or syrup.

Every now and then, our cistern that held our drinking water had to be cleaned out. Papa had a ladder that would reach to the bottom. After taking a bucket and rope down inside the cistern, he would scoop up a bucket of "stuff." There would always be someone willing to draw the bucket up, dump it, and lower it back down to

Papa for another load. Finally, it got down to where Papa could take a broom and sweep up the junk that had somehow gotten down in the cistern. Even though it was kept covered, debris seemed to creep in and down to the bottom.

None of you reading my story have a clue how much I hated to see Papa down there in that hole. I'm not sure, but I imagine the cistern was about eighteen feet deep and maybe six to eight feet wide. Now keep in mind, I wasn't very old, and I was afraid the walls of the cistern would cave in and bury my Papa. I suppose I was worrying needlessly, but I've always been a worrier. A good part of the time, all it does is make your hair turn white.

Back then we couldn't even imagine having electricity. Right after my sister, Wilma and Oscar Woody, were married, they got electricity and a refrigerator. I loved to go stay all night with them and open the door and just stand there in the cool air. Wilma told me Mama would go to the icebox and pretend to be looking for something. Wilma said she thought Mama was trying to get cool. You can't fool me. I'm sure that is why she was standing there. Cool!

My parents didn't get electricity until about 1945. Mama sold strawberries to make the money to buy a Frigidaire refrigerator. She was so happy and proud. I know of no one who deserved that refrigerator more than my Mama.

I still have the old butter churn and telephone our parents had when they got married. Back then, everyone had a certain series of long and short rings on their telephone, but it would ring in several homes. It was called a party line. The telephone would ring one long and two short rings for our house. If we heard the phone ring someone else, we could pick up the receiver and listen to the conversation. I wouldn't do that, would I? (I was too busy churning the cream into butter.)

When we churned, we took turns on the dasher. One would do one hundred dashes and be tickled pink to turn it over to someone else to do it for awhile. Mama had a butter mold that had an imprint of a cow on top. That was cool, too. The butter with home-baked bread is something you couldn't or wouldn't turn down. Actually, there isn't a word in the dictionary to describe "homemade bread and butter." I'll use "um, um good!"

Mama would bake six or eight loaves of bread every time she was baking. With so many mouths to feed, those didn't last too long. If Mama would let me, I would slice off the heel (first slice) and devour it while it was still warm. Of course, to spread some of Mama's homemade jam, jelly, or homemade butter on it didn't make it taste too shabby either. We always had plenty of her jelly in the pantry. Preserves and honey were plentiful, too. It's no wonder we all grew up healthy and sassy. Once she cut into that loaf of pure fantasy, it wasn't long before I could have the other heel and it would be all gone.

Papa did his plowing (walking plow) and harrowing with horses. He would come in after a hard day's work, so tired he would kick his shoes off and stretch out on the porch to rest before eating supper. Long about that time is when some of the beer he made tasted pretty good to him.

One time he told us he was plowing way down north of the house and plowed up a bull snake. It was so big he was afraid to try to destroy it. If that had been me, I would have unhooked the horses, mounted one and vamoosed out of there in nothing flat. Snakes and I have nothing in common. They may be more afraid of me than me of them, but I doubt it. I certainly hope they are.

Since I started writing this, I was told Papa had a Fordson tractor while at the Usta Place. I don't understand why, but I simply can't remember it. I remember so much from down there that it surprises me that I would forget a tractor. I would imagine I could remember being afraid of it, too. I was afraid of my own shadow, especially if I had "night horses."

Please let me add this little memory here. Up until I was about three years old, I had scary dreams. I called them "night horses." They were mostly about snakes, high water, mad dogs, and sometimes falling off a barn or house. As busy as I was as a little kid, I'm surprised I had time to dream. I would wake up scared silly and shaking. I would run to get in bed with Papa and Mama because I felt I was safe there. Although there wasn't much room in their bed, they made room for one more. You see, there were usually three or four kids already there.

In later years, around 1936, Papa took out a loan and bought a Farmall tractor, and Mama bought a pressure pan to do her canning. It sure saved her and him a lot of "sweat of the brow." You see, Mama had always had to do her canning either open kettle or hot water bath method. This pressure canner cut down on the "hot old time in the kitchen" for Mama.

I must tell you about the chickens and eggs. You know that gross gristle on each side of the egg? I think it's called the Chalaza. Several years ago, Vena, sister number three, told me she takes all that yucky off the egg before she uses it. So does this old girl, as do my children. When my grandchildren started cooking, I believe they started doing it too.

Mama always had old hens for laying the eggs we used. Naturally, if you have old hens, you needed old roosters, too. I just loved to hear them crow. I still do, but not too early. Mama had an incubator heated with a kerosene lamp for hatching baby chicks. I helped mark an X on each egg, and every other day I would help Mama turn them. We were like the two old hens, don't you know? In just a few weeks, we had baby chicks start popping out of their cozy little place, and before long they would be hungry like all other babies. There were just darlin'.

Mama always saved the eggs to sell to help out on groceries. If one of us was feeling poorly, we got to have a treat of a fried egg. It was fried in lard, of course. Now they tell us that eggs and lard aren't good for us. They sure were a treat back then.

I used to go gather eggs, and every time I went to the hen house one or two old hens were sitting on their throne. Since I was afraid of them biting me, I would hold a little board over their heads and reach in under them. I wasn't taking any chances of gettin' chicken bitten. I would always find eggs in their nests.

In all my years, I have never told anyone about this incident, but I feel I should put it in my story. Although I feel guilty, this is a little part of my life and I hated myself for what I did. As I mentioned before, Mama would save up eggs and would hatch them in her incubator. She had a lot of baby chicks hatching at the same time. These chicks were housed in a brooder house, heated with a coal oil lamp, until they were a little older. One time I went inside the brooder house to play with the baby chicks and accidentally stepped on one. Now I was a little tad, but I must have felt as big as a dump truck to that little chick. Naturally, I mashed him. I really don't remember if I told Mama what happened. I would hope she would have known it was an accident, don't you know?

Have you ever seen a hen lay an egg? It is quite a sight! It makes you wonder how anything could taste so good and have so many uses. Mama would sell a hen or two to help on grocery money. It was the job of my sister, Margie, and me to hook the old hens and tie their legs together so they wouldn't vamoose away. It wasn't our favorite thing to do, but someone had to do it, and besides, the sooner we anchored the old hens, the quicker the young chicks got to go to Moundville. Now this was a big time.

Papa would take his drinking water to the field in a glass jug. He would try to keep the water cool by wrapping it in a burlap bag and setting it in the shade. It wasn't like ice water, but if you were thirsty, you didn't think about ice. There was no such thing as a thermos bottle.

When I was real little, about six years old, my baby sister, Meryl Darlene, had to go to the outdoor throne early one morning. Being the big sister that I thought I was, I took her down there. I was carrying her back to the house, since she was so little.

On the way up the hill to the house, I heard a pitiful sound, like moaning, coming from the barnyard. I looked and saw my Papa walking towards the house, with both hands holding his chest. He could hardly walk. I put Meryl Darlene down and ran to the house to tell Mama. In the olden days, you could call a doctor, but we didn't know anything about hospitals. Naturally, I hadn't seen one, but there were several things I hadn't seen, being from the Usta Place, don't you know? Anyway, Old Dick, one of Papa's horses, had kicked him in the ribs.

The doctor came out to the farm, examined Papa, and found several broken ribs. I'm not sure how many. Dr. Carter used adhesive tape to tape around Papa's chest. I suppose that was the only kind they had back then. Now all of you know what adhesive tape can do if you apply it directly to the skin. Papa had to wear this stuff for quite a spell while the ribs healed. Finally, it was time to remove this "tape" bandage. The pain and hurt was unreal. It was just like raw flesh when Dr. Carter peeled it away.

I went through surgery in the mid-sixties, and when Dr. Aldis came to check my sutures, he said, "Who taped you up like this?" I told him, "When all of this was done, I was out like a turned-off light." (Still under anesthesia, don't you know?) He located the nurse and got this squared away fast. You can bet your bottom dollar they had a doctor-nurse talk. Yes, I was allergic to the adhesive tape, and my skin was a mess.

I must jot this little bit of excitement down before I forget, because it was so much fun. If we were lucky enough to get to go to a carnival, my sister number three, Vena, would always be there and pay for our rides on the bumper cars. It was so much fun for just ten cents a ride. This was a rare treat for us, and it was so good of Vena to do this for us. Papa and Mama had taught us to share, and she was doing just that.

While Papa was slaving in the fields, Mama was doing her share also. On wash day Mama would heat some water on the kitchen stove. While the water was heating, she would cook a pot of beans or bake something, trying to save wood, don't you know? She scrubbed the laundry on a washboard, using the lye soap she made. She kept the white clothes white by boiling them in a wash boiler with some bluing added. I don't suppose there was such a thing as bleach in the olden days. If they had bleach, Mama couldn't have bought it. There was no extra money for luxuries.

Naturally, without electricity for a washer and dryer, we hung the clothes outside. That was my job. I liked hanging them outside on the clothesline. If the temperature was zero, they still had to be dried. I would come in and warm my hands, then go out and hang another load. Those were the days.

Mama always insisted that our cotton clothes be starched and ironed. She, of course, made her own starch out of flour and water. After making a paste of the two ingredients, she then added it to a pot of boiling water. When the starch was just right, she would add some cold water. We would then dip the clean clothes in the starch, wring them out, and hang them on the clothesline outside. When they were dry, the clothes still had to be ironed.

Mama had flat irons and would plan to iron and bake bread or a cake the same day to save wood. You could bet your bottom dollar the house was warm on those days. Another use for the flat iron was to heat them at night, wrap them in an old shirt, and take them to bed with us to keep our feet warm. Those hot irons worked pretty good. We didn't have cold feet.

The starch we used on the clothes would always build up on the flat irons. To clean those irons, Mama would have us get a branch off a cedar tree and rub it on the bottom of the iron. I don't know how it worked, but those cedar branches cleaned those irons right up.

If one of us went somewhere, you know we needed to go clean and dry. Mama always taught us to change our underwear if we were leaving the house, in case we were in an accident. This seemed strange then. Know what? I still do.

The only time we had ice water was during the threshing season. Mama bought one or two blocks then so the crew could have iced tea. We had to wrap it in newspaper and burlap bags to keep it from melting. We little ones would go out and sit on it if we dared. Since it was the middle of July, it sure made a nice cool place to sit. That seat was more pleasure than occupying an electric chair, don't you know?

In the middle thirties, sisters Ruby and Pansy graduated from Totten School and, as usual, the commencement was at McKill Chapel. (All of us except Margie, Gayle and Meryl graduated at McKill Chapel.) It was raining, but we had to go. Now Papa had a hard time keeping the 1924 Model T Ford radiator full, so he carried a can of water to fill it up before we started home. He had to make several trips to the well and back to the Ford. Now remember, it was dark and raining. He filled the radiator and we were ready to start home. He had filled the wrong car! Someone else apparently had the same problem with their car radiator. In the dark, they all look alike. He goofed! Someone else got the benefit of a filled radiator when they got ready to leave. I bet they were surprised to find it full. He had a hard time living this one down.

Sometimes this little 1924 jewel wouldn't start, so Papa would jack up the back wheel and crank it. It would usually start when he did this, but if not, two or three of us would shove it down a little ridge and bingo! It worked every time. Papa would drive back up the hill, load all of us back up, and off we would go, probably to Moundville. We little ones would sit on the laps of the bigger children, sometimes three laps deep. We had that 1924 Model T loaded. There were a couple of hills to get over between home and Moundville. If the load was too much for that little darlin' Ford, we would all pile out and help shove the auto to the top. After getting to the top, Papa would reload all of the "pushers" and us little ones (only the big people did the pushing), and we would start down the other side of the hill. He would turn the key off and coast to the bottom. I was a little child, but I remember being afraid it wouldn't start when we got to the bottom. After all, I was anxious to get to Ashbaugh's.

Want to know why he coasted down the hill? He did it to save gas. In the olden days, gas was from ten to fifteen cents a gallon, and he was saving that precious fuel. Now all those pennies, nickels and dimes he could save meant more times we could go to Moundville. Getting to travel to Moundville or anywhere for that matter was a big time. This sounds dull, doesn't it? Those were the good old days.

Now you can talk all you want about the good old days and there were a lot of them, but I wouldn't necessarily want to go back to them. I just want to remember them and I sometimes find myself comparing them with what we are and could have today. The opportunity is there, if we are willing to search and work for it.

You may wonder why a child would worry about the Model T starting. Well, to climb Ben Martin's Hill, he would have that thing wide open and make a run for the climb. Just minutes before we got there, he had jacked up a back wheel and cranked it to get it started. It seems like he pushed the clutch in and turned off the key. When he reached the bottom, he let the clutch out, turned the key back on, and if you were lucky, that little black darlin' would take off and away we would go until we came to the next hill, which wasn't quite as steep.

All of us in the Ed Clark family really enjoyed getting to go places. We loved that little black Model T. Now eventually you had to buy gas for the gas tank and when it came time to "fill 'er up," it wasn't as easy as it is today.

Sometimes when we needed to go to Ashbaugh's, the old Model T would be low on gas or Papa low on cash. He would get Dick and Dock hitched up to the famous grain wagon, and off we would go. It was a little rough, but as the old saying goes, "If you dance, you must pay the fiddler!" (We got to ride in the wagon to school if the weather was really bad.)

In the olden days, the gas was pumped by hand. You would pull into a station and there would be an attendant on duty to fill it up and wipe the windshield. All of this would be done for ten cents a gallon. You had to first unload everyone riding in the front seat. The seat would be lifted up, and there is where you would find the gas tank. The attendant would put the requested amount in or the tank would be filled, if Papa had enough pocket change. They would then load us all up again and away we would go.

If it was raining or cold, we had side curtains that could be snapped on. Of course, you couldn't see out at all with these curtains on. If the weather was right, the curtains were removed and this would be our "air conditioned" ride.

Now, I would love to tell you about the flat tires on that little darlin'. Yes, we had them in the olden days. The tires were a tad bigger than bicycle tires. Papa always carried a jack under the front seat. In those days, we had inner tubes that fit inside the tire. The inner tube was inflated with air, using a hand tire pump that was used manually. That was a big job and I never mastered this one.

Papa bought patching material in a round tin can to patch the inner tube. This rubber material came in the form of a flat sheet, from which Papa would cut a piece to fit the hole in the tire needing to be patched. There was a tube of cement and the top of the lid had a rough surface, which he used to scratch around the hole to "rough-up" the area to be patched. After removing the backing from the cut-out patch, he applied it over the hole and pressed it tight. I just loved to smell this "yucky" cement. Can you imagine that? I always wanted to help, so Papa would let me tear the backing off the patches.

I guess it was a good thing I didn't help with too many tires, don't you know? Oh, my goodness. I felt so grown-up helping him in so many ways. I doubt if he would have ever gotten those jobs finished if I hadn't helped. I suppose I thought the sooner we get the patch on and the tire pumped up, the sooner we would get to go to Ashbaugh's.

Naturally, if you have a car you have to have a battery. This little black Model T was no different. When you had to check the battery, you would have to raise the floorboard in the front seat. This is a strange place for a battery, but that is where it was. Once in awhile those old batteries would wear out and have to be replaced. I wish I could remember what Papa paid for one. You can bet your bottom dollar they were bought for a lot less than now.

I think now you buy a battery and it's a certain price, with a trade-in. Would you be interested in knowing what happened to the worn-out ones at the Usta Place? Papa and Mama took a weekly newspaper. I think it was one from Kansas City. When it came time to renew the subscription, it was sometimes hard to have enough pocket change to pay for it. The paper carrier would take an old car battery or something else lying around the house for a payment. Isn't this incredible? This not only helped Papa financially, but would also help keep the Usta Place neat and clean of junk.

Most of the time Papa and Mama went to town alone. After reading about some of the problems in the last few paragraphs, you can't wonder for very long why they went alone, can you? What Mama and Papa didn't know is that this was a perfect time to take a sample of Mama's shredded coconut. I just loved it and still do. I take a pinch now and then. The seventh sister, Margie, liked to raid the hiding place of the chewing gum. It didn't make any difference how well it was hidden, she was able to follow that sweet fragrance and find it. We weren't allowed to get into stuff, so we had to take advantage of the opportunity and make hay while the sun was shining.

The minute our parents would leave, I would go get Papa's old fiddle and pretend I was playing it. The bow was badly worn, but still had strings. The fiddle was given to my first brother, Herman, after Papa was gone. I offered to buy it from Mama, but no sale. Later I tried to buy it from Herman. Again, there was no sale. He said to me, "After Ma is gone, you can have it, because I don't care anything about it." Well, it was a sad deal. Herman died before Mama. I didn't get the violin, but it was promised to me.

Years ago, Papa and Vernie Davis went duck hunting together. They needed to go over a fence, so Papa laid his single barrel down and climbed over. When Papa started to pick up his gun, it fired and shot the end off his middle, ring, and little finger of his left had. He continued to play this priceless instrument. The accident didn't stop him a bit.

When Papa was playing the violin, it was music to my ears. It really was. The *"Peek-A-Boo Waltz"* was my favorite. Now when I grew up and started working, I bought new strings for the fiddle and new hair for the bow. Papa was so proud. I would come home on weekends and after supper, Papa and I would get in there at the piano and I would chord while he played. Now we are talking hour after hour with our instruments, but he loved to play and was happy to have me accompany him. I got so tired, but this is really a sweet memory. The way he enjoyed this time together, I bet he really looked forward to Saturday nights like I did.

All eleven of us played the pump organ and piano by ear, of course. Ruby got to take violin lessons when she was in high school and played in the senior high orchestra and in the second orchestra. If any of us knew a song, we could play it. It is fantastic how blessed we were with so many things. In reading my story you know what all of these things are.

A few years after the Model T days, Papa, with help from Herman and Dana, bought a blue 1934 four-door DeSota Sedan. It rode like a big boat. I had never been on a ship or boat, but this is what I imagined it would be like.

Dana was working for a family by the name of Strode, close to Ft. Scott, Kansas. She would come home on weekends, and Papa would take her back on Sunday evening. Sometimes Papa would let me ride along, and I would always sit on the left side in the back seat of the car. I wanted to be ready when the motor started because it was a big deal to me. Because I didn't get to go anywhere very often, I knew I better get aboard and not miss a chance to get to go somewhere.

Somewhere along the trail, someone gave me a red hat. I felt rich. I've always loved hats and still do. I guess I wore it all the time; probably even when I was sleeping. When I was a year or two years old, I would put on any cap or hat I saw lying around. It didn't matter if it belonged to a man or woman, I would wear it until the owner wanted it back. I have proof of this hat business. You'll see a picture of me on one of the pages in this book.

I wish hats would come back in style. I'd buy one of every color. I still have the last hat I bought. It is a small black straw hat, the style you could wear anywhere. As a matter of fact, when my son saw it the first time, he asked me if I was going to a fox hunt. I told him I was going to church. Now there is quite a bit of difference between the two.

When we were all little youngins' at the Usta Place, we didn't get to go to church and Sunday School. Our parents taught us right from wrong, and you can bet your bottom dollar I've never forgotten any of it.

As we were getting ready to leave school one evening, my cousin had some words with Miss Hester. As she excused us, Junior Taylor made a sassy statement about her. She asked him to repeat what he said. Instead of answering her, he started out running towards home. About eight or nine children were walking the west road, so we started running with him. We cut across the meadow and just kept running, maybe one-half to three-fourths of a mile. Miss Hester was right behind us. We finally stopped and, needless to say, we had a teacher-student conference right there in the meadow! She then excused us the second time.

For our punishment, because we all ran, we had to stay inside for lunch and recess for a full week. We got to go to the outhouse, but never left the school building for anything else. We ate our lunch at our desk, too. Now here is the big one. We all had to learn the Lord's prayer. We all thought that was a steep punishment. Not! Now you can't even have a prayer before class time. Quite a change, isn't it?

There was a lot of musical talent around the Clark household, and in the yard and up the road. Wherever you would see a Clark, there was singing or you might hear an instrument. If it was inside, you could bet your bottom dollar there would be someone at the pump organ. When I told my second cousin, Lois, about writing my story, she told me she could remember being at her Grandma Etta's house and seeing us Clark kids walking by. Some of us would pretend like we were playing a guitar and the rest would be singing: Tee-Tee Dee Dun, Tee-Tee Dee Da, Dee, Dun, Dun. It sounds like *"How Great Thou Art,"* doesn't it? We may not have had the lyrics down pat, but you could bet your bottom dollar we were carrying a tune without a burlap bag.

Please let me add something else here that is really cool, to me anyway, with all the talent floating around the Usta Place. I found out years after Mama died that she taught our cousin, Blanche Davis, music lessons on the piano. Mama never mentioned this to me. When I was going through Mama's things for her auction, I found the schedule of the time and day the lessons were given at Aunt Etta's house. (This was the same house where I found that great big quarter.)

My sister, Wilma, my nephew, Paul, my niece and her husband, Dean and Donna, went out for Mother's Day lunch one time. Wilma had a sore finger, but said it was getting well. Want to know what she was putting on it? I'll just tell you. Fat meat and turpentine is what she had been using. I guess Wilma remembered using this remedy from the Usta Place.

I could never find out where Mama and Papa found the name Beatrice. Anyway, they hung it on me. A woman in our neighborhood was named Beatrice. She had freckles everywhere you could see any Beatrice. In thumbing back through the pages of our family tree, there was a Beatrice on my Great-grandfather Clark's side. I hope she liked her name as well as I do now. I found out about this relative Beatrice when we had a family tree "grown" by our cousin, Marion Miller. Cool!

At the Usta Place, the only carpet we had in the whole house was located in our parlor and one floor with a linoleum covering. We had throw rugs that Mama made by first braiding strips of scrap fabric. She then sewed them in oval and round shapes. When it was time to wash them, Mama would scrub the throw rugs on the wash board with lye soap and squeeze them by hand. They would then be put on the clothesline to dry. When the big parlor rug got dusty, three or four of us kids would roll it up, carry it outside, drape it over the clothesline, and beat it with a broom or mop handle to get the dust out. While this was being done, one of the other kids would

This is the picture of me standing barefooted on a big tree stump, in a white dress and black hat, with dimpled knees showing. This time it was a man's hat. This picture was taken in front of Aunt Etta Davis' home. You could bet your bottom dollar Mama made that dress. I guess you could have called me a "little blue-eyed, barefooted darlin'. I looked just that. Now here is living proof I loved hats and still do.

scrub the floor real clean and then the rug would be put back down. I guess you could say we were the "Clark Cleaners."

Sister Ruby told me about a precious photo she has and I was going to share it with you, but the quality of the old picture was too poor. Ruby said she thinks of all the Clark photos, this picture makes her more sad than the others. What she was referring to is some of the kids were barefooted and some wearing a jacket or coat. We will never know the answer to that. Maybe it wasn't his or her day for the shoes. Beats me. Those were the days, don't you know?

When we lived at the Usta Place, it seemed like almost every year we had this ritual of hedge tossing between Uncle Tude and our Mama. There was a row of hedge between Mama's garden and his cornfield. When Uncle Tude trimmed hedge, the trimmings were tossed over on Mama's side. Yet today, I think of him as "Rude Tude." Now Aunt Etta wasn't like that. By the way, Aunt Etta made the remark a long time ago, "It's a good thing we don't all think alike. I might not have gotten Tude." She never knew how lucky I felt that we had several choices! He should have burned his hedge mess and not made more work for Mama. Agree? I don't know who won the toss. It might have been a "toss-up."

Now being the hard-working Mama she was, she didn't want that brush on the ends of her fancy peas, beans, onions, and potatoes. Now you must remember she needed those potatoes and onions for soup and my fried potatoes. Who could forget the onions? Not me! Had I been a little taller, I would have been in there fighting for those potatoes, too. Baked, fried, scalloped or mashed potatoes are always welcome here.

When we were little children at the Usta Place, Mama did her best to see that we had the same things as other kids. We didn't have our own room, vanities or certain drawers in which we could put our "under lovelies" and personal belongings. After all, we didn't have enough room like other families, but we needed a place of our own to keep our pretties. Being the thoughtful loving mama she was, she started to do what all mamas would do.

She got her saw, hammer and nails and started to work. She took two strips of lumber about two feet long and fourteen inches tall and made sides for a box. She cut out two pieces for the ends. I guess she used scrap lumber to close the bottom and for the lids. Of course, there were hinges that fastened the lid on. There was a screen door hook to hold the lid closed. Now for the finishing touch. The boxes needed a little paint, don't you know? There were too many boxes to paint them all, so some were left plain old boxes. My box was red, (perhaps to match the red lips I got from drinking my five-cent bottle of strawberry pop at Ashbaugh's), and now I had a place of my own. We shoved our boxes under our bed, so we could keep watchful eye on it. After all, we had sisters and brothers around there that might be nosy. (Not me.)

I wonder how many of you remember going into a big store and there not being a cash register or scanner to make your change? Way back yonder in the olden days, I remember going into a big store with Mama to get an item we could not get at Ashbaugh's. I would stay right there by Mama, afraid I'd get lost if I didn't. You see, Moore's, in Nevada, was a huge store, with a second floor. I had never seen anything like it. It seemed as though I was in another world. When Mama bought something, the sales clerk would write down the purchase price of the merchandise, put it and the money in a small container, like a long cup, and attach it to a lid that was stationary on an electric cable. This cable was strung upward to the second floor where the store's office was located. She then pulled a lever that would then start the cup upward to the second floor. As a child, I could never understand what kept that cup from falling off. Perhaps this outfit was in a groove? Anyway, the lady in the office would make the change, put it and the sales slip in the metal cup, reattach it in the ring holder, and this was let slide back down to the sales lady. Guess what? The change and sales slip were in there. Isn't this absolutely confusing? It was then, for a little girl like me.

I was so little, it's hard to imagine I can remember these beautiful memories. After we finished at Moore's, we would come back to the Model T. We would have to cross the street at the southwest corner of the square. Since we were just a little tads, Mama would take our hands so we would be safe crossing. We didn't have mittens and I can remember in the cold weather, Mama's hand would feel so warm.

When we would start back to the old T-Ford, we would pass a coffee store called Buckners. I can't remember if they had groceries, but I certainly remember the aroma of all the coffees coming from the front door. I just loved to walk past the entrance and smell the aroma of the coffee. Mama would occasionally stop and get a pound of coffee for eighteen cents. They would grind it fresh right there in the store.

When Mama would trade and spend just so much at Moore's, she would get a gift called "a doll box." This was given in appreciation for shopping at their store. The box was white, about 14x8x4 inches. She never knew what the contents of the box would be. There would be eight or nine items like shoelaces, soap, a thimble, needles, bias tape, a pair of socks or gloves, a comb or tweezers. Quite often there would be a celluloid "cupie" doll, which would usually end up on one of the Clark clan pie boxes and taken to a pie supper.

When Totten School had the pie supper, I imagine there were at least five beautifully decorated boxes filled with a lot of goodies, brought from the Usta Place to be sold. The auctioneer did just that. No wonder District #83 was in trouble in 1936, when the Usta Place youngins' and Papa and Mama had to leave the Usta Place in search of greener pastures.

I guess you could say they were a tad greener just east of Nevada, but it just seemed like lean times followed us every mile of the way. You can bet your bottom dollar they made the best of what they had to work with every one of those miles.

When I was about seven or so, I went to Nevada with my sister, Wilma, and her husband, Oscar. We were in Scott's Five and Ten Cent Store on the south side of the square. I asked Wilma for ten cents to buy a small red comb for my hair, not realizing it was a hardship for her. She searched her pocketbook and finally found a dime so I could buy the comb. I was so proud of it. Money was also real scarce at the Woody ranch, but I didn't know it. I wish I still had the comb.

Now this is changing the subject completely, but I must write this new flash. After Papa, Mama and all of us "wee ones" moved from the Usta Place, Papa started milking more cows. That meant more chores for all of us. He bought a cream separator. Now all of you who have lived on a farm know it's a big job to turn one of those machines, and also a big job to wash and dry it. Guess who got to turn the handle? I've spent a lot of my growing-up years turning handles on cream separators and grindstones. They were hard jobs, but jobs needing to be done. I looked at it like this. Even though I was only twelve years old, I was helping Papa and Mama earn a living. The older sisters and brothers helped so much in other ways, helping with the big people's work.

No matter how hard or bad circumstances sometimes get, you can always find happiness. Want to know where? In the dictionary, of course! Cute, huh?

When we enrolled in Stanton School, east of Nevada, Missouri, we found out that there were so many people who were poor people besides the Clark family. I remember one family in particular who suffered some lean years. After all, we were in a depression. They had four or five children, and one little girl was very ill. I can remember when it was time for lunch at school, all that these children had in their lunch box was one-half of a grapefruit. They were on a government program called Relief, like welfare now, but it surely didn't go far enough.

This little daughter died shortly after we moved there. The school was dismissed for the funeral. They had a graveside service and the little casket was opened. The wind was blowing and moving her little blonde curls. Now I wasn't but twelve or thirteen years old, and the death and funeral of that little girl bothered me so much. I couldn't understand how and why someone could die so young. This precious little girl was about three, I suppose.

We had about thirty students at the Stanton School. It was quite an adjustment to change schools. It was at this same school where I met my first love, who gave me a picture of himself. Elmer, a red-haired freckled-face boy, was so cute, but he had a temper. He made me mad for some reason one day, so I tore up his picture in so many pieces it would take longer than recess to paste it back together. I never found out because I didn't have any intention of doing just that. That was the last of Elmer. I wonder if he remembers me? I bet he does.

Margie and I were singing together in those days. When it was time for a pie supper, we were supposed to sing on the program. There were two more students, who were brother and sister, who also sang. She played the guitar, Hawaiian style. After the pie supper was over, things were going pretty well. Bingo! Miss Frances and the Clark kids had a meeting. Now mind you, Papa and Mama always told us kids not to start fights, but to always stand up for our morals, standards, and what we believed in. We did just that.

Well, this meeting was held. Miss Frances said she was told that Margie and I had said that she, Miss Frances, had used the pie supper money to buy a fur coat. What a lie! Guess what? Alice and Bob had told the lie and told our teacher we had said it. She believed them. (I think their dad was on the school board.) Things were never quite the same with our teacher and us, and definitely not with Alice and Bob. They had lied, big time!

As it turned out, our parents believed us, but I can't remember for sure if they went to school to straighten out the mess. I do remember when it came time for the last day school program, our precious Mama told all four of us, Margie, Gayle, Meryl and me, that if we didn't want to be in the program, we didn't have to. That suited us all just fine. Our parents stood behind us and that is all that mattered, don't you know? I give our parents a lot of credit for what we are today. Papa and Mama taught us good morals, standards and good old-fashioned values.

I really must tell you a little more about this Bob I mentioned. He, for his size, was a little "bully." He would try to fight anyone who was a little shorter than he was, which weren't too many. Now Stanton was a good school, with a lot of good kids, and Miss Frances was a good teacher. I was thirteen going on thirty and I felt pretty brave. I felt I needed to take care of sisters seven, eight and nine: Margie, Gayle and Meryl Darlene.

One day during our break for lunch, Bobby was being a bully, hitting and pushing Margie. As I said, I was older and realized I needed to step in and help her. I punched Bobby in the nose, and the blood started running clear down to below his chin. He said, "I'm going to tell Miss Frances!" I made a simple reply of, "If you do, I'll hit you harder next time!" Guess what. He didn't tell. He also kept his hands off my little sisters after that. I guess you could call me "the champ of 1937" at Stanton School!

My first experience with a radio was down at Harry Beisley's house, our good friend. They had an old Philco. I was so young and back-woodsy, I thought you could turn the radio on and turn to whatever music you wanted to hear. Remember, this was the Usta Place days. I told Herman to turn on to "*Somebody Loves You.*" You see, this is the first song I learned to play on the organ. Papa and Mama finally got a radio later that we ran on a car battery. My, that's been a long time ago.

Nothing went to waste at the Usta Place. There were seldom any leftovers, but if there were any, they were saved and a little more of the same thing was cooked to make more servings for the next meal (like gravy, potatoes or soup). Mama just could not afford to waste any food.

If you haven't already read about Mama making her own soap, you will. When the cakes of soap got too small, Mama would put them in a can of some kind and when there was enough, a little water was added to them and they were melted to make a liquid soap. The liquid would then be used in the laundry water. Mama had to skimp and save to make ends meet. I would imagine some of you can identify with all of these precious years that we shared at the Usta Place. Am I right?

I'd like to go back to the olden days for right now. I've heard several times we had it rough and they were the good old days, but I don't ever want to go back to them. Well, we all had it rough back in those lean years. I haven't forgotten them, but my goodness, we had so much to be thankful for. Our Papa and Mama made do with what they had available, and they didn't miss what they had never had. We were just rich and didn't know it then.

Our Papa loved his five-cent (yes, I said five-cent) cigars. He was a saver also. When this cigar got down short enough that it was a little hot to the lips, he put the little "stub" in his smoking pipe and salvaged the rest. He really enjoyed his old pipe. I still like the aroma of a good cigar — outside of course.

We always lived on a farm, either owned or rented. Papa rented a small place close to Pawnee Station, Kansas. It was a very friendly neighborhood with a lot of young people and a two-room schoolhouse. We had pie suppers, picnics, ball games and church parties. Nothing was too wild in those days, but we all had lots of fun.

Sometimes at these gatherings we would have two or three games of Chinese checkers going at the same time. There was this young lady who loved to play and played to win. If she saw she was going to get beat, she would "accidentally" shake the board. Some people will do what it takes to come out ahead. She tried.

She had a beautiful sister. This sister didn't like games and didn't like to participate in them. Want to know what her big hang-up was? I'll tell you. She would sneak around and try to find someone doing what he or she shouldn't be doing and then could hardly wait to go "tattle" to anyone that would listen. She liked to cause trouble. I think you call someone like that a troublemaker. I wonder what happened to Corine? Remember I said she was beautiful? Well, her little hang-up really ruined her outer beauty.

A close friend and I were at one of these pie suppers one time, standing up along the wall of the schoolhouse. (I believe it was the same one that I was voted the most popular young lady.) We were nodding our heads and talking with our hands, don't you know? Before I knew it, I had bought a pie box. I had brought one, you see, to be sold and shared with someone, so I sure didn't need to buy another! When I bought the pie box at the pie supper auction, everyone had a good laugh. It sort of embarrassed me, but I laughed right along with the rest. I've been told I talk plenty, and I guess that last story proved it's always been true. You must keep in mind that while I like to talk, I'm also a good listener.

We were at another pie supper and program when we lived at Nevada, Missouri. I was about eleven or twelve, and being the show-off I am, my teacher wanted me to sing on the program. She played the piano and I sang *"The Skater's Waltz."* It would have been fun if it could have been taped back then so I could hear how I sounded. There's no doubt I gave my very best.

I was sitting here this morning thinking about winter starting and how I'll miss all our flowers and the green plants growing. We don't have as many birds in the winter either, but then we don't have bugs, flies and snakes.

It reminded me of when my brother, Herschel, and I were little and we climbed trees a lot. (Now I get dizzy if I get up on a ladder to wash windows.) Anyway, we were playing in the front yard at the Usta Place and saw a huge black snake crawl into a big hole in the fork of a tree we had climbed dozens of times. We ran and told Mama about seeing the snake crawl into the hole. Now when she saw a critter that might endanger one of us little ones, that critter was dead meat.

I bet you are wondering how she got that snake out of the hole. Mama heated some water real hot, and I believe brother Herman (he was taller) poured the water in the hole. The snake came out of that hole real quick! Mama was waiting down below with her garden hoe. If that snake had known Mama was waiting on him, maybe he wouldn't have been quite so quick to respond to the hot water. Either way, that snake was done, and this is the end of the snake story. Snakes and I don't hang out at all, don't you know!

There were so many things that we Clark children didn't have. One of the items we didn't have then that is really considered a necessity now was a toothbrush and toothpaste. Mama had us take a piece of cloth with baking soda on it and wipe our teeth. We would sometimes use salt instead of soda. (Now they have baking soda toothpaste.) Our method must have done some good. I'm seventy-three years old and I still have pretty good teeth. I don't even have dentures.

I wonder how many of you who are reading my story remember when you lost your first tooth. I remember just getting used to one vacancy and bingo, another would start to wiggle back and forth. The teeth were so little, but when I lost one, there was quite a space. I looked like a baby jack-o-lantern.

When the little "chopper" got loose enough, Papa took a piece of twine string, made a loop, slipped it around the tooth, and worked it back and forth. If he thought your mind wasn't on the loose tooth, a little jerk would usually do the trick. I had a little blood, but you would have thought I was dying.

We didn't know about the tooth fairy. If there was ever one around the Usta Place, you could bet your bottom dollar or the evidence of the tooth fairy money, she didn't knock on any door at our house, night or day.

Now days, children have been taught to expect a good-size piece of pocket change under their pillow. Then after these little ones grow up and have the keeper teeth, then comes the dentist office, with cleaning, check-ups, etc. You have to dig below the belt for another big piece of pocket change. You just can't win!

CHAPTER 3

AS CHILDREN GROWING UP in a family without much income, our toys and gifts were homemade. Papa took spoke rims from wagon wheels and made a paddle. We would use the paddle to shove the rim forward. We called this precious toy "my hoop and paddle." Sometimes we would push our hoops the two miles to school.

At Christmas, we might get three or four pieces of candy. "Santa" chose licorice, chocolate mounds or ribbon candy. If he had enough, we each got a peppermint stick. You can bet your bottom dollar each item was dropped in those stockings with all kinds of love, don't you know? Usually, there would also be a small gift in our stocking from Santa.

On this one particular Christmas, I woke up and heard paper sacks crackling. I thought that at last I would get to see Santa Claus. Surprise! What a surprise! I wasn't hurt or disappointed. There was a sock for each of us on the table. Mama was as busy as a little bee trying to finish before Christmas morning. This is true love.

Papa or Mama would chop a limb from a cedar tree in our yard, anchor it in a bucket of rocks and tie it securely in the corner of our living room. All of our decorations were homemade. We popped popcorn and strung it to make decorations for our tree. We also colored strips of tablet paper, separated them and pasted them in a circle to make a ring chain for our tree.

When I was a little girl, we started getting excited about four nights before Santa Claus was due. Oh, my goodness! Those last four days seemed longer than the last two months. Seemed like it would never get there. We had to hurry and get to bed, but who could sleep knowing the little old man in the red and white suit would be slipping down the chimney this night? (It certainly was a puzzle to me how Santa came down our chimney without getting covered with soot.) If one ever needed a sleeping pill, that would have been the night. Those definitely were the days.

Suddenly the night turned into Christmas day and we all headed for that row of stockings (all sizes) that were filled by who else but Santa. You can bet your bottom dollar each item was dropped in those stockings with all kinds of love.

One year Margie got a toy stove, and the same year I got a china tea set with little orange flowers. Mama made me a little wooden cabinet to put my dishes in. The cabinet was purple and had a piece of purple floral cloth hung on the front. It was so neat!

When we left the Usta Place, Papa rented the farm near Nevada known as the Fleshman place. Each Christmas, Mr. Fleshman brought a big basket of fruit (apples, oranges, bananas) and candy for the family. They knew we were poor and noticed that there were eight kids still living at home.

Our gifts were items that were useful and needed, but sometimes gifts that were questionable. Herschel would always wrap up the pepper shaker and put my name on it. I always liked pepper on most everything I ate. Every year, someone would get a corncob all wrapped up in red or green paper. We never found out just who the guilty giver was, and we didn't know just which one would get the cob until it was unwrapping time. However, we all made it okay and looked forward to having a delicious dinner later.

Mama would start early planning the menu for Christmas day. Besides the traditional baked chicken or hen and homemade noodles, the menu would usually be mashed potatoes, gravy, dressing, rice pudding, pumpkin pie and the famous fruitcake. Delicious it was! Mama was really a good cook, but she had lots of practice.

We would wait patiently for Mama's famous fruitcake. Now let me tell you about this fruitcake. It took priority over everything else. Mama would start about three weeks early and bake this beautiful cake. After cooling it down, she wrapped it in cheesecloth and a tea towel. It stayed in the big wooden box until time to slice. In this time period, she would brush the cake with a little "bubbly." You talk about yummy. I never did know just where she kept that bottle. It sure wasn't in sight. I'll tell you right now, there wasn't any of that cake left over.

Sometimes coming home from town, Mama would be kind of hungry, so she would mash some banana and spread some on a cracker. Gayle, Meryl and Margie couldn't understand why she liked this snack. It could have been it was the only snack handy at the time.

As I mentioned a couple of times, money was so scarce during this time that it became an issue. Mama tried in every nick and cranny to save wherever she could save. If she didn't try to save here, there and everywhere, it meant there would be a shortage of food. She couldn't and wouldn't have that.

Here is another of the many ways she made the most of what she had. After the Christmas gifts were unwrapped, the paper and ribbons were saved. After the holiday, she would press the paper and store it away to be used next year. I still have one piece of paper with holly design and two bows that were on two of my gifts years ago.

As I grew up, with a home and children of my own, I found it hard not to save all this stuff, too. Know what? I pressed our paper for several years. Sherri, my daughter, says she remembers me showing her how to press the wrapping paper and ribbon after the gifts were unwrapped at Christmas and put it away for next year. It was just part of the clean-up job. My children and grandchildren teased me about doing it, and I felt guilty for being so conservative. Know what? They are also saving bows, boxes and the best of the paper now. We have some tags we have used for eighteen to twenty years for the grandchildren and some we used for our children longer than that. When Marcus and Trenton, my grandsons, unwrap their gifts, they leave the tags with "granny" (that's me), to be used again and again.

All of us Clark kids were all so happy Christmas morning. After all, we got to go to our hanging stocking. We didn't expect a lot like children do now. I suppose we didn't know that some families got a lot more material things. I'm sure there was love and sharing in the other families, but I know for a fact that in ours there was plenty of just that to go around and be shared.

Just think, if Mama could have had just a portion of what we have now, she would have made it go so much further. You can bet your bottom dollar we spend way more for gifts now than we ever thought of back then. But, oh my goodness, how we loved everything we got on Christmas day.

You will notice that so far in my story I haven't mentioned birthdays. You will not hear about birthday parties, cakes, candles, balloons, cards or gifts. There wasn't money for birthdays, and it was a full-blown struggle to get through Christmas. There is no doubt in my mind, Mama would have done something for our birthday if she could have. There were just so many of us, she couldn't do for all, so she didn't do for any.

I just wonder how many people, like me, get depressed through the holidays. I know it's supposed to be a joyous time, but I feel really sad, and I really believe that thinking about the Usta Place years, plus the Christmas music all combined, makes me dread the holidays just a little. Isn't that just far out?

I would love to write this post-script here. Have you heard the saying "cheaper by the dozen"? Dana, sister number one, said, "They aren't cheaper by the dozen." She would know, and I'm sure Mama and Papa figured that out somewhere along the line, too.

In 1934 we were still students at Totten School. During the Christmas program or shortly before, Cousin Blanche Davis carried two packages into the schoolhouse. We never dreamed they would be for us. There was a beautiful doll in each package. One was for my sister, Margie, and the other one was for me. I named my doll Billy Ray, and if I wanted to dress her like a girl, she was Mona Marlene. I still have Mona. She has on a dress and is much older and in played-with condition, but as beautiful as she was then. (She is stuffed with "excelsior.")

I remember so many times and places from way back in the olden days. One thing I can remember is eating from a tablecloth every day. Mama had an oil tablecloth, and the top of the table was always covered. This type of tablecloth was wiped clean with a damp cloth and didn't need ironing, don't you know?

When Sunday or threshing time came, Mama would put a linen cloth on the table. That thing sure was hard to do up, but someone had to do it. We used flat irons, and it would take three or four to finish the job. I'd bet my bottom dollar today the hungry threshing men didn't even notice what was under all those mouth-watering dishes. You can believe there weren't enough leftovers for our sup-

This picture of the Clark family was taken at the Usta Place. As far as I know, it is the only picture we have of the entire Clark family together. Left to right, back row: Herschel, Wilma, Herman. Middle row: Vena, Pansy, Ruby, Dana. Front row: Mama, Meryl, Gayle, Margie, Helen, Papa.

per. Mama would sometimes have to cook for the threshers two days. The men worked hard and worked up a hearty appetite.

I wonder how many of you remember in the olden days the men ate first when we cooked big family dinners and the meal was ready. This always puzzled me. The ladies would slave over the coals or flame and worked really hard to prepare those really famous dishes. I just imagine they worked up an appetite, too. I just never did figure out why it was this way. As I grew up and had the family get-togethers, the tradition continued. I guess that was one of my pet peeves. Somewhere along the line, we ladies finally got this little problem taken care of. (At least in our family, we did.)

I have a bushel of pet peeves. If you don't mind, I would like to mention a couple of them. You may find we share the same view. When you go through the check-out line at the supermarket, nine times out of ten those who pay by check wait until it is all totaled to start writing out their check. This causes me to have to wait on these people longer than if they had it all done, except for the dollar amount. It throws the checkers behind, too. Another pet peeve is for people to spit "hocky" on the sidewalk or parking lot. Besides being unsightly, it's very ill mannered and unsanitary. I get just plain "huffy" if I experience it, but I keep smiling and go on.

CHAPTER 4

AS I SAID BEFORE, Papa and Mama were married way back in 1911. Of course, I wasn't here then, but I've heard them and a lot of other people say times were rough and managing finances didn't take long. Want to know why? Well, what little "dab" they had needed to go for food and clothes, and when all of us came along, it didn't get any better. There wasn't much income, but you could bet your bottom dollar what they had was spent wisely.

We were getting ready to leave for school one morning. I was just six years old, but I remember this day, December 11, 1931, like it was yesterday. Dana and Wilma made the lunch buckets that morning for us and bundled me up for school. I knew something was going on, but was just too little to know what.

We started back into the living room and saw our precious Mama walking behind the stove to the bedroom to get back into bed. She had both hands cradling her body, trying to be brave. I was so little, but I knew she was in pain. Now you can bet your bottom dollar, if I had been a little older, I would have helped her.

School was long that day, longer than usual. Finally, we were excused and we didn't waste any time walking home. I was worried about Mama, not knowing what was wrong. Guess what! I had a new baby sister, Meryl Darlene Clark, number twelve of the Clark siblings, when I got home! She was so tiny. Mama let me lie down beside her, just for a little bit. After all, I might hurt her, me being so big and grown-up, don't you know? Do you suppose this is why Meryl Darlene and I love each other so much and I miss her when she is so far away?

Now, Papa and Mama had another helper to replant corn and pick beans, strawberries and blackberries. This would be when she got bigger, so it would be a little while.

Sister number five, Pansy, told me when she was born, Mama tried to nurse her, but the milk didn't agree with her. She became under-nourished and frail. Mama couldn't find any canned milk that agreed with her and thought she was going to die. Pansy was so near death, Mama had her little white dress and stockings all laid out ready for her burial. Well, they wouldn't give up. They decided they didn't have any thing to lose but Pansy, so Papa got milk from our family cow, Babe, and started her on it. That milk must have been just what she needed, because she started getting better and gaining some weight. She had pneumonia three times while she was a very young child.

There is another good reason to be thankful for all the medicines we have available for our illnesses now. Haven't we come a long way? Thank God for the lift!

Looking back, now that I'm older, how did they keep up their faith and courage? I'll throw in sanity with the rest. With all the hardship, worries and doing without, I believe it would have been easy to give up. With all the little mouths open and ready to eat, they just couldn't give up.

The folks didn't have a paycheck. They raised a whole lot of what they ate. I don't suppose they really knew when the depression started. They were living those years back in the teens. I wasn't born then, but I've heard them talking about it. Things started looking up in the late forties and early fifties. By then, there were just the two of them living on the farm.

Hey, don't you suppose they were pretty lonesome by then, after having so many little ones running around in red hats, no shoes or hand-me-down shoes, white beads, and all colors of homemade dresses? Of course, the handsome little boys would be in overalls.

While visiting with Patty, my niece, she told me her mother and dad, Dana and Earl Winter, had a big date on April 23, 1935, when they attended Pansy's graduation. Pansy graduated at McKill Chapel, as did eleven of the Ed Clark children. Shoot! Since we spent a good part of our time coming and going, we should have just moved there. Then they had another big date on June 13, 1935, and went to a movie show. Do you want to know the name of the show? It was *"Two Heads on a Pillow."* I would bet my bottom dollar you would have liked this one.

There was always something to be done at the Usta Place. There were the kerosene lamps to be filled with kerosene, chimneys to wash outside, wood, kindling and corncobs to bring in for the cook and heating stoves. I really didn't mind any of it, but I had a hard time splitting a chunk of wood. I would carry in the cobs and kindling to start the fires. I was pretty good at starting the fire, but I never had to put one out.

Hold on to your dentures! When I was five or six years old, I asked Papa the biggest question of them all. I asked him, "If Jesus' last name is Christ, is God's last name damn?" You know somewhere I must have heard some language I should not have.

Like I have written in the first part of my story, I was very close to Papa. We liked the same foods, except fat meat and frosting. I could write his name like he signed it. Because we were so close, we had a very special relationship.

I kept all my grade cards for years. Somewhere along the way, they got lost. Speaking of grade cards, I even signed mine a few times. Have any of you ever done this? Papa had so many to sign, he probably didn't miss this little girl's card. While we were bringing these cards to be signed, we were busy going to Nevada to attend the country chorus. This was when I was about eight or nine years old, and one of our big times was when the chorus was held and we would all get to sing. Several schools would be there to sing together. We sang in "rounds," with three groups singing at the same time. The most popular one was "Row, row, row your boat, gently down the stream. Merrily, merrily, merrily, merrily, life is but a dream." This sounds boring now, but it was a big time then. We sounded real nice when we all got in gear. After all, we didn't have too much invested.

With all the "have-to" jobs Mama had to finish, she always seemed to have time for flowers. I don't remember too many houseplants, but there probably wasn't any room inside the house for them. She had peonies, roses, morning glories and marigolds in her flower garden outside.

When Papa got the ground ready, it was then time for Mama to start planting. They had saved seed from tomatoes the year before. They would plant them about the last of March in buckets and keep them inside the house. By the first of May, they were big enough to set outside. Later in the summer, when those plants produced ripe, red and juicy tomatoes, they sure tasted good. I guess this is one of the ways we survived the Usta Place days. We had plenty of good food and a lot of faith and hard work.

In her garden at the Usta Place, Mama had dill, garlic, winter onions and a huge strawberry patch just west of the house. I don't actually remember how big her garden was, but I do remember it seemed really big. Even with everyone picking, it seemed like we would just finish picking, start to leave the patch, and there were ripe berries right there where we started out. Those berries seemed to ripen faster than us little Clark pickers could pick. I loved to eat those strawberries right out of the patch. This patch was on a slanted side of the field, so the berries and vines were nice and clean.

One of the vegetables Mama had in her garden that I remember well was cabbage. She used the cabbage to make sauerkraut. After making the kraut, she would put it in a big stone jar in the Usta Place cellar. If we were lucky, it lasted all winter. We always had this canned kraut, potatoes and lots of home canned fruits and vegetables to get us through the winter. Believe me, it took a lot of food, and our parents prepared for it. Oh, yes, they always had turnips, too. My, they were good!

Not long ago, I cooked a big pot of turnips. Before I started cooking them, we had called Harley's brother, Ray, to chat awhile. I asked him if he had ever cooked turnips. He said, "I sure have." He told me that you cook them until tender, set them on the back of the stove to cool, and then throw them out to the hogs! I guess he doesn't care for turnips.

Papa hauled corn to Waco, Missouri, to have it ground for cornmeal. He also grew cane for molasses. When it came time to harvest the cane, we all pitched in and helped Papa strip the blades and load the stems on a sled. It was then hauled to the Les Woody farm. With Mr. Woody's vat, his old horse and three or four bosses (Clark kids), Papa came home with some good stuff. There is nothing like a bit of molasses right out of the vat.

Papa loved to work with his bees. I believe he had three or four hives. When it came time to rob the bees, he used a smoker and a screen mask. As far as I know, he was never stung. We little ones liked to chew the honeycomb, but Papa always left plenty of honey in the hives for the bees to last all winter. Of course, the next summer the bees would start work again.

There wasn't any way we would go hungry. For instance, when Papa butchered, Mama would grind up all the lean meat, season it, and fry most of it in patties. These were layered in a big stone jar and covered with hot drippings. She would then cover it with a towel tied tightly and store it for winter use. This was carried into the cellar to stay cool with the other winter food. Then when the winter months came, she would take out a platter of the patties, heat them and make gravy. If you didn't have an appetite right then, you would have one right away, with the delicious aroma coming from the Usta Place kitchen.

Please let me insert this news flash! Since Herschel was my little playmate, we did little things together that all little boys and girls like to do. Well, little girls make mud pies and things like that. We climbed apple trees and robbed the birds' nests to get eggs. We had to have eggs in our pies, don't you know?

During the real lean years (teens, twenties, and thirties), if there were all kinds of medicine for each ache or pain, Papa wouldn't have had the money to take each of us little Clarks to the doctor's office for treatment. When one of us would get over an illness, another one would come down with it, then another and another. Besides the expense to see the doctor, think of all the gas it would take. (Gas varied in price from fifteen to eighteen cents a gallon.)

Mama would get out the coal oil, Vicks and turpentine and grease our chests. Now if we were bad enough, out would come the onions for the traditional onion poultice. Papa would be there to help doctor us, too. He mixed in a little turpentine, sugar and water, and we would gargle with the mixture. I had a hard time learning to gargle, for that stuff tasted so bad. Sometimes you were sicker than before gargling, but we eventually got well.

I'm not really sure how Papa paid the doctor when all of us little ones arrived into this old world. Some people paid with a dozen eggs, an old hen, or maybe a sack of turnips or potatoes. The doctor would have to buy these items anyway, so it just saved him a trip to Ashbaugh's.

Those were the days. I find myself thinking more about them as I have gotten older. I'm not sure I would want to exchange times; however, we had a lot going for us back then. We have more financially now, but this just makes you want more. At the Usta Place we had trust, honesty, good neighbors, and a handshake was as true as a man's word. If you shake on an agreement now, I have to admit you might wonder how long the handshake would last.

Our parents didn't have very much furniture. They had an oblong table in the kitchen. Papa made a bench that would seat about five of us. The rest of us had to sit in chairs. They were nothing fancy, but they served their purpose. I remember the old wooden folding bed that had to unfold twice and would sleep about three. I believe the three oldest girls, Dana, Wilma and Vena, got to sleep in this neat bed. I slept in one like all the rest of the clan, clean and warm. I couldn't ask for any more than that.

We, at this time, didn't have a clue of the luxuries just waiting for all of us in the coming years. Getting electricity and plenty of water to drink and use was certainly a blessing and made living a lot easier.

In the middle thirties, we had to pick up pecans to earn extra money for groceries. Papa would climb a tree and with a mallet would shake them down. We would pick them up like crazy so we would have plenty to crack and pick out that evening. When we got in the full day of picking, we would head for home to get supper over and start picking out the nuts. Two or three of us would start supper, one or two would help with outside chores, and one would be on the handle of the squirrel pecan cracker that Dana had bought for Papa and Mama. He or she would have enough of the nuts cracked for us to start picking out after the dishes were done. I usually helped with the pecans, because I was never impressed with dirty dishes. (I'm still not.) I don't know how many pounds we would pick out each night, but we all hung in there and helped get the job done.

When it came time to haul the pecan meats to town, they were sold to a candy store. Now, I'll tell you right now that this was the best part of this job. Does seven cents sound like enough pay for a big job like this? I didn't think so either. It was a big job, but someone had to do it, don't you know? I still love to pick out pecans and walnuts.

My second cousins, Doris and Junior Taylor, were everyday playmates of Herschel and me. They lived with their aunt and Granny Etta. We were playing one afternoon and I found a quarter. (In those days, it was like a small jackpot). Anyway, my Aunt Etta took the quarter and decided to divide it among us. She gave Junior and Doris ten cents each and gave me five cents. That little experience never seemed quite fair. What do you think?

Papa and Mama and all of us children, of course, did a lot of fishing in our creek at the Usta Place. Sometimes we got supper over early, and everyone who wanted to fish would grab a pole and head for the water. Once in a while, this precious little creek would flood and our crops would be threatened. Anyway, some of us would carry the old lantern so we could stay after dark. If they were going to fish all night, we would take a tub, probably our round galvanized one, to keep the fish alive until the next morning. We would then take our catch to the house and dress them. It was lots of fun and lots of good eating, if we had fisherman's luck and the big ones didn't get away.

One day, when we were all down there at the fishing spot, a large tree had fallen and this made a good playground for all of us who were afraid of worms or too young to land the big ones. Pansy, Ruby and I were playing on the tree, and somehow I fell to the ground and hurt my tiny little back. I was afraid that Papa or Mama would switch me for being where I shouldn't have been, so I told them Ruby and Pansy pushed me. Needless to say, it upset our fishing party, and Papa carried me about a mile or so to the house. (I bet it seemed like five to Papa, having to tote me all that distance.) I don't think my sisters got in trouble. If so, dear sisters, I'm sorry about seventy years late. Seventy years too late!

Now I don't know for sure just how it happened, but around 1931, I went to Nevada with Papa and none of the other children went along. When I think about why I was the only one to get to go, it really boggles my mind. While in Nevada, we ran into Uncle Jimmy Whiteside and his daughter, Norma. Uncle Jimmy had bought Norma a hollow chocolate bunny that was about twelve to sixteen inches tall and cost twenty-five cents. I asked Papa for twenty-five cents to buy one. He searched all his pockets, but didn't have a quarter. I just wanted a rabbit and didn't realize it would embarrass him. I was just a little girl and wasn't aware of it being a problem for him, don't you know?

Well, Uncle Jimmy reached into his pocket, pulled out a quarter and gave it to me. I got the chocolate rabbit and when we got home, I broke it up in pieces and shared with all my brothers and sisters and Papa and Mama. The bunny didn't go very far with all those little mouths ready for bites. This is one of my favorite childhood memories.

Down at the Usta Place, Papa did his own horse-shoeing. Being so little and naive, it puzzled me how the horses could stand so still while Papa tacked the shoes on. I know now. I've seen and learned a lot of things since then. Some good, some not so good, don't you know?

Papa had a mare named "Old Molly." We had her at the Usta Place, and she would let all of us ride her. Because she was so gentle, she was a nice riding mare. One day our neighbor, Fred Currier, said he saw a bolt of lightning with three tails strike. One tail struck in a field east of our house, one struck our house, and the other struck Molly, killing her. We were so scared. Papa and our brothers were away baling hay, so we were the bosses and caretakers of our home. We imagined hearing crackling up in the attic for weeks!

We didn't lack food, clothing or a warm place to sleep, but there was something we little girls at the Usta Place lacked. One was knowledge of the things little girls, beginning to grow up, need to know. Mama was busy doing all of her chores, and I suppose there wasn't time left to prepare us for what they now call "becoming a woman."

When I got to this age, around ten I guess, sister number four, Ruby, got me out alone one day and explained all of it to me. She didn't leave anything out. As a matter of fact, she told me more than I wanted to hear. I just couldn't imagine having to go through this every month.

When that awful time arrived for me, being the big girl I was, thought I was ready. Not! Ruby helped me make the famous belt and the procedure of tearing old rags to make a pad, which was held in place with a safety pin. Now if they had sanitary belts and napkins in those days, we didn't have the choice of one or the other. We made our pads from scratch, don't you know?

Well, we weren't blessed with a basket of rags, so when we had to change pads, they weren't thrown away. We had to wash, dry them and use them again and again. What a time that was. I remember seeing the rags hanging on the clothesline, long before I made my debut, but I thought nothing about what they were for. Boy, was I in for a big awakening!

As you have guessed by now, I grew up very timid and shy. Well, I was very modest, too. When I did my laundry, I dried my valuables by spreading them out flat on top of my wooden box under by bed. (You remember the wooden box Mama made for each of us to keep our things in?) Eventually, they would get dry and I would fold them so they could be used again the next month. Those were the days. The only good thing I can think of about this whole ordeal is when you worry about that big white bird with a long beak making a sudden stop!

Many years later after I had grown up and had a daughter of my own, I prepared her for the things little girls need to know. I explained to Sherri that it would take place each month and what to expect. She said, "Mom, you mean this is going happen every month? I'm not sure I'm going to like that." Cute? I believe the school had a film on this subject when she was in the sixth grade, but since she developed at an early age, we had already had our talk long before then.

In the early forties, we lived in a neighborhood close to Pawnee Station, Kansas. There was a two-room schoolhouse that we went to. Gayle and Meryl, my two youngest sisters, attended school there. Meryl reminded me recently that she, Gayle and Margie used to sing at Pawnee socials. They sang *"Pretty Kitty Blue Eyes"* and *"Surrey With the Fringe On Top,"* among many others. Estelle Keeney played the piano for them.

For any of you who don't know what a pie supper is, I'll tell you. We would have a pie supper to raise extra money for the school to have picnics and wiener roasts. All the young ladies would fix a box of fruit, sandwiches and two pieces of pie for a nice supper. The boxes were all decorated with crepe paper, just any color, cupie dolls on top, with pretty color bows to make them beautiful.

At this particular pie supper, they had a box of chocolates for the most popular young woman. Two young ladies, both named Helen, were nominated. It cost one cent for each vote. Her father, brother and boyfriend spent their pennies on their Helen. My Papa, brother and boyfriend spent all their pennies on this Helen. I can remember the chocolates brought $24.50. I bet you are wondering who won the contest. Well, I'll tell you this, the chocolates were delicious, especially the ones with the maple centers. I still favor the maple middles. Papa, Hubert and I ate the whole box at the pie supper. Afterward, Hubert told me he made up his mind his Helen was going to have that candy.

When I was dating Hubert, it was getting pretty icy this particular night and I was waiting on him to come pick me up. Papa bet me $2 he wouldn't come. I took Papa's bet and I lost. Actually, it was a good thing, because it really was getting bad outside. You see, back then he couldn't just call me and let me know he wasn't going to come, because we didn't have telephones like today.

At the Sunny Slope pie supper, Dar Johnson and I got a tiny "potty" for the couple who would most likely get married. People would nominate a boy and a girl for the contest, and everyone would vote for the ones they wanted. I guess it was Dar. He had a twin brother Dare Johnson. I hadn't ever dated either one of them, but we somehow got nominated that night and won. Guess we proved them wrong, but it was just a game anyway.

A little while after that, I worked for a short time at Ben Franklin store in Ft. Scott. For a good part of the time, I was behind the candy counter. How did I get so lucky? While I was working at Ben Franklin, a customer came in and purchased an item for one dollar. He gave me a ten-dollar bill and I gave him his change for the ten dollars. He said, "I gave you a twenty." I said, "Sir, you gave me a ten-dollar bill. I'll call my manager." I said, "Mr. Waite, would you come here for a minute, please?" I told him about the customer problem. We checked my register. Know what? My register was right on the money. Now he didn't have a gun, but he was trying to rob the store. I suppose he thought I was a "green horn." You can bet your bottom dollar, he didn't pull that trick with this popular young lady again.

Getting back to pie suppers, when we went to them at Totten School, it seemed like every year a certain young man, Merle, would always buy three or four of the boxes, but was always too drunk to eat with anyone. My box was usually one of them. You see, I wanted Harold William (Bud) to buy mine, so I would tell him how it was decorated and the colors. He was about my age, and besides, I wanted someone sober. It didn't always work out my way.

When Miss Hazel was teaching, her father, John Ames, would buy six or eight boxes and give them to the young boys or men who didn't have a lot of money. He was not only helping them, but was helping Miss Hazel to make money for the pie supper.

It was a real big deal to get to ring the big bell at the Totten School. Our teacher always let us take turns. I wasn't very big, so it was a tad heavy for me. When it was my turn, I always gave it all I had because I wanted to do it as well as the big kids.

One time at school, we were outside playing and Herschel decided he would raise a block of cement that was a well covering. We never used the old well, so he was curious as to what it had inside. He found out! He got the block up about a foot or so, and Miss Hester said, "There are snakes in there and one is coming out!" Well, Herschel did what came natural. He dropped the block, and a corner of it landed on his big toe, splitting the toe in half. Miss Hester and one of the students, I think Junior Taylor, lifted the block and freed Herschel. Let me tell you right now, there was one sick lad. Someone ran to the closest neighbor, Jack Hope, who came and got Herschel and took him to Moundville. He then went to tell our parents, who took care of everything. Let me tell you right here, we were never to go near that well again. No one wanted to.

As I said, we never used that old well. We had drinking water from a well just outside the schoolhouse. There was a hand pump that was all boxed in. You had to turn the handle clockwise to bring up the water.

Every morning a bucket of water was drawn from the well and brought inside for drinking water. It seems we all used the same water dipper for drinking. A little later, tin drinking cups were provided. I suppose our teacher thought this would be more sanitary.

I remember Miss Hester (Holman) Boone asked all of the parents to get their children a cake of soap and towel for hand washing. I imagine all of the little Clarks used the same one. We used the same one at home, don't you know?

When we moved from the Usta Place in 1936, that meant Papa took at least five students a year out of the District #83. Well, you can guess what happened. Know what? Our precious old one-room school just lasted two years after that and closed in 1938. Without the well known "Clark Clan," there weren't enough kids in District #83 to support a school. You see, we really were valuable and important. We didn't realize it then.

It was a sad day for all the students who were still going to school there because they left the old school and were transferred to Moundville and Bronaugh, Missouri. That old schoolhouse burned down in 1995, I believe. It makes me sad to think about it not being there.

I remember the day Papa and Mama left the Usta Place and moved east of Nevada. Papa had a new team of horses named Ribbon and Blondie, some baby colts and a mule colt. I bet those babies got tired walking, don't you? Meryl Darlene told me that she, Gayle and Herman rode in the rumble seat of Wilma and Oscar's two-door Ford when we left for our new home.

At the Usta Place, we little ones never had a real sled, so Papa pulled us in the snow in a big grain scoop shovel. He also made us a swing with a rope and an old tire. Now those were fun times for the

Clark clan. Of course, the fun times were after chores were done.

There were several of us to swing on the old tire, so Papa made a second swing. He took a burlap bag, filled it two-thirds full of straw and tied it in the same manner. Before long, you could look out and see a yard full of "swinging sisters" and brothers. We had good trees in our front yard, and they made for some nice swings for us to play on.

I wish Mama could have had a porch swing, but then she probably wouldn't have had time to swing in it. She didn't have much leisure time, but she could have enjoyed it while cutting or peeling vegetables or maybe while embroidering. I'm sure it was cooler on the porch than in the kitchen. I do remember seeing her sitting on the steps of the porch paring her vegetables.

One summer Papa's brother, Uncle Bill, and his wife, Aunt Minnie, came to visit us during the hottest part of the summer. Mama had to cook extra food and was probably expecting another baby. Aunt Minnie complained about it being too hot to cook and went outside to sit under the shade trees, while Mama slaved over the hot stove. To me that didn't seem quite like it should be.

I believe Uncle Bill worked in a dress factory or knew someone who did. He brought a box of quilt scraps for Mama. The pieces were stacked five inches tall, for there had been two dozen dresses cut out all at once. I think I still have one of Mama's quilts with one of those pieces in it.

I still don't know how Mama held up the way she did. It would be a real big task to try it today with a family the size of ours, even with electricity, gas and indoor plumbing.

I can remember when the ground was extremely dry and we would experience dust storms. I especially remember when we were living east of Nevada, Missouri, the ground being dry and a lot of it had been plowed. When the wind would blow hard, the dust would start flying. A big storm would come from the southwest, and you could see it coming about a mile or so away. The dust was so thick, it was like a cloud on the ground and you couldn't see more than a half block. The dust was so thick it blocked the sunlight and would make everything feel gritty.

When I was around six years old, still living at the Usta Place, my older siblings met a young man who owned and flew his own air ship. Yes, I said air ship. It was a two-seater, carrying the pilot and one passenger. Although Clyde O'Bannon didn't do this for free, he did take people for rides. I don't know how much he charged for these trips, but I do know that sister Wilma got to ride once. Her future husband paid for her to get to go. She really enjoyed seeing the country below from above. She said they flew over the Usta Place. I said, "You mean, like the Clarks' nest?"

I'd almost bet my bottom dollar, if I was a betting lady, this was the first and only time any of the Clark clan ever "looked down" on the Usta Place. You see, we as a family didn't look down on our home even when we weren't flying above it. We were just a big happy, healthy bunch, happy as could be to have a roof over our heads, even if it did leak. When it did, Papa, being the man of the house, got the ladder, climbed up on the roof, and would patch where the roof was leaking. He didn't want us to be wet and cold.

Getting back to Clyde O'Bannon and his little flying machine. He would land in a field where he would be able to take off easily. I never got close enough to hear the price of the ride. I remember being afraid of that noisy thing. After all, I was only four or five years old. Like I said before in my story, we didn't get out and away from the house much, so we weren't used to planes, fast cars and bright lights. When anything like these showed up, we little ones always tried to stay clear of them because it might mean danger. We never knew how the other half lived and we didn't care too much. We were taught we should stay away from things, and we did just that. We were taught the danger of everything, and I guess you could say Papa and Mama kept us pretty well sheltered. I suppose that's okay, but maybe too tight isn't good either.

That little flying machine couldn't even be compared to what we have in the air today, you know, the ones that seat two or three hundred people. Those would make Clyde's little two-seater look like a plaything. I reckon it was just that! We've come a long way since. If someone back then would have told us we would be going places fast and doing the things we do now, we might have thought, "get real."

Once in a while, I will take a rest and get a cup of decaf or a Pepsi and park in front of the television for a few minutes and watch Oprah. This rest is usually every day during the time her show is on. One day awhile back, I flipped the remote, and it just happened a band was playing *"America."* You can bet your bottom dollar this brought back a memory or two.

At our old Totten School, we sang from a soft-cover yellow

songbook with "Favorite Songs" on the front of it. At the beginning of every school day, our teacher and all the students repeated the Pledge of Allegiance and sometimes the Lord's Prayer. Every morning we sang "*America.*" I told you earlier in my story how I learned the Lord's Prayer. It was a good thing I learned it, so I could say it with all the other students.

I got along pretty well in all the games we played at noon and recess. I liked English, spelling, arithmetic and history. Geography I did not like. I did pretty good learning the multiplication tables. Some of the games we played were "red light," softball, and "fox and geese." The big people wouldn't let me play ball because I was too little, couldn't seem to hit or catch the ball, and couldn't run very fast. I guess that's why Maurice grabbed my stocking cap. He wanted to tease me and get me to chase him.

I can understand now why they didn't want a little whippersnapper like me on the diamond. I didn't understand then why they wouldn't let me play with them. I didn't know how they expected me to learn if I had to sit on the ground all the time and just watch. (In the olden days we didn't have benches.) I wonder if the older kids at Totten were glad when Papa and Mama moved us little Clark kids out of the way? I doubt it very much, since the school had to close after we moved.

Once again in the thirties, we had all kinds of dances. There were dances that were held in houses and there were barn dances. Once there was a big platform that would take care of about four squares at once. They did just that. This fun place was built on the southeast corner of the state line road, as you are leaving Garland, Kansas. There was a concession stand and plenty of dancing. This place was called "The Green Parrot."

One Saturday night, we were getting ready to go. I was little, but as I was taking care of myself, I lifted the teakettle to pour my bath water. Somehow, I spilled hot water on one of my feet. Ouch! It didn't keep me home, but I didn't get to waltz with my Papa because I couldn't wear a shoe on one foot.

The year following our move to Nevada, Papa, Herman and Herschel were all in bed with pneumonia. On February 10, 1937, my brother, Herschel, died at home of pneumonia. I remember this night distinctly. Dr. Wray had told Mama the night before that brother Herschel wasn't going to make it. You see, Herschel had been really bad a while earlier and, being an energetic child, got out too soon and took a setback.

When I woke up the next morning, he was breathing hard, gasping for life. He was put on morphine for pain, as his precious life started slowing fading, and finally it was over. As I said before, I was only twelve and had lost my brother. This was my first encounter with a death of someone so close. I had lost my playmate and hunting buddy.

I went in and lay across the bed and cried and cried. I needed someone to hold me and explain why I had to give up my brother at such a young age. Mama was at the bedside of Papa and another brother, Herman, for all three of them were bedfast with pneumonia at the same time.

Of course, Mama contacted the funeral home to start arrangements for Herschel's services. When Mr. Ferry, the mortician, came to our home, he noticed that I was alone back in a bedroom, crying myself sick. I was sitting on the side of an old folding bed when he came in. I needed to be comforted, but no one was there to do it. Mr. Ferry felt so sorry for all of us. He had been around this type of sickness and death, so he knew I needed someone. He sat down beside me, put both arms around me to comfort me. You see, there were three children younger, and Ruby and Pansy weren't much older than I was. He could see someone had to take care of all of us little ones and he volunteered for the job.

I remember feeling secure when he held me. He let me know that someone cared and he was so sorry that my little playmate was taken away so unexpectedly. From that day on, I started growing up. I knew that all of us would have to do the outside chores and housework, because Mama was being doctor to Papa and Herman.

In the olden days, when someone died, the body was kept at home until the services were held. I couldn't stop crying and didn't go to Herschel's funeral, because I was afraid people would laugh at me for crying.

Dr. Wray knew Papa was failing fast and told him, "Mr. Clark, you have lost one son, another one critical and you are very sick. You have to get in there and fight. You have to live. You have small children in there. Mrs. Clark and the children need you. You must get well!" Papa was very ill, but thank God, he recovered. We all know God had other plans for Papa, so he healed him that year.

Old Buss, our dog, knew there was something wrong going on

and stayed on the front porch for several days after Herschel died, just lying there. After all, he had lost his hunting buddy and was missing Herschel.

When they all got sick, the onion poultices were made and the Vicks, turpentine and tea were gotten out of the cabinet. This was all Mama needed to help them get well. When this illness hit our home, it meant Mama would be the nurse and doctor. Dr. Wray from Nevada helped some. Pansy and Margie took care of the house with the help of Gayle and Meryl Darlene. Ruby and I did the outdoor chores. We fed the hogs, cattle, chickens and horses. We got wood for stoves. Now this job was not my favorite thing to do. It was a tough job, but someone had to do it. What a terrible experience we endured, but we all pitched in and with God's help, we made it.

Earl Winter got the news of the illness at the Clark home. There he came with two twenty-five-pound bags of onions. You can bet your second bottom dollar, there was someone starting to peel onions for a poultice right away. Now I am going to tell you right here, those onion bags work. I've used them myself a time or two, and I've made it to 73 years old, so far.

A good neighbor, Raymond Griffiths, told me at the first school reunion the coldest day he ever lived was the day he dug Herschel's grave. Back in the olden days, men volunteered to dig the graves for friends and neighbors. Raymond was definitely a good friend and neighbor.

I recently learned that Mama and Papa didn't have the money to buy a headstone for Herschel's grave. Mama started saving her nickels so she could buy one for him. I don't know exactly when she was able to get it, but she did finally save enough to purchase the headstone.

When I was little, twelve years old or so, I thought I wanted to grow up and marry a truck driver. I liked big trucks with tall racks, the kind you could haul cows, pigs and lots of hay. (Looking back now, I should have had my baby blues set on the owner of the freight being hauled on those big trucks.)

Long about 1939, I graduated from the eighth grade at age 14. My teacher then was another Helen, Miss Gordon. She was an exceptionally nice person, too. I not only had good teachers, they were always kind to me. One of them told me recently that as a child I was very shy. Can you imagine me being shy?

As I was saying, I had to get ready for my big night. Like all

other young ladies, I wanted to look nice. Ordinarily, Mama would have made my dress as fancy as she could because this night was very special. Know what? Because it was so special, sister number three, Vena, who was working for the Fred Thompson family in Bronaugh, bought me a new dress for my big night. It was blue with three-quarter-length puffed sleeves. It was so beautiful. The dress cost $1.98 and I believe it came from Chicago Mail Order. (Does anyone remember that one?) Of course, back then that might have been a week's wages. I don't remember having a new or hand-me-down store-bought dress before. I consented to Margie setting my hair for my special night. She set it the Shirley Temple style (long curls). Margie had gotten a new dress from Vena, too. It was a fun time. The school purchased each of the girls graduating a pink rose corsage. Anyway, in my new store-bought dress, my rose corsage, and my hair fixed so pretty, if there had been a beauty contest that night, I would have won, hands down!

That winter, Vena bought Pansy and Ruby boots and tablets for school. What would all of us little ones have done if the older sisters hadn't helped Papa and Mama financially, when they started working for pay! I had such a beautiful family. Every last one of them was always anxious to share and do anything to help the others. Our dear parents taught us to share a long time ago.

After I graduated from the eighth grade, I wasn't too anxious to go to high school. I really hope you won't laugh at the reasons for my lack of interest. I thought all of the other girls in high school were prettier, had nicer clothes, would be smarter and would make fun of me. This is one of the reasons I didn't want to go on. Another reason is that our parents had moved to a farm that was about two and a half miles from the bus stop. It seemed like our parents didn't encourage any of us kids to go on to school. I suppose money was the biggest factor.

In 1939, when I finished my last year of school, I was more interested in sewing and learning to cook. I started getting my "hope chest" ready, just in case some handsome young man came along who wanted to talk with Papa. I see now that I should have tried some way to go to high school, but like I said before, my parents just didn't have the means to help. I didn't want to make it any harder on them. As the years cruised by, my three youngest sisters, Margie, Gayle and Meryl Darlene, finished eight years, and by this time Papa and Mama had moved again to a farm that was only about half a mile from the bus stop. Our parents were starting to see a little daylight by then and that helped. Gayle and Meryl Darlene worked in the school cafeteria to pay for school lunches. This helped to make it cheaper for Mama and Papa.

I suppose some of you are wondering why I didn't find a job in town and work my way through. Well, Mama wasn't the kind of a mama who would let a fourteen-year-old girl go live in town. She kept a tight rein on all of us. It was out of the question.

Since I had to be sixteen to work in the public, I did housework for some people and cared for some people in their homes. When I was about fourteen, Mama let me go stay with a lady who had just had a baby. These people weren't real rich, but they had enough to get by pretty well. Their cupboards were full of everything. I had never seen anything like it before. I remember this was the first time I got to taste mayonnaise. My, but it was delicious! I'd get a spoon and dip into it when I wanted a bite. Now isn't that strange? Mama never had anything like that. We had plenty of homemade spreads, but this was really good.

Papa and Mama and the last four of us little ones were still living on the same farm real close to where this lady with the new baby lived. I finished the job there, and immediately an elderly man asked Papa and Mama if I would come and work for him and his wife. Margaret was such a lovely lady, but she was very ill with cancer and he also needed help with the house and taking care of her. Margie, sister number seven, and I took turns staying with them. I would stay two weeks, and then Margie would take over and give me a rest.

Well, let me say right here I wasn't much of a cook yet, but Fritz Klockson liked and ate everything I cooked. He loved fried potatoes, beans and soup, so he never went hungry. Margaret practically lived on juice. We always had toast for breakfast, and this old man would dip his toast in his coffee, then eat that "soppy" bread. That's where I learned to "dip." I guess it was bad manners, so Fritz told me not to tell my parents where I learned to do this. I guess he thought they would think he was teaching me bad table manners. Shoot, I didn't see any harm in it. People without teeth sure wouldn't have any trouble eating it. Anyway, too bad if it is bad manners.

Margie and I slept upstairs, and about halfway to the top there were about three or four shelves built in the wall. An urn sat on the third shelf, and like any nosy kids we looked inside. We thought it was a flowerpot, but I suppose it was someone's ashes. They didn't say and we didn't ask. We were so young and naive, and we never had a clue it might be a loved one's ashes.

You learn a lot with age and some of us learn something every day. Now when I was a lot younger than I am now, I thought I knew just about everything. As the years passed by, I found I didn't know everything and, as a matter of fact, I found out I had a lot more to learn.

At one of our school reunions, I displayed a lot of old school pictures of Totten School students and teachers. Now here is the grand finale. I showed all of my classmates my pink pressed rose the school had bought for me the night I graduated from eighth grade. Honest! So I'm a pack rat and I still don't throw anything out. That's why my house looks like it's the maid's day off.

I hope you will let me write this little bit of news. It's such a cute story. At one of the school reunions, each student was asked to tell a joke. I didn't know many jokes, but I did know a cute one that I had clipped from a magazine a long time ago. Here it is. Two little mice appeared in Heaven. St. Peter asked them how they were getting along. They said "Fine, but Heaven is so big, we are having a hard time getting around." So St. Peter gave each of them a pair of roller skates. The next day a couple of big black cats appeared in Heaven. St. Peter asked them how they were getting along. They replied, "Heaven is really a big beautiful place, but we especially love your meals on wheels." Poor little mice! However, I could easily get along without them!

I imagine most of us have done some little and big things that we shouldn't have. Herschel and I were coming home from Totten School one day. Having been in school all day long and ready for something to eat, we stopped and picked up an apple for each of us. This man, Marion Kendall, told us to get out and let his apples be. A great big part of this apple story is the tree wasn't his. It grew on the shoulder of the public road, close to his fence line, but still not on his property. Do you suppose he could have enjoyed all those apples later? Or do you suppose he could have gotten a tummy ache for being so selfish of two apples, which weren't his anyway? I felt sorry for him because Papa and Mama had taught us to share.

I must add this to my story. Mama was funny at times. She would crack a joke and never smile at it. If someone pulled a joke on her, she would say, "You big ike." I don't know where she came up with that, would you?

I know most of you have heard "kids say or do the darndest things." Well, kids, after they grow up a little, still do some of the darndest things, even worse. When brother Herman was still living at home and dating, he went with some of the neighbor girls and most of them had a brother my age. I was too young (said Mama) to start dating. Herman was seven years older, so Mama thought it would be all right for me to go to church with big brother. Not! Boy, was Mama in for a big surprise! Big brother didn't want me tagging along, so I would leave the house with Herman. He would drop me off at a house where this boy, his sister and her boyfriend would be waiting for me. We would go car riding. Now, to keep this all looking legitimate, we would meet Herman at a specified corner about a half-mile from home. I would then get back in the car with Herman and, of course, go on home with him. We had quite a system worked out. I was about fifteen, but Mama thought I was too young to date.

Years later, I told Mama about this system Herman and I had. Do you want to know her reply? She said, "You big ike!" Papa would have said, "That's uphill business."

I may have told you this before, but if so, please forgive me. I like to go down to the Usta Place and just walk around where we used to work and play and where the garden grew. It brings back so many memories. I can still almost hear the laughter of my sisters. It seems I can hear Mama calling us to come set the table for supper. I can even almost hear the old organ. My memories of the Usta Place are so vivid it doesn't seem possible that it has been so many years.

Papa had a mowing machine to go over the yard at the Usta Place. There were more weeds than grass, so that meant stubs. Now if we ran through there barefooted it sure was hard on our feet. You can bet your bottom dollar we would find a new route next time. Those big weeds left a stub up out of the ground, stiff as a nail. Sometimes if you stepped just right, that stub would go into your foot. Now it hurt terribly bad at the time and would stay sore for quite awhile. Out came the fat meat and turpentine and bandage. It didn't stop you though. You had to keep going.

Ruby, sister number four, was telling me when she was a little one coming home from school one day, the boys were showing off. (They were bad about that). The boys walked together and the girls walked a little ways ahead of them. The boys had killed a big black snake and thought they would scare the girls. They started running to catch up with the girls to throw the snake onto them. Naturally the girls ran from the boys. Ruby said she knew she couldn't outrun them, so she and some of the others cut across a field. There was a barbwire fence across the path instead of a gate. Some of the girls ducked under the fence, but Ruby didn't see it in time. She ran right into the fence, cutting her chin and mouth. It scared the boys so much they threw the snake away and stopped chasing the girls. They behaved themselves for awhile after that.

Dana told me about the time that she and the other older sisters had to do field work because there weren't any boys yet to help Papa. He got three daughters, then a son. Can you imagine finally getting a "free" field hand after waiting all those years?

Since Dana was the first one, she fell heir to all of these jobs. She hitched horses to a cultivator and would go a half-mile to cultivate corn. Now down at the Usta Place, you started early and stayed late. Wages were the same, no matter how many hours you put in. Dana helped, as did all of the other children, in stripping cane. We were all taught to pitch in and get the work done. She mentioned pulling the sulky rake to rake hay to the baler, then hauled the baled hay to the barn loft.

Those days were before my time, but Dana said she and Papa were bringing a load of hay to the barn, with Papa driving the team. (I got pretty good driving horses when I helped Papa shuck corn. He should have had little me out there). Anyway, Dana was on top of the load at the back of the hay frame. They started to cross a ditch, and the weight of the load caused the front of the hay frame to give.

Papa and some hay ended up on top of the team, Dick and Dock. I guess she grabbed hold of a limb and hung on, then eased herself to the ground. Papa ended down between the horses covered with hay. The next time he saw Dana, she was in front of the horses trying to get them settled. I just wonder what kept them from being badly hurt. Maybe someone up higher than Dana atop that load of hay was watching over both of them, don't you know?

First one thing, then something else. Papa told me once that one of his neighbors at the Usta Place bought a bushel of seed corn from him and, as far as I know, the person never did pay Papa for it. He had promised to pay at the end of the week. I won't call him a man, because anyone that would do this to someone doesn't deserve to be called a man. I'd rather it be this person owing Papa than Papa selling bad corn. If that corn didn't yield big, maybe this person was getting overtime for his deeds. It seemed like Papa was left holding the bag (no pun intended) so many times. Yet today, some of the grandchildren are still big farmers. I guess you would say our Papa helped them get started. It always seemed when Papa's pigs or cattle were ready to sell, the price was always down, and he needed the money yesterday. Just seemed like he couldn't win for losing.

Speaking of hogs, I remember when the mamas-to-be pigs were getting ready to farrow, it seemed to always to be at night. Papa got the old kerosene lantern, some cloths and heated rocks and headed for the barn. You see, the babies needed to be kept warm, and these heated rocks were placed between these little "porkies" to keep them cozy and warm. The mama was busy having babies, one right after the other. It kept Papa busy helping her. Sometimes the sow might have twelve to fifteen, sometimes more or less. There was always a "runt" that needed to be cared for.

Our Papa loved to play with and take care of his livestock. When the pigs got a little older, he would take a stick and scratch them on the back. Sometimes he would have them so relaxed they would be practically lying on the ground. I would say "Ed had the touch!" He called all of his baby colts jackies, the little calves bolivers. Please don't ask me why, but I suppose he had a good reason.

Papa used to have a five-dollar gold piece. Through the years, somewhere along the trail, it disappeared. Do you suppose he at one time got into some hard times and had to use it? Maybe some "con" came by and borrowed it, promising to pay him back? Beats me! I really doubt if anyone needed it more than my Papa.

Seems like Papa and Mama always had chores to do at the Usta Place. If it wasn't farming, there were tree stumps to dig out. Since dynamite was a little easier, he used it. It would scare me half to death when it went off. I guess I was a little coward in a lot of ways.

Sometimes when he would be working away from the house, I would ask Mama if I could take him a cool drink of water. This one afternoon she had told me I could, so I headed down to where he was plowing. I was walking along in the furrow and stopped a minute to rest. I looked back and there was a snake right behind me. I started running to get to Papa. When I turned around again, that snake was right there. I was probably around six or so. I didn't know what a blue racer looked like and I still don't. I suppose they are blue and they move right along. I don't know what kind of snake this one was, but I was sure glad to get to where I was headed. I stayed with Papa the rest of the day just in case that critter was still somewhere waiting for me out there.

Know what? Papa let me drive the team to the house. I did pretty good with that team as long as they weren't hitched to a wagon or plow. After all, if I was big enough to carry water a half-mile, I was surely big enough to drive a little old team of horses. Don't you think so?

As I mentioned a way back in my story, we didn't go out much, but I imagine we made every minute count when we did leave the house. Vena, sister number three, was working in Bronaugh, Missouri, for Mr. Thompson. She bought gifts for us little tads at home. I loved nail polish then and still do. She had bought some and brought it home with her one weekend. She painted my nails. Back then, nail polish was a thicker consistency. You put on one coat and when it dried, you could peel it off. Well, this polish did just that. When my polish started to peel off, I thought I was losing my fingernails. I'm not teasing. This is what I really believed.

You may have noticed as you have been reading my story that we seemed a little "back woodsy." At the time though, we really didn't know that we would be classified that way. We lived close to the timber at the end of the road, very close to a big creek. Aunt Etta's house was the only one between the Usta Place and our mailbox. I never measured how far it was to our mailbox, even though I walked it several times over an eight to ten-year period, but I suppose it was a half-mile to a mile.

When we saw a wagon and team or maybe headlights at night

on a Model T coming west down the slope, they had to be coming to the Ed Clark house. Now remember, not too many people traveled that road, so when we saw someone coming, we little ones would go somewhere to hide. I guess we were afraid of our shadows. I suppose we were afraid of a lot of things. Any little shadows I saw were probably just another sister or brother running along beside me. I always had lots of company around the house, but not many strangers.

The razor strap was one of those things I was afraid of. Once in awhile, Papa would use it to sharpen his straight-edge razor, what it was actually meant for. It was always right there ready to be used for something else. That something else was, well, you know. I actually think the razor strap is more famous for being used for spankings than it is for sharpening razors.

Brother Herman nicknamed me "Freckles." It used to make me so angry when Herman called me that name. I knew better than to attack him, because I wasn't tall enough to beat him up. If I had tried, I would probably have had some help from Papa. He took care of and watched out for me.

It seems like I keep jumping back to the Usta Place, but you must remember there were several of us and a lot was going on down there. I was a little tike, but I was right in the middle of a lot of it, good and bad.

When sister number two, Wilma, was dating Oscar, he would bring her flowers when coming to pick her up. Some of the younger children would meet him out at the car and carry them inside. I'm sure he intended to get to hand them to her himself, but being the kind of person he was, he let the little ones help. There's not a doubt in my mind that one of the younger ones was sister number nine. Figure it out! I've always loved flowers and Oscar, too, so I just wanted to help out.

When the older ones would be taking pictures, I would go get between Oscar and Wilma to have my picture taken. She probably still has them. She doesn't throw anything away either. I used to love to go to Wilma's house, especially when the peaches were ripe. They had and sold bushels of them and other fruits and vegetables. They tasted so good. I can still almost taste them. They also had an apricot tree that was a nice place to visit. Everything tastes better when you go to the garden, orchard or barn to get it. I believe they sold peaches for fifty or seventy-five cents a bushel.

It may seem to all of you that I'm bragging a lot about our parents. Well, I guess they were the best. As I said previously, they were "top drawer." Just like Vena had written in her poem, "The Best Parents Any Kid Ever Had." She couldn't have described them any more clearly. They could have been referred to as "King and Queen." The only difference is that there weren't any jewels, servants, velvet robes or tiaras. What they had, though, were hearts of gold. In my eyes, they would have passed the test and they had my vote.

Ruby and I were talking recently about the time some of the children played a joke on Papa. He was feeding the cattle at the barn. One of the children yelled at him and told him someone wanted to talk to him on the telephone. Naturally, he came to the house. He answered, not noticing the kids were giggling behind him. He kept saying, "Hello, hello"! He thought there was something wrong with the receiver. We told him it was an April fool's joke. He looked at all of us sort of angrily, and not saying a word to anyone he turned and went back to the barn. Knowing Papa, he probably chuckled all the way back to the barn. Mama would have said, "You big ikes."

In the 1920s and 1930s everyone was short of money and tried their best to get along. We did just that, but still we had some fun times, too. What we considered fun times back in those years was so different from "fun" today. We spent time with family, friends and neighbors and did things that didn't cost a lot of money.

Now I'm not too sure where the money came from for the canned oysters, but the neighbors would sometimes get together and have an oyster supper. Now days, I suppose they would call it an oyster feed. Since Papa had Old Roan and Old Pat, we had lots of milk. Maybe someone else brought the oysters. Beats me! After all, I wasn't doing the cookin'. I didn't like oysters, so I just ate crackers and the soup.

Sometimes at these suppers, we would have a "grab bag." This is a box filled with little presents brought by the guests, with a long string tied to it. Each guest could pull out a nice little treasure to keep. Usually, the adult gifts were separated from the youngins'. I'm glad, because we little ones had a better chance of getting a gift suited for our age. The last little package I remember getting was a china dog with three baby puppies. I played with them for awhile, then sister number two, Wilma, let me put them in her china cabinet to keep them safe. She kept them for me until I got big enough to "dog sit," and I then took them back. I later gave them to my children with some other keepsake treasures.

To most of you these days, this kind of entertainment is boring and drab. Just think, if we hadn't had the grab boxes and oyster feeds, barn dances and pie suppers, there wouldn't have been too many reasons for taking extra baths. Since we didn't have television or movies, we didn't miss anything then that we have now. You must remember this. You don't miss what you never had!

I suppose you could say we are blessed with the luxuries we have today, but I think neighbors stopped being neighbors and friends when we all got televisions. It's so easy to flop down and watch the "tube" instead of stopping next door to chat, don't you know.

I have mentioned sister number nine, Meryl Darlene, several times in my story. I'm just six years older, but it seems like more. We were very close when we were growing up and still are. If either of us would get into a little trouble, no matter what it was, you could be sure the "good" one would be there to bail out the other one. When Meryl Darlene was born, Mama was forty-three years old. I guess, since I was a big girl of six, I could help Mama take care of this little sister. I would say the reason we were so close growing up is because I took care of her, doing the things a mother would do.

CHAPTER 5

FOR SEVERAL YEARS I took Mama to the K.O.A.M. television station in Pittsburg on her birthday. Because she loved to get dressed up and show off on her big day, I would always get her a corsage to wear. I would get Dana and maybe one or two of the other sisters, and we would all drive down to Pittsburg. We would have a big time and always go out to lunch after the television appearance.

Mama just loved a young man on the show who played the fiddle. His name was Shorty Pruitt. I want to tell you right now, he knew how to play. Shorty was so kind to Mama. He would tease her, make over her and wink at her now and then, making her feel special. I'm sorry to say little Shorty was killed in a car accident not long after our last visit to K.O.A.M. Mama was so sad on her next birthday when I asked her if she wanted to go to Pittsburg to be on the program. She told me if Shorty wasn't going to be there, she didn't care if she ever went again. You see, Shorty would always fiddle a tune and dedicate it to her. Anyway, after that year and each year after, her birthday celebration didn't include the trip to the television station, but I continued to take her to lunch.

As I mentioned before, I had my own beauty salon. I could and did book my appointments and change them around so I could take Mama places. I took one day a week off, for just that. It didn't make any difference what day it was, Mama was always ready any time to go any place. Mama, like many women back then, never learned to drive a car.

If Mama sounded down, I'd lock the house (the kids knew where the key was hidden), and I would get her and take her somewhere. She loved to go to the places that had bushels of fabric. We both liked to sew and we could almost always find the kind of materials we wanted. When we went to Nelly Don Fabrics, it wasn't unusual to bring home eight or ten pieces of fabric. The minute we hit the door, we both felt like we were in seventh heaven. When we finished shopping there, we would go out to eat somewhere in Nevada. You can probably realize what a treat it must have been. She had been tied down for so many years having all of us children at home and working so hard in the olden days.

When Harley and I got married, twenty-seven years ago, we had two bowls of punch. I asked Mama, "Do you want a cup with or without?" What do you suppose she said? You got it right if you said "with." She told me my wedding dress was too short. It probably was, but something worked, since we've had twenty-seven anniversaries. Our children were going to take us up town for a ride like all newlyweds do. I asked Mama if she wanted to go. I meant in the first car behind us, but she said she would go if she could sit between us in the front seat. By now, after hearing all these good things about Mama, I bet you can guess where she got to ride.

Harley and I used flowers from Mama's back yard to decorate for the wedding. Mama had all kinds of flowers growing back there. This was in May, so everything was in full bloom. Mama was living in Ft. Scott, so I went there and picked a huge box of cut flowers, then placed them in the refrigerator. These "pretties" would be ready for decorating the altar the next day. Mama was so happy to think I was using the flowers she grew and loved so much. She has at times grown sunflowers that measured eleven inches in diameter.

When Mama planned to go to her school alumni reunion, she asked me to do her hair. When the time came, I went down and got her and brought her to my beauty salon. I changed her style just a tad, and she looked so pretty. She later told me she had a lot of compliments on her hair at the reunion.

One time Harley and I took Mama to the Red Barn, a restaurant in Ft. Scott, for Mother's Day lunch. Harley opened the car door, escorted her in, pulled out her chair and seated her at our table, like gentlemen do. She felt like a queen with all this. When they served our lunch, she pulled her paring knife out of her purse to cut her meat. Pansy had given her a beautiful pink floral dress with a pink ribbon hanging down from the neckline. It kept getting in her way, so she unsnapped it, folded it, and put it in her purse. I wonder what else she had stuck down in there? I doubt there was too much money. She said she felt like a queen that day and was a queen in my eyes.

I loved to go visit Mama, not just to see her, but she liked to hear me play the piano. I sat down one time and played *"How Great Thou Art."* When I finished, she asked me to play it again. She really liked that old hymn. Since it was one of her favorites, we had David Freeman sing it at her funeral.

We all learned to play the pump organ, and when our parents got "rich," they bought a used upright piano. If we heard a tune or knew the song, we could play it by ear, of course.

When we lost our Papa, well, words can't describe the loss of a parent. Unless one has been there, they can't know the pain that won't leave. When Papa was killed, I thought my world had ended. I then remembered we still had Mama. But when our dear Mama was gone, too, there wasn't a home anymore. A home is a place to grow up in, to leave from and come back to. I like to go back down to the Usta Place and just walk around.

Mama told me one time she wished she had a lot of money to leave all of her children. I said, "Mama, let me tell you something. You and Papa are leaving me more than any kid could ever want or need. I have the ability to work, take care of myself and make a living to survive." She didn't think it was enough, I guess.

Since I completed the "college of hard knocks," all of this skimping, learning and saving hasn't been easy, but they both left us with a lot of love to share. Mama told Pansy she hoped that she (Mama) died before she had to bury another child. You see, she had already buried three sons and Papa.

This was May 17, 1970, and Mama had been in failing health. I lost my precious mother on August 5, 1970, just two and one-half months after Harley and I got married. She had told me so many times that if she could live long enough to be able to go to Frances, her granddaughter, and Larry Richmond's wedding, then she would be ready to go. She was in the hospital, and Dr. Basham had released her in Pansy's care to go to the wedding she wanted so badly to go to before she died. I took her picture as she was ushered out after the wedding. That picture was the last one I have of her. As she walked by me, she slapped me on the shoulder. After the wedding Sunday afternoon, Pansy had to take her back to the hospital. Harley and I stopped by the hospital before we came back to Pittsburg. She was so tired.

She was lying there talking to Harley. All at once she reached both arms up toward the ceiling and started talking about the white horses and a carriage coming. The following Wednesday at 4 a.m., Wilma called from the hospital and said that Mama was very bad and that I had better come. I got Harley up, and he was dressed in minutes. I grabbed my clothes and dressed on the way.

Bless his heart, he tried to get me to the hospital to be with Mama, but I was too late. (It's about thirty miles to Ft. Scott.) Wilma said Mama passed away about 4:10, just awhile after she called me. Mama was tired, and I believe God decided it was time for her to come and take a rest.

Papa was very generous. He gave me a nickel when I learned to tell time. He also paid us three or four cents to replant corn when some of the crop failed to come up. He paid me one cent to wash his feet. Kids will be kids. If I had it do over, I wouldn't do that. His foot-bath would be "on the house."

Someone asked Papa one time how many kids he had. He said, "Two boys and rest are girls." I don't know if he ever told the person how many girls or not. Can you imagine having eight sisters? I did and was blessed with a ton of love for each of them.

We all had so much fun growing up. We all had plenty to eat and a warm place to sleep. It might be three or four in a bed, but we kept each other warm, don't you know? We all got up and ready for breakfast, but I don't remember ever being hungry when I went to bed. (I've gone to bed hungry since then, when I was dieting.)

When we were all at home, Mama always cooked a lot of beans and cornbread, pancakes, potato soup, chili and fried potatoes. These were foods that were filling and good for us, too. Mama had to make foods that could be stretched to feed us all.

In later years, Herman bought a good used guitar. I'm still not sure how I learned to play, but I did. Just talented, I guess. I started using this big bunch of talent playing the guitar and singing duets with Margie. We sang at picnics, community meetings and the Durkee Margarine Colonial Theater Amateur Hour in 1941. We were one of the finalists there. We often sang with A.J. Cripe and the Town Talk

This picture of (left to right) Meryl, Gayle, Margie, and me (Helen) was taken in 1942. We were dressed up and ready to go somewhere, probably to a talent contest or pie supper.

Boys from K.O.A.M. Radio in Pittsburg. They played at picnics, and we sang with them at different times. We also did some yodeling and should have stayed with it. Maybe we could have ended up in Nashville. We were good, but didn't realize it then.

We auditioned previously for the amateur hour. After we finished, a young man came up to me and said, "You girls are good. Loosen up and if you will shake a little more, you will have a better chance of winning. It can't hurt anything!" If I had known then what I know now, there would have been so much shaking going on while the Clark sisters had the microphone, you might imagine you were going through an earthquake. There seems to be a lot of shaking in the music field these days.

I must throw this in while I'm bragging. I was recently looking through my scrapbook and a clipping I put in it back in the thirties. The clipping read, "El Dorado Springs held the annual picnic Saturday. Music was by Lester and Inez Murphy, Tom Jones and Helen Clark." I don't remember if I played a guitar or the drums. I would have been about thirteen or fourteen then.

I was twelve years old when Mama gave me my last haircut. She had a one-pattern cut. It was the same style, using the same bowl every time. Now that style wasn't me, especially at twelve. My brother-in-law, Earl, made fun of my hair. I didn't care for him much after that. It was then I decided to do my own trimming. I can honestly say I haven't had more than three people cut my hair since I've learned to cut my own.

Three girls out of nine became cosmetologists and owned their own salons. Mine was called Helen's Beauty Salon. The state inspector told me one time Margie and I looked more professional than any operators in Ft. Scott. We never knew when the inspector was coming, so sometimes operators wouldn't be dressed appropriately. I guess she would find some in jeans or housecoats, but when she dropped in on Margie or me, she would always be impressed with the appearance of our salons and us.

I don't remember much crime in the olden days. In the '20s, '30s and '40s, we didn't have to lock our doors when we left our home. We might hook our screens at night. There was one occasion when one of our neighbor girls was murdered. She was dating two boys and one became jealous and shot her. After the killing, he carried her into her house and called the sheriff from the girl's home. A third young man was also in love with Merle. He was slightly retarded, and after the murder he committed suicide. Johnny was missing for awhile, and his body was found later in a cornfield. I was quite little then, and everything that happened there were things to which a child should not be exposed.

I remember, when we were really little children, my Aunt Etta Davis called and told Mama some gypsies were coming down our way. We lived on a dead end road at the Usta Place. Papa and Mama were afraid the gypsies would try to buy or steal one of us. Mama got all of us in the house and hid us. We didn't have clothes closets, but our clothes were hung on the wall on nails with sheets to cover them. It served for a hiding place. I was so scared. I was little, but I remember it very clearly and was so glad when they left.

We lived a little less than a mile from our mailbox, so there would be two of us children to go instead of one to get the mail. No one ever went alone and we took turns. I don't know why it was such a big deal to walk after the mail, but I guess we were just tired of playing.

One day Mama told Herschel and me we could go get the mail. When we got back, she had forgotten she had promised us. Yes, you guessed it. We got the worst switching anyone ever experienced. Believe me, I haven't forgotten that one. Never will. Another time when we got into trouble, we had to cut our own switch. I guess the first one had been used too many times. It took us quite some time to find that switch, don't you know? Finally, after cutting the smallest one we could find, we returned and let me say right now, we learned the hard way. I'm sure there were many switchin's after that.

We really were pretty good kids. We were never in trouble with the law, just in trouble with Mama. But looking back, I can see our parents loved us very much. When we were ill and feeling a tad puny, they were both sympathetic. Sometimes they made an ointment of Vicks, turpentine and coal oil, heating to lukewarm, and applied it to our chest and throat. This really helped us get relief fast. This is the only relief we knew. In the olden days our parents used only natural medicine. They didn't call the doctor for every ache, pain, cut or sprain.

One time after I was married, I was really sick, and my husband, Hubert, was in the Army. Mama had insisted I take off work and come home so she could take care of me. Shoot, I was twenty-one years old, but that's what Mama did. She made the famous onion poultice. I was in bed with this thing on my chest, and you guessed it. Hubert came home on leave unexpectedly. He came in my room, and there I was with that onion poultice and all. Can you imagine what a homecoming that was? My "bathroom with lid" (galvanized bucket with a lid on it) was there handy also. What a sight!

Papa was always bothered with boils. For his home cure, he would boil shaved wild cherry bark and make a tea. He would drink this two or three times a day, which would always cure the boil. It's amazing how they came up with ways to treat various illnesses and problems.

Mama had nine of us in bed with the measles all at one time. Can you imagine how much work this must have been for her? Not only because we were sick, but she didn't have any help with all of the daily work needing to be done. I thought I wanted some potato soup when I was sick with the measles. I told Mama, but after she went to the work of making it for me, I was too sick to eat it.

Meryl Darlene, my youngest sister, had whooping cough, mumps and measles all in her first year of life. I guess the older kids managed to expose her to these childhood diseases while she was just little.

It seemed like our parents had a cure for everything. We would gargle with salt water for a sore throat, or maybe eat a little salt. She gave us sugar to calm a cough. It really did help and was so soothing. If the cold started to go down into the chest, you could bet your bottom dollar you would get the famous onion poultice immediately. This poultice was a real experience. Mama would fry a pan of thinly sliced onion until nice and juicy. Then she would place them in a cloth bag and stitch the onions in place. While the onions were still warm, this bag would be placed on the chest area with a cloth on top to hold in the heat. Now you wouldn't smell all that whoopee, but you could bet your second bottom dollar your cold would break and you would feel fit as a fiddle soon. It works! It really does. I know because I've been there. No matter what your age, if Mama thought you needed it, you got the onions.

Nothing healed cuts any faster than a slice of fat meat dipped in turpentine. Place it on the cut and maybe change it a time or two. Cover with a clean bandage and wait. Then you would be back to the grindstone.

Speaking of fat meat, I never liked any kind of fat meat and still don't. When we were all seated at the table, you might have guessed, I always sat next to Papa. I was lucky, because he always ate the fat and I ate the lean. They should have named me "Jack Spratt." Now the second streak of luck was that Papa didn't like frosting on his cake. Guess who gobbled down his frosting?

A jar of Vicks Vapor Rub was a must in the Usta Place bedroom, living room and kitchen. We used it all over. Papa kept a jar under his pillow, and if he needed some at night, he would put some in his nose and he breathed easier. You see, our parents didn't have money to buy medicine then, even if there had been all kinds of medicine like we have today. Those home cures worked though. As I write my story, we have living proof something worked.

We always had water to drink, but had to haul it now and then. We were taught at an early age to save, and that also included water. Our bathtub was a galvanized wash tub, and if you were lucky enough to be one of the third or fourth bathers, you got a warm bath. I'm sure some of you reading my story find this hard to believe, but we really did have to share bath water. That galvanized tub we had to use was not anywhere near the size of the bathtubs you all are used to these days.

I have heard many years that men aren't supposed to shed tears, but I believe tears are meant to be shed. The only time I ever saw Papa cry was in 1942, the day he suffered a broken leg from a farming accident. A young man, Calvin Allen, helped him cut oats. As Calvin was backing the tractor to connect the binder to the tractor hitch, Papa took a step at the wrong time and his leg was jammed between the two couplings. He had a complete break between the knee and ankle and his foot was just hanging there dangling. To get him to the hospital, we slipped his leg into a burlap bag and got him in the car. There is pain, and then there was my Papa in pain. We got him to the hospital and admitted. When he was told he would be in the hospital at least six weeks, the tears started. You see, they had just started cutting grain and Papa was concerned and upset about how was he going to get the harvesting finished. I'll tell you how.

The word spread like wildfire about the accident. We had about ten or eleven neighbors who jumped in and finished the job. Are there neighbors like this out there today? I haven't heard of any, but I'm sure there could be some left somewhere. (When Papa was released from the hospital and until his fatal car accident, he walked with a limp.)

Papa didn't always have good brakes on his car, so when the accident happened I needed a car to get Mama back and forth to the hospital. Well, I was dating a neighbor boy who happened to have a big heart, with a car that happened to have good brakes. Guess what? You probably guessed it. He let me have his car for as long as I needed. I married that boy a little later, and it wasn't because he had a car with good brakes. By the way, this boy was one of the twelve who finished the harvest for Papa while he was down with the broken leg.

A long time after Hubert and I were married, my cousin Jessie asked me if I knew Papa cried at my wedding. I didn't know it, but I

These men are the "harvesters" who came and helped Papa after he got hurt. They were truly good friends and neighbors to come help the Clark family. Most of them had crops of their own to harvest. Back row on porch are from left to right: Hubert Rhodes and Bob Anderson. Seated on porch, left to right are: Perry Keeney, Loyd Sydner, Wes Bailey, Lawrence Sydner, Alf Lytal, Walter Kelloge and John Madison. Seated on ground, left to right are: Fred Killian and Johnny Succoni.

have wondered since if they were tears of joy or if he was sad to see me go. I'll never know, because I found about the tears several years after Papa's death.

I have spent too many hours to count turning the grindstone for Papa to sharpen the mowing machine sickle. We would rest awhile if I got tired, and then I'd get my "nose back to the grindstone." Because I so much liked helping my Papa, this is a good memory.

I just read my last paragraph to Harley. He said, "You know, when I was a boy, this one time when the days work was done, my dad was sitting there in the yard resting. I walked by the grindstone and gave it a turn and walked on by. My dad told me to come back and turn that stone "until I tell you to stop." Harley said he turned it thirty minutes. Just think of the sickles he could have sharpened.

Harley and I don't have a lot to do this time of year, so we sometimes sit and talk, reminiscing about hard times, lean years, and how thankful we are. Harley told me he had to go barefooted to get the cows before first light, tramping over stubs and rocks. He has told me this so many times, and this evening he mentioned it again. He said, "It looks to me like they could have managed to find me some shoes somewhere." Now that line brought tears to my eyes. We went barefooted sometimes, but we were blessed with shoes as we needed them. They may have been hand-me-downs or resoled, but that was all right. Poor little boy!

As I've mentioned before, we didn't get out too often to know how other folks lived. I guess you could have called us "back-woodsy." Papa and four or five other men owned a threshing machine. They would thresh one man's field, then go on to the next, and then to the next. We had an uncle who ran the machine and would "toot" the whistle when they were coming down the road and driveway. We little ones would go hide because we were scared of it. Pretty soon, we could come out of hiding and be excited it was there. Uncle Stub would "toot" it just to tease us little ones.

Uncle Stub had this bad habit of trying to hug us or kiss me. I definitely didn't like this one bit. When I went to his funeral, you can just imagine what went through my mind. He may have been teasing, but I didn't like it at all and that memory has stayed with me all these years.

Down at the Usta Place, we always ate breakfast together. We all ordered the same thing off the same menu, and if you were hungry enough, any breakfast tasted pretty good. When Mama would make pancakes, she would have two griddles going at the same time. The idea was to get enough cooked first, then we would all sit down together. You must remember there were thirteen of us to eat, so that meant thirteen pancakes were stacked on one plate. Now I like my cakes right off the griddle, so I wasn't too excited the way we did it then. They were "soggy," but still being a growing child, I ate my soggy cakes like all the rest. I made it just dandy.

When I became a parent of two beautiful children who liked pancakes, I fed the little darlins' and their father, and then since Gary was older, he cooked them for me. That made everything work out fine for me to have fresh pancakes, too. I make pancakes from time to time, but not as good as Mama's were. Hers were made from scratch, using a cup of this and a pinch of that.

Both of my children, Gary and Sherri, were so helpful around the house when they were growing up. Both of them are good cooks. I'm so proud of them. I'm not sure if all of my grandchildren like to cook or not. I know Rusty, my oldest grandson, likes to cook if the fish aren't biting.

When Gary was about six years old, he took a cardboard pill box and made a precious little box for me in which to keep my postage stamps. (Back in the olden days they dispensed pills in little boxes.)

It was just the right width and length for the stamps. Of course, I still have it. You don't think I would throw it away, do you? One year Sherri made a holder for my yardsticks. She used burlap material with clusters of grapes made out of pom-poms. It was so sweet and so useful. I didn't have it when Gary said I used a yardstick on him.

It seems like I had a lot going on down at the Usta Place. I keep thinking of more happenings I want to share with you about my life during and after the Usta Place days.

My cousin, Doris Taylor, and I played together a lot when we were young. We grew up still sharing a close relationship. I was with Doris, who had been ill for sometime, a little while before she died. I told Doris I wanted to tell her something now, before we were both gone, but not to let it go to her head. I told Doris when she walks into a room where I am, I feel like her presence lights up the room like sunshine and she made everything seem bright and alive. She said, "I know." We laughed at that for quite awhile.

I'm going to admit right here that I've never told anyone before. This will probably make you gag. I certainly hope you don't think I'm the type of person who would eat just anything. A long time ago, Papa decided out of nowhere, he wanted to dress and eat a sparrow. You all know sparrows are small, so to get a sample it took a lot of hunting. I don't know how many he dressed for cooking. He salted and peppered them, then fried them like chicken. I wasn't sure it was the thing to do, but Papa was there and if he was dressing them, it must be all right. As near as I can remember, they were good, but you wouldn't want to eat it every day. Boy, what some Papas will do for pleasure or to put food on the table.

I was sitting here having my morning decaf coffee, thanking God for all our blessings. When I glanced out the window, I saw four sparrows taking a bath at the same time in the birdbath. I had just cleaned and filled it with clean water. They were all splashing around and having a good time. This sort of brought back memories of the Usta Place baths. You know, the same tub and same water for three or four of us.

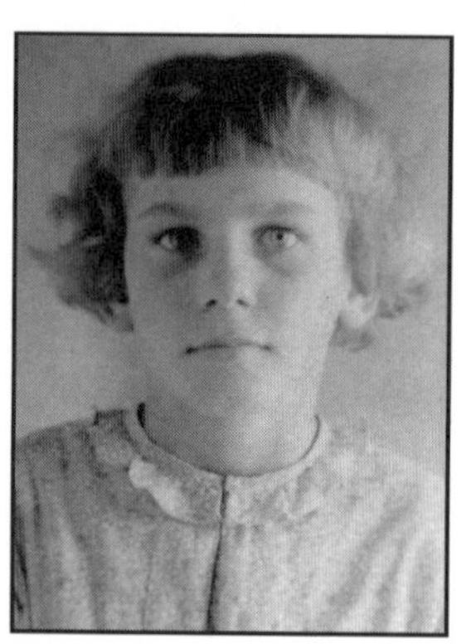

Helen Clark, age 9
This picture of me was taken at school when I was in the third grade.

CHAPTER 6

IN THE EARLY FORTIES I had a close friend in Ft. Scott, Kansas, whose parents owned a roller skating rink, so Susie and I went skating often. I couldn't skate too well, but I met a handsome soldier from Camp Clark, Missouri, who was more than anxious to teach me. He had patience and I had plenty of time to learn. When he was with me, he was a perfect gentleman, but I didn't date him for very long. He later got married to a young lady and they had twins. Just think, that could have been me. From what I hear, he got mean and often beat his wife. It's a good thing I learned to skate and skated far away from this loser. (He lost me.) It's unbelievable. If he had hit me one time, I would have decked him myself, or one of my good buddies would have done it for me. I wouldn't tolerate a spouse or anyone else being mean. Life is too precious to be wasted on violence or hurting someone.

In later years, Mama would buy margarine instead of making it. Back then margarine was white when you bought it, but each pound came with a packet of coloring that had to be mixed into it. That was my job and I didn't mind doing it. You can bet your life savings that no one fought me for the job either.

Sisters number two and three, Wilma and Vena, had nicknames. Dana tried to say sister to Wilma and it didn't come out right. It ended up "Tis." Vena's nickname was Tad. When she was little and trying to crawl, it reminded some of the kids of a tadpole, so Tad was hung on her. But I always called them by their proper names.

Down at the Usta Place, we didn't have fans or any other way to keep cool, so we would get a piece of pasteboard and used it for a fan. Our homemade fans helped some, but I can remember I would sometimes go to sleep while still fanning. Using those little homemade fans was obviously not like the electric fans that came a few years later.

When my sister, Margie, and I first started working in town, we liked to go home over the weekend. The Frisco Railroad had a little one-coach passenger train that ran from Ft. Scott, Kansas. We would jump on that little noisy train and ride out to a little berg called Pawnee Station. When it pulled into the station, Papa would be right there waiting for us. Mama would be up early Sunday morning, maybe take out some fried-down ham or sausage, and make gravy and biscuits for breakfast. Around four o'clock, my Papa would taxi us back to the station. When we could hear the train coming around the bend, he got out on the track and started waving his arms to let the engineer know he had two more passengers. We got aboard, shook and rattled all the way back to Ft. Scott. It was better than jogging or hitchhiking. I just wish I could remember how much the round-trip ticket cost. Since I never had to borrow any money or walk, I guess it wasn't too steep. Anyway, I always dressed up in high heels and a hat, so I wouldn't have made it very far walking.

My brother, Herman, was stationed at Ft. Sill, Oklahoma, for basic training in the early forties. I don't know who thought of it first, but it was probably me. I've always been ready to go on the bus, train, car or plane. Anyway, one weekend we decided to jump on a bus to Lawton, Oklahoma, and visit our brother. My advice to all of you young ladies is this: If you ever visit an army base, you won't necessarily need anyone to show you around. There are plenty of soldiers waiting to do just that.

Herman had made reservations for us to stay in the home of his Master Sergeant and his wife. We wanted to go out on the town, so she gave Herman the house key, making us feel welcome. We went to a club close by and had so much fun. You can bet your "dog tags" we stayed close to Herman. We danced with some soldiers, but we stayed near to our table, as Herman told us to. I noticed a soldier across the room who kept watching me all evening. Warren finally came over to our table, introduced himself, and asked me to dance.

What a surprise! He was a boy from Ft. Scott. Warren's sister worked with me at Key Work Clothes! He wanted to take me home, so he took us all back to the home where we were staying. He asked me for a date, but I explained Margie and I were there just for the weekend. He was a very handsome young man and treated me exceptionally nice.

Warren spent all his time in the service without getting hurt and when he came home, he was killed in a car accident five miles from Ft. Scott. It was a very bad accident and was not a very pretty sight. It was such a shame for it to have happened after he had served his country.

While we were living east of Nevada, Missouri, Herman dated one of our neighbor girls who had an identical twin sister. Herman always wondered if he was actually going out with the right twin. I guess if he couldn't tell the difference, it didn't make any difference.

Our brother, Herman, was born in 1918. Mama told me she was glad Herman was little when the war broke out so he didn't have to go to the service. Well, the very next war got him and a lot of other young men in 1941. I knew many of them who had to go in the early forties. (My husband, brother, cousins and several friends.) There were three boys from this one family I knew who were in the service. The two boys that were in the Air Corps were both killed, but the third son made it home.

Another old memory just popped up in my mind. When Herman was drafted into the service, that meant he was taken from the farm where he helped our Papa make a living. Now some of the young men who were farmers or married might qualify for a deferment. Well, Herman left for the service, and that meant Mama could draw an allotment of $50 a month for each of us four little Clark girls still at home, Margie, Gayle, Meryl Darlene and me. Mama had to get all our birth certificates for proof of her eligibility for the allotment.

She needed a set of dentures so badly and was now able to get them. You see, there never was enough money to take care of our precious Mama. I'm really not sure if Herman had to fill out a form to get the dentures or if they came out of the $200 allotment. Anyway, it was through the Army and I don't know how it was done.

Herman was in the army for several months and, like many young men sent overseas, wasn't allowed to write to let us know anything of his whereabouts. We all hoped and prayed he was safe. I know Mama did a lot of worrying. It was really hard for her not knowing where he was or if he was all right.

One day when I was walking home from work, just for kicks I stopped at a place where a lady read cards and could tell your fortune. I had never put too much faith in this type of thing, but fifty cents was all I had to lose, which was about an hour's pay back then. (You must remember, he was our only living brother!) I went in, not telling the lady anything. I asked her this one question, "Can you tell me where my brother is and is he all right?" Well, she did her thing, you know, reading cards, and she said point blank, "I see him somewhere on the coast of Venezuela." Now that didn't tell me a whole lot, but we all kept hoping and praying harder that he could or would write to Mama. Finally, Mama got a letter and it was postmarked Trinidad. He had been stationed there for some time. How about that?

As I mentioned before, I always walked to work. When I wanted to look pretty for an evening out, I would put my hair in pin curls before I went to work so it would be ready for the evening. It would always be soaking wet when I started my walk to work. No matter what the weather, my hair must look nice. In the really cold weather, I would have ice in my hair when I got to work. At 4:00 when I got off work, it would be dry. That's all that mattered!

When my brother, Herschel, and I were still little tikes, we didn't have lots of toys like children now days. The toys we had were homemade, using items from around the house. For instance, Mama would save the empty wooden spools left from her sewing thread. Papa would take a piece of wire and fasten a large one for the back and a smaller one for the front and make each of a us a two-seated car. We pretended they were cars, don't you know? We made hills, ditches and bridges while playing in the dirt. We used sticks and rocks to make a building for our cars. We had a good time playing with those spools. Sure, we got dirty, but it was the kind of dirt that would wash off. Our toys were very simple, but entertained us for hours.

Kids do the darndest things, and here is more proof they do. As I probably mentioned before, Papa used to raise hogs, not only for meat for us, but he would sell one now and then. It always seemed when it was time for market, the price would be down. There also came a time when the little boy pigs had to be castrated. We weren't allowed to view the occasion, so Herschel and I sneaked up in the hayloft and peeked. We were so young, we had no idea what was going on. After I grew up, I found out.

I think a lot about the olden Usta Place days. They tell me that is a bad sign, like I am getting old. I wouldn't know about that. I just know most of these memories are as clear today as they were when they were being made so many years ago.

When I was a little girl, I was never told I was pretty or ever praised for the little chores I did. Do you suppose I didn't have to do little things since I had a lot of help above me or just maybe I charged for all the little things, like washing my Papa's feet or combing Mama's hair? Our dear parents were so busy making a living for us. I'm sure they didn't think it was necessary to praise or thank us.

I've talked to Harley about the olden days. He has lived them also, about seventy-nine, and can identify with almost everything we discuss. Harley's mother died when he was three months old, so he has certainly lost out on a lot in his growing-up years. Even though he had a granny to help raise him, he surely needed his mama. He knows this now.

Dana took care of all of us when Mama would be busy doing other chores. Believe me, there was always something to do. While Mama did the work only she could handle, Dana ended up doing for the younger ones some of the things a mother would do. Since she was the oldest, Mama depended on her to help out in so many ways.

When I started growing up, I wasn't any different from other little girls. I liked little boys. News flash! I've liked little boys since I found out that they weren't little girls. I had this silly idea that no one would want to date me, because I was ugly. Another news flash. I found out later that I wasn't ugly. I was pretty. I've been blessed with beautiful hair, nails, skin, standards and a personality that won't quit. It just keeps racing on. I know I was loved, but grew up thinking otherwise. Thank God, I truly know better now. It makes for an unhappy childhood when parents don't take time to praise their children and let them know they are loved. All parents should realize this. It takes perhaps eighteen to twenty years to prepare a child to go out on his own. It takes only a matter of seconds to say, "I love you." God gave you a gift of 86,400 seconds today. Have you used one to say "thank you" to Him?

Cosmetology helped me build confidence and wade out of that knee-deep self-esteem. When clients would call and specifically ask for Mrs. Rhodes, it made me feel special, with a capital "S." One gentleman, an instructor at the college, always asked for me to do his manicure. My husband said, "Get real, honey, he just wanted to hold your hand." (He was just teasing me.) I'll tell you more about cosmetology school a little later!

I keep remembering precious moments that must be written in my story. Years ago, several of the sisters and their families got together for a family dinner. Mama kept the idea that the coffee she used was the best flavor and no coffee could come to the top step with hers, so she took her can of coffee to make coffee for dinner. I don't know who came up with this idea, but Papa was in on the joke, too. Someone switched the coffee with what Dana had in the canister. After dinner, something was said about how good the coffee was. Mama agreed. Someone accidentally let it slip about the trick that was played on our Mama. It was a nasty trick, but it was all in fun. When she found out, she said, "I don't think that is very smart." I don't know if she spoke to Papa on the way home. She probably did, because you absolutely cannot keep a Clark quiet for very long!

Have you ever worn a garment, like a knit sweater, blouse or dress and get stuck in there, unable to free yourself, especially something over your head? I have, and it is a terrible situation. As I said before, Mama loved to get in the car and go, just anywhere. I was going to pick her up and go, probably to Nellie Don dress factory in Nevada. She told me when I got to her house how hot and sticky she was when trying to change her dress. She tried to undress, over her head, and was perspiring so badly that she couldn't get out of her dress. She got worried, there all alone, and got panicky. Bless her heart. She said she was so frightened because she thought she would smother. She got to her sewing machine, found the scissors, and cut her dress enough she could free herself. Poor Mama! There just wasn't much left of the dress. I sew for myself and I don't make too many garments I have to slip over my head. I button them down the front or make a lower cut neckline. When I go shopping for ready-made clothes, I don't even try on outfits with high necklines or tight clothing. I want to be able to move. Besides, I don't want to mess up my hair.

A few years ago, Harley and I were watching it snow. We thought it was so pretty floating to the ground. All at once, the snow came down in lengths instead of flakes. We saw some three or four inches long. It looked so strange to see the snow falling that way. Certainly our weather is changing.

Our parents moved to a farm south and west of Eve, Missouri. Now this farm had a two-story rock house with a fireplace and a storage room upstairs. It was a pretty old farmhouse. You know how kids like to explore? Margie, sister number seven, noticed a door leading off to somewhere from our bedroom. There wasn't anything to do but unhook the door and see what was behind it on the other side. We were in for a big surprise. This room was sort of an attic, darker than pitch. We got a lantern and explored all around the room. We found a dressmaker's dummy lying back in the corner. Being young and inexperienced, we thought that thing was a corpse lying there. This was so silly, but we had never seen anything like it before. I don't know about Margie, but I was glad to get out of that dark place and back into fully lit rooms.

Someone asked me just recently where and how I learned to drive. I don't know if they were curious or questioning my ability. Well, this enormous task took place at this same old two-story rock house. We had plenty of yard and, believe me, that big yard came in handy. I was about fifteen and a half years of age and I suppose big brother, Herman, thought I should learn to drive. The doors of his little V-8 two door Ford swung open from the front on the car. I don't know the year of the car, but this was in 1945. I suppose it was a piece of cake to him, but to me it seemed more like a slice of "hard tack." This little car was a darlin'. After quite a few starts, jumps, and stops, I got the hang of the clutch and gear shifter. I still drive a stick shift in our pick-up.

I was sixteen when I got my first driver's license, costing me a big twenty-five cents. I have never had a wreck, but I got a speeding ticket once that cost me $24.10. I tried to talk the officer out of it, but I still hadn't had enough experience talking. (It didn't work.)

I'm sure some of you have had a cup or two of coffee in your lifetime. If not, you have missed a lot of gossip or conversation, and at the same time missed enjoying a few minutes of pure relaxation. When this old girl was about three or four years old, my parents gave me a cup of coffee. They filled the cup about half-full of coffee, then filled it on up with cream. Yes, I said cream. I'm not talking non-dairy. I mean the fat stuff you take off of the crock of milk that you have brought in from the barn earlier. Oh, yes, there were about two teaspoons of sugar poured in the cup also. This was regular coffee, because we never heard of decaffeinated back then. Now they say coffee, cream and sugar aren't good for you. Whom are we going to believe? I guess you might say I've been drinking coffee since I was knee-high to a grasshopper.

This is another picture of me as a teenager, not smiling.

When Herschel and I used to play with our cousins, Doris and Junior, at their house, we would always get a treat. I remember Aunt Etta almost always had a cake baked. She would give us a dish of canned peaches and a piece of cake. The snack wasn't any better than at home, but the idea the peaches came out of a can bought at the store, instead of a glass jar home canned, made it better. It was just fun to have something different. We really loved the store-bought fruit.

A wise monkey is a monkey who doesn't monkey around with another monkey's monkey."

CHAPTER 7

IN THE EARLY 1940s, Papa and Mama moved back to Kansas. They lived in a two-story house with a vegetable cellar. They still had four little ones at home. I was one of those little ones, but the oldest of the four.

This is the farm where there was a two-room schoolhouse for us to attend. Oh yes, they had lots of picnic and pie suppers. Also, when school was out for the summer, they would have a last day of school picnic and a big softball game in the afternoon. The boys would play against the girls. I never understood why, but they put me on first base. Well, Hubert, whom I later married, had gotten a hit and was coming to first base. When he got there he shoved me off of the base and out of the way. I never knew for sure if he had the right to shove the first-base woman out of sight, don't you know? Other than that little incident, he acted as though he liked me, and we sat together at lunch time. He asked for a date to go to church. Since we were headed for church, I guess Mama thought it would be all right. From then on, if we went to a movie, we had to take his sister and my sister with us to chaperone. It's so easy to find something for little sisters to do, if you know what I mean.

We started dating about once a week. From our first date until our wedding day, I kept a memo in a book of what we did, where we went and the name of each movie we went to. (I gave this book to

Sherri a few years ago.) I don't actually know why I did this, but I started writing it down and just kept it up until we got married.

Now this sixth daughter of Papa and Mama Clark had a certain hour to be home. I don't know the set hour for all the older sisters to be in, but it seemed like my time was set up sort of early. I knew if I stayed out later, that I couldn't go out again for some time. Today, I believe they call it grounded, don't you know?

About the time I began seeing this young man, I started working for Key Work Clothes. Sometimes some of us girls would go out to eat lunch. We had to walk across about three railroad tracks to get there. After they started drafting our young men, you would see "troop trains" on these tracks every now and then. These young men were not allowed to get off of the train, so they would have us mail letters for them. I have no idea how many letters I dropped in mailboxes for these dear boys. I never asked any of them if the letters were "Dear John" letters. If so, it surely would be the girl's loss. They seemed like very sweet young boys to me. Of course, if we hadn't mailed their letters for them, they might have shown their true colors.

When it's time to turn on the lights at night, do you pull the curtains, close or draw the draperies? Do you sit and read, eat dinner or watch television with the windows all open so any one can see inside? I don't. I cover all the windows and then turn on the lights. When the sun sinks, I close the doors and windows and make sure that no one can see in.

When I was sixteen or so and went to town to work, my Papa gave me some good advice. He said, "You lads keep those windows covered." He knew there were "peeping people" out there. He knew we would be safer at home, but all children grow up and want to leave home and get out on their own. He was trying to prepare us for that great big outside world. Up until then, we were all somewhat sheltered, not knowing too much about what was going on out there with the birds, and the bees and the cigarette trees.

In the meantime, I applied for a job at Key Work Clothes. I was hired a few days later and was requested to report to work at 4 p.m. the next day. That meant that I would have to work nights. My hours would be from 4 p.m. to 12 a.m. Mama wouldn't hear of it. Well, she hadn't heard yet, but I knew there would be no way she would allow it. My parents wouldn't let me out on the street that time of night. I lived about nine blocks from work and walked both ways. Well, part of these blocks didn't have any extra lighting and I was only sixteen years old. You could bet your bottom dollar right then that I would not be working the evening shift. That suited me just dandy, because I didn't want to work nights either. You see, when you are sixteen, there are a lot of places to go and things to see. If you get your day's work in early, you are free until 7o'clock the next morning!

When I grew up, got a job and earned a paycheck, I bought gifts for Papa and Mama. These gifts were for their birthdays, Christmas or just because they were special. Sometimes Papa's gift would be a big bag of salted peanuts and Mama's would be something feminine, like hosiery or dusting powder. One year I got Papa a nice pair of leather gloves for Christmas. He laid the package on his table, unopened. I told him if he didn't open it, I was never buying anything else for him. I was lying, of course. I bet he was shaking in his boots. Well, he opened the package and liked the gloves very much. I've thought so many times since then that the reason for not opening the package that day was probably because he didn't have a gift for me. Believe me, I didn't give him gloves because I thought I would get something from him.

I gave my heart to Jesus Christ in 1944. Margie and I were baptized on October 8, 1944, in the First Christian Church in Ft. Scott, Kansas. We had been going to church there since we had moved to town to go to work. Hubert and I were later married in that same church by the same minister, Rev. Dunlap.

Way back in the olden days, when I started dating Hubert, I had younger competition. I still had three siblings younger. As I said earlier, we all liked potato soup at our house when we were little. Well, anyway, when my boyfriend got there to pick me up, my being a young lady all dressed up ready to start my big night, I couldn't understand why he was always hungry. After all, we would get a five-cent hamburger after the ten-cent movie. Gayle and Meryl Darlene would ask him if he wanted a bowl of soup. Of course, he didn't mind that. They liked Hubert and wanted him to stick around and have a bowl of our famous soup. He would most always take time to eat what they had fixed for him. My little sisters fell for Hubert like I fell for Oscar Woody.

Somewhere along the way they nicknamed him "soup." Wonder why? He eventually went back to his old nickname, Bub, which is what his father called him. I don't really know where he got it. Al, Hubert's father, was a sweet old man. He was also good to me, his daughter-in-law.

One year at Christmas, Hubert gave Meryl Darlene a set of tin dishes. I'm not sure what he gave Gayle or me. I can only remember the dishes. This young fellow who liked the soup and bought gifts for my little sisters is the same one who helped finish the harvesting for my Papa. Remember? He was the one with the good heart, good car and good brakes.

When I first started dating this young man, I naturally wanted to make a big impression with my cooking. I decided I would try my best and make dinner for the two of us, Hubert and me. My first thought was what I should serve for the entree. Now, I did really well cooking for me, but trying to show off, I was going to have to do better than that, big time. I knew it had to be something special. Well, I finally decided on baked guinea, with dressing and all the trimmings. I can't remember what I served him in the dessert line, but it was probably pie.

We had finished eating and talking about how good everything tasted. He said, "I have never liked turkey, baked guinea or duck." I just couldn't spoil his dinner, so I never told him what he ate, nor have I mentioned it since. That's a long time to keep a secret as precious as that. I suppose after over fifty years, if he reads my story, the secret will be out. You can bet your bottom dollar if he could eat guinea and not know the difference, you could feed him anything and he would eat it. He was always easy to cook for, don't you know?

Now this is the young man who shoved me off first base at the last day of school picnic. You know, the one who loaned me the car with brakes, the same one who helped me get the chocolates for the "most popular young lady." That's him! Well, it came time for him to go into the service.

His mama and I took him to the bus. He was in the states for awhile and was sent to Ft. Meade, Maryland. He sent me a musical powder box from there. When the postman brought it to my house, I set it down on the table. Would you believe that little package played a few notes before I ever opened it. The melody the box played was *My Wild Irish Rose.* The tune fit me pretty well.

He was sent to Italy and served most of his time there. Hubert told me later that when he and his outfit were on their way from Italy to Japan, he made a promise to God. He told God that if He would be with him and let him get home safely, he would, when he had children, raise them in a Christian home and always take care of them. Well, on the way to Japan, they got word that the war was over. God answered Hubert's prayer, and Hubert has kept his promise to God. That has been over fifty-five years ago, but Hubert kept his vow to God to always have a Christian home and take care of his kids.

I was working all the time he was gone and trying to save up for the future and special needs. My boss at work tried to discourage me from getting married. She was an "old maid" and besides, she would be losing a good sewing machine operator, don't you know? He returned to the states in early 1945. While he was home on furlough, we were married. He was stationed at Camp Campbell, Kentucky. After we were married, I worked for a while and then went back to camp with him.

Since Hubert and I were going to get married, I needed a wedding gown. I went to Pittsburg to Little's Store and bought my beautiful gown. I brought Mama and Stella Rhodes, my future mother-in-law, with me to help pick it out. I tried on three or four of them, but we all liked the one I finally decided on. The price for the gown was $25, but you must remember this was 1945. That much was a lot back then. It was almost two weeks' wages. My train was three times longer than I was tall, so I "snipped" enough from it to make myself a beautiful veil. It worked just fine. I was just as married in it as I would have been in one that cost several hundred dollars.

Hubert and I lived in a mobile home on the base and had store and laundry privileges. We had a male clerk at the store, so when I ran out of you-know-what at the end of you-know-when, Hubert went to the store and bought a box of them for me. I was too shy to buy them from a male clerk.

While living on the Army base, we met some very nice soldiers and their wives about our age. Some were older and some younger. They were from the eastern states and some came from as far west as Idaho.

Hubert and I had just gotten married. So he could see what a good cook I was, I thought I would surprise him with a double layer chocolate cake. Well, if you look and wait a while, you wouldn't or couldn't find a cake any flatter if you searched the world from one end to the other. To this day, I don't know what happened. I hurried and dumped it in the trash. I didn't mention the cake to Hubert, and he didn't ask. We left it at that.

I just happened to remember three or four things about our wedding. My husband's Aunt Thelma lived just across the street from my apartment. He was getting dressed over there. Naturally, I was getting dressed at my place. I didn't want to leave until he left, because I just couldn't let him see me before the wedding, don't you know? We kept waiting and waiting. Finally Hubert left for the church. The wedding was at 2 p.m. I mean it was supposed to be at 2 p.m. You have probably guessed by now that we were both late. My friend, Art Witt, sang *"I Love You Truly."* We weren't there, so he sang it the second time.

My wedding dress had about 18 inches of buttons up the back, but I had plenty of help getting all buttoned up. When I was getting dressed, my pastel bra showed through my gown. I had to borrow a white one from my landlady. Good thing she was my size. At least I had something borrowed.

Papa gave me away that day. I never thought to ask him if he got tired waiting. He did all right because I don't suppose he had any better place to go or anything any better to do. I bet I was beautiful coming down the aisle on the arm of my papa, as Sherri was on the arm of her daddy. Dad Rhodes said many times our wedding was the nicest place he had ever been!

When my husband and I were still in Kentucky, we would get a three or four-day leave and come back to Kansas. We would have to drive all night and day, so we could have more time at home with our parents. It was a good thing we were young and could handle those long hours.

Hubert was a cook in the Army. Sometimes he would bring our dinner home from the Army kitchen. It usually tasted almost as good as the Usta Place kitchen. With all the practice he got, he became quite a good cook. Of course, he was used to cooking for several hundred.

One time as we started back to camp, we noticed two soldiers hitchhiking along the highway. They were about two miles out of Nevada, Missouri. We stopped and asked them where they were headed. They told us they were headed for Camp Campbell, Kentucky. My goodness! We were headed there, too. We asked them if they wanted a lift. We had a two-door 1937 one seated Pontiac. We told them they could ride all the way, but would have to take turns sitting on each other's lap. No one mentioned me taking a turn. Please let me say right here. It was so crowded in that one seat that the trip seemed three times farther. They were so grateful that it was worth the inconvenience. Since they were hitchhiking, had we not

This picture is of Hubert (my first husband) and me at our wedding on September 9, 1945.

picked them up they could have been A.W.O.L. We never did ask them where they were from, just where they were headed.

While we were stationed at Camp Campbell, we used to go to the Grand Old Opry in Nashville. One night when we were coming home from there, I saw a falling star. I kept watching, and another one fell very close. Then I saw another in about the same area. I must have seen six or seven fall. I tried to make a wish on every one of them. I guess they all came true, because we got home safely and have been loaded down with all kinds of blessings, visible and unseen ones, don't you know? When we got back from Nashville that night, we pulled into camp, were checked through the gate and were on the way to our home. We were both very tired. Hubert thought the guards were asleep, I suppose, so he may have been speeding a little. The guard said he was anyway. He told Hubert to "hold it down," and he didn't ticket us. Maybe the guard was just half-awake. It was late!

When I lived there on the base, I could go to the commissary and buy everything that was scarce off base. Sugar, meat, coffee and lots of other items were hard to find at grocery stores. The soldiers had first choice. I would buy some of the hard-to-get items and take them home to Mama and Papa.

For all of you reading my story, I want you to know times were very hard for everyone. After the war was over, it took quite awhile for everything to get back to normal. For those who lost loved ones, I don't suppose life ever returned to normal.

A lot of you remember that during the forties there was a shortage of various articles. The government issued books of stamps to people to use to purchase these necessities. I was entitled to a gas stamp. During this time gas, sugar and meat were rationed by the government. All of us little Clark kids would give Papa and Mama our stamps. I want to know one thing. What good is a stamp for gas, if you don't have a tank to put it in? It was no good to me, so I gave my stamps to Papa Clark.

While in the service, there were four or five couples we hung around with, and we all became good friends. We were there a few weeks, and most of the soldiers had to go to Chicago to march in a victory parade. The war was over and this was a celebration parade. All of the husbands in our little group had to go. We had one man and wife whom we hung around with sometimes, but since he didn't have to go, he helped us while our husbands were away.

Being afraid to stay alone, all of us girls stayed together at one of our homes each night. One morning five or six of us girls decided to go into Clarksville, Tennessee, to eat breakfast. We all had scrambled eggs. I never saw so many scrambled eggs on a grill at one time in my lifetime. (Not even at the Usta Place.) I bet they had four dozen all being cooked at once. We stayed in Rhoda Miller's house that same night. Next day for breakfast she tried to scramble eggs like our chef at Clarksville. She didn't even come close. Maybe because she wasn't cooking four dozen or maybe the reason might have been because she hadn't learned to cook eggs just yet. I was a good cook, but that two-layer chocolate cake I told you about was a disgrace.

When Hubert was in training, he would get a leave, go to town and try to buy me some nylon stockings. Now some of you ladies can remember how scarce they were and how you had to wrestle, knock down and grab to get a pair of those nylons. We couldn't get them anywhere. Anyway, Hubert would stand in lines, sometimes an hour and a half, to get me a pair. He knew how happy I'd be to pull a pair of those lovelies out of his duffel bag. It was like Christmas, any time of the year, don't you know? One time he had been in line for an hour or so and just as he got up to the front of the line, they ran out. This was not cool!

We became real good friends with Rhoda and George, who were from Idaho Falls, Idaho. Some time later after we were out of the service, they invited us to come for a visit. They didn't have to ask twice or twist any arms. I'll tell you more about them and Idaho later.

The day finally came when it was time to leave Kentucky. There were a lot of tears and hugs exchanged that day, because many of us had become good friends. While in the service, you go through a lot together, and the friends you spend all of that time with sometimes become more like family than just friends.

When we came back to Ft. Scott, Hubert still had to go to Leavenworth, Kansas, to be discharged, so off we went. For two nights we stayed in a big hotel. While he was busy doing official business, I stayed at the hotel drinking coffee and riding the elevator up and down, up and down. This was a great way to pass the time, since I didn't have to clean, cook, etc. Besides, being a little back woodsy, I hadn't been on too many elevators in my whole lifetime, so it took a while to learn which buttons to push. Do you believe this? It's true.

For dinner the first evening, Hubert and I ordered fish. We both like fish and have eaten a lot of it, but these were served with the head still on. Now where I came from, the head was taken off before the insides were taken out. I removed the head and hid it in a napkin. When I saw those fish eyes, I wondered what kind of a place we were staying in anyway.

We finally got out and away from Leavenworth and needed a home to start housekeeping. Hubert's parents, Al and Stella Rhodes, had an old farmhouse needing a lot of fixing up, without electricity or running water. I can remember snow blowing through the cracks around the windows along one side of the old house. Actually, it was not much of a house and had only three rooms, but we could live there until we could do better, don't you know?

Well, Hubert and I decided to wallpaper our old farm home. Boy, did we have a lot to learn and a long way to go! After we hung the first ceiling, we weren't speaking to each other. We figured it would be to our advantage, being newlyweds, to hire it done. You see, we didn't know how to hang paper, so it didn't go very well.

We had saved a little money from my allotment and my check

from Key Work Clothes. To get started out, we bought seven young heifers that were ready to calve. When it came time for our baby calves to be born, every last one of the new mamas had a very hard time giving birth. Now remember, we still hadn't been married too long. I certainly knew how babies were made and how they were born, but I never knew you had to pull them out of the mamas. There was one baby calf that died out of the first seven we bought.

After seeing these little babies born, I wasn't too sure I wanted to have any little babies myself. I changed my mind somewhere along the line, and they are both worth every pound I gained and every contraction I had.

I had bought twenty-five hens for our fresh eggs. Boy, they were fresh! I knew how to get those eggs from the nest. I had plenty of experience down at the Usta Place. I can't tell you how many eggs I got from those hens each day, but I know it was plenty.

There was a small spring for stock water, so we hauled water from there for drinking. We really struggled out there that summer, as did several others along about then. We had started from scratch, so it was especially rough for us.

Hubert, Gary, Sherri and I went to the branch to go fishing one afternoon. Somewhere along the path I got into some poison oak. One minute I wanted to die and the next minute I felt like I was going to. I went to the doctor and got a shot and some medicine. I lived, but it took quite awhile to get rid of that poison oak. I suffered so badly because it was hot and we had no electricity for a fan. It not only itched, but was extremely painful. I haven't had it since, and probably won't, if I stay out of the bushes.

Papa came over to visit us one morning, and I made him a sandwich lunch. It was just too hot to cook. I have no idea how hot our kitchen was, but the heat was terrible and made the poison oak seem even worse.

It was not only hot that summer, but it was really dry, too. We had no water for stock and none for drinking. What an experience! I thought I had hauled the last water I would have to haul while living at home with Mama and Papa. Guess I was wrong! Now I hadn't told Hubert yet, but I didn't plan on spending another summer at that place.

When we were first married, we went out to Yellowstone Park and stayed there three weeks. We pitched a tent, slept on Army cots and used a kerosene stove for cooking fish and warming toes. We certainly had plenty of fish to cook and eat. It was plumb scary to hear the bears out there looking through the trash at night.

Rhoda and George, our friends from the Army, had again invited us to Idaho Falls. Well, we made that little trip out there to visit them again. When we got home, we decided to move out to Idaho. We got rid of all the stock and chickens, loaded up our old '37 Pontiac and headed for Idaho.

Now you could bet your bottom dollar our parents hated to see us leave. My second mama, Stella Rhodes, said, "Honey, you have to go where the money is." There wasn't that much money, but there was plenty of water, cool air and electricity. Papa gave us a dollar for gas. It cost fifteen cents a gallon back then, so that dollar went a lot further than today. I can still see him standing there as Hubert and I drove away.

This was about "spud" picking time, so we contacted our friends there. George took us out to meet his dad. Well, this was where it all started. We picked for his dad, and the farmer next to him, Mr. Burggren, wanted us to pick potatoes for them. I guess by now we were getting to be good "spud pickers." One summer we picked up over 420 bushels of those Idaho potatoes. You could take about a step and fill your basket. My goodness! We were paid eight cents a bushel. You can bet your bottom dollar, if you worked all day, you put in a hard day's work.

This farmer's brother-in-law, Mr. Beckman, also hired us to work for him. Well, I guess he liked us well enough to give Hubert a permanent job. We stayed with John until 1950, when we moved back to Kansas, but I'll tell you more about Idaho first.

As I mentioned a while back, this was just after the war ended. Well, I had to sign up and wait in line for a refrigerator. I signed up for a Norge. We waited for months and didn't get one. I then went to Montgomery Ward and signed up a second time. In a short while I got to buy my fridge. Twenty years later it would still freeze ice cubes in thirty minutes.

Farmer John was really nice to us and to work for. He never married, but took care of his mama and ran the farm. He loved children. A man like him would have made a good daddy.

He had a cottage with two rooms where we lived. We also had to go to an "outside throne" when we started to work for him. Sometimes there were seven-foot drifts of snow between our cottage and the throne. After we had lived there and worked for him awhile, he built on a small room for a bathroom and an extra bedroom. That room got put to good use. Having a bathroom in our house made us feel so rich.

Both of our children were born while we were there with the Beckman's. Gary was born first, and when he was a toddler, John would pick him up, wet diaper and all, straddle Gary around his neck and carry him around in the yard. Of course, Gary loved the attention.

Yes, I did try to keep that child dry. It was useless, especially when they would irrigate their yard. The water would be about four inches deep in parts of the yard. Gary liked to play with his sailboats in the irrigation ditches.

Just before Gary was born, President Harry Truman was campaigning through Idaho. We found out his caravan was coming within one mile of our house, so we jumped in the 1937 Pontiac. We had to wait awhile, but finally they came. There were about six or seven cars. President Truman saw me standing there and waved great big at us. They all "tooted" their horns. Being as big as I was right then and due anytime, Mr. President couldn't have missed seeing me.

I really want to add this little memory before I go any further. I bought a lot of things at J.C. Penney in Idaho Falls. While I was pregnant with Gary and Sherri, I still did the grocery and other shopping. I had always thought I'd be embarrassed for anyone to see me so big. I felt like I got bigger faster than anyone. I was in J.C. Penney's one day and a sales lady told me that a lot of women let themselves go when they become pregnant. She told me that I always looked so neat and clean and I kept my hair and nails done so pretty. That really made me feel good to hear a compliment like that. I felt good all the way through with both children, and that does really make a difference.

When Gary was about two years old, I started potty training. Just awhile before this, we had to walk over seven-foot snowdrifts to get to the outdoor throne. We got lucky and that summer our landlord built us a bathroom in our little cottage. We felt so rich and on top of the world, don't you know? Well, little Gary felt all grown up and would take his place on the stool to do his thing. To keep him interested, I would let him flush the stool when he finished. He would say "bye-bye" and wave to the stool. Cute, huh? He thought flushing was big-time fun.

When Gary and Sherri wanted me to get them ready for bed, they would say, "I'm sheepy." (You don't remember this, do you, children?) It seems like only yesterday. Those were the days.

We always had a lot of snow in Idaho with big high drifts. Sometimes they delivered our mail by snow plane. The year Sherri was born, our mail was just delivered to a pick-up point where we would have to go pick it up. One time when I went to get it, there was a package from Mama. She had pieced ten quilt tops, one for each Clark child. When I opened the package, I found mine was the "double wedding ring" pattern. That was true love. I finished up my quilt, lined and bound the edges. Sister number one, Dana, machine-quilted it for me. (I have given this beautiful quilt to Sherri now.)

As I mentioned before, it was time to pick potatoes and we were hired on this farm by Mr. Burggren to pick potatoes. After we finished his fields, we met his wife and family and were invited to have dinner with them. Oscar and Hannah had a son and daughter who were both pretty young.

Now remember, we were from Kansas. After dinner, we were visiting over coffee when their little girl asked me, "Helen, what do hillbillies look like?" She had to have heard that somewhere, don't you know? I asked Fern to get a pencil and paper. I then told the little girl to first draw my profile and then draw a front view. They laughed about that for a long time.

While we were waiting to go to the hospital to have Sherri, we had reserved a snow plane to come for me, just in case the car, our 1937 Pontiac, couldn't make it through the snowdrifts. Anyway, that plane was on standby. This was in January of 1950, so we never knew what the weather would do. Mrs. Beckman, John's mother, told me when we first went there to always keep our pantry and cupboards full of food like flour, sugar, coffee, lard and salt because sometimes they get snowed in. I already knew that. Mama always told us to stock up. One winter we were snowed in for two weeks and one day. I had two tablespoons of flour left when we were finally able to get out.

My mother-in-law, Stella Rhodes, came to Idaho Falls to stay with Gary while I was in the hospital having Sherri Ann. When I got home from the hospital and she saw Sherri, she cried. Tears are made to share and are shed to show joy!

We lived in Swede country out there, so you can bet all of your bottom dollars we would stock plenty of coffee. They take coffee breaks at 10 a.m. and 4 p.m. every day of the week, so I began to drink more coffee than I did when I was a little tad.

As you have read in my story, I always grew and canned barrels of fruits and vegetables. Out there in Idaho it was no different. John had another nice man working for him who helped with the irrigating. Ed always took care of watering my garden for me. Another thing that stands out in my mind about him is that when their cattle or sheep would be "making out," he would be speaking Swedish, of course, and he would say, "Rid'em, cowboy!" It was so cute. Could any of you reading my story tell me why I would remember something like that?

When we first got to Idaho, we saw lots of jackrabbits. I asked Hubert how there could be so many rabbits without a mama. Surprise! I thought the jackrabbits were the bucks. I should have known that. I was from the country.

We all loved to fish, so George, Rhoda, Hubert and I fished a lot. We spent a lot of our weekends on the Snake River or Yellowstone Lake. One time when we were on the lake, we all had our lines in the water troll fishing. Soon Rhoda felt a hit. She had one. I said, "Hold him, Rhoda!" She was reeling him in, and the reel went all silly and wouldn't work. Her line looked like she had a whale; her rod was bent in half. She carried her extra lures and tackle in a cigar box. When this darn reel went haywire, she started wrapping her line around the cigar box. She was so nervous. I just knew she was going to lose the battle. After all, we didn't want to have to the say "the biggest one got away," did we? If the biggest one got away, he would have had to be a dandy, because she caught the prettiest salmon you ever saw. It was probably twenty inches long. I don't know how much it weighed, but it was a beauty!

The boys thought we needed gas for the boat, so Rhoda and I got out on land and planned to start lunch and eat when the boys got back. They had been gone about ten minutes. Now, you will never believe who came for a visit, or maybe you might. He wasn't grown, but a good-sized bear cub appeared. Naturally, he was starved. Now you can bet your bottom dollar I did some deep thinking. As I said way back in my story, Papa and Mama taught us to share. I was more than willing to share our food, and that's what it was going to take. He was big, and if you are out there alone with no protection, he looked much bigger!

This little visitor stayed around and got started early on our loaf

of bread. I gave him half slices to make it last longer. He liked that. He didn't know it wasn't a full slice, don't you know? He ate that first slice like it was yesterday's news. I gave him another and another and another. After all, bears don't get baker's bread every day. He acted as though he liked it almost as much as I did when I got it out of Uncle Jimmy's breadbox. Anxious to know what happened? Well, I'll tell you. After he ate all the bread and started on the sandwich fixins', the boys were coming and "teddy" heard the motor. He stood up and looked around. That bear was taller than I, but just about everyone and everything is taller than me.

Teddy ran into the woods. We didn't waste any time getting into the boat and left. There wasn't any use staying. Our food was gone, and there could be a bigger bear, several bigger bears being told about the good food being offered at the side of the river at the "Rhodes-Miller Buffet." The scenery was just as beautiful viewing it from the lake as it was on shore, and we were much safer there.

When Gary was born and we came home from the hospital, I

wasn't expecting to find everything so in order. When I came in the house, there sat a new baby buggy, the one I used in the pea field later. The fridge was full of steak, roasts and chops. There were two sets of clothes for Gary. Hubert couldn't decide on one, so he bought both. He had also bought me a set of silverware. The pattern was "Eternally Yours."

When we brought Gary home from the hospital all dressed up in blue, our neighbor held him and gave him back to me. Mrs. Beckman, who was about seventy-five years old, thought he was so precious she started crying and used her apron to dry her eyes and her nose. This seems like just a few days ago. Do you know what I mean?

Now when Sherri was born, we didn't get a new buggy, but this first one was practically new. Sherri loved to ride in the buggy, too. (Granny didn't have a buggy to "drag" in when I was a baby. I had to learn to walk early to make room for sister Margie.) Sherri was just beautiful in her little pink hood and sweater, booties, lacy dresses, anklets and white shoes, of course. Yes, they both had shoes. Times had really changed from the time I was born at the Usta Place to when my children were born. It's amazing how life or time just keeps going on and on and is so different from the Usta Place.

My sister, Gayle, and her husband, John, moved to Idaho Falls and lived there at the same time we did. Of course, we lived in the country, and Gayle's family lived in town. Now when I went to town, I always took the buggy because it was just easier to care for the children. We would also put her son, John Edward, in the buggy.

One time when we went to town, we got thirsty so we went to the fountain to get a root beer. I lifted Gary out of the buggy and set him up on the stool. Gayle picked John Edward up, and I picked Sherri up out of the buggy. A little girl about three years old stood there watching. She leaned over the side of the buggy and said, "You got any more in there?" It was so funny and cute, too. Gayle and I laughed about it for a long time. I suppose she thought we had a "day care" tucked away in there.

I always cut potatoes for planting. Gary was a little biddy baby the first year I cut seed. I took him with me to the potato cellar in his big baby buggy, warm bottles and blankets. He slept most of the time.

The farmers there grew peas for seed. Our friend, John, told me I could go around the edge of the field and pick in about ten or fifteen feet from the edge. By now, you have realized old hard-headed,

hard-working Helen wouldn't let those peas go to waste. I'd wheel Gary to the field, buckets and all, pick two buckets of peas, go to lunch and go back in the afternoon to do the same thing.

You are probably wondering how I carried two buckets and pushed a buggy? I hooked them on the sides of the buggy and wheeled everything and baby Gary to the house. I hulled the peas at night. That year, I canned seventy pints of peas the hot water bath method.

When we lived in Idaho, I didn't have a washing machine. I had a wash board and tub. I washed Birds Eye cloth diapers every day. Since Gary and Sherri were eighteen months apart, I would have twenty to thirty diapers in the laundry each time. It was a big job, but someone had to do it. I didn't have the luxury of disposable diapers when my children were babies.

Away back when we were in Idaho, we went shopping one day. I should have left Hubert at home. He wanted me to try on a full-length fur coat. I liked it, but we couldn't afford something like that. It was big money then. Now it is still too much for me. I took it off, but it was fun to dream for awhile.

We came back to Kansas a short time later, and I mentioned the coat to Papa. I think most of us have asked our parents for advice and not liked to hear what they have to say. Oh yes, it has happened to me a couple of times. I asked him if he thought it would be silly for me to buy a fur coat at that price. His answer was, "I think that would be uphill business." This was the end of the coat. I wasn't about to bet my bottom dollar he would agree. His "bucks" were always hard to come by also.

Mother-in-laws are like seeds. They come with the tomato.

CHAPTER 8

I'M SURE YOU HAVE HEARD of mothers-in-law, and I'm sure most of you have had one of these precious ladies in your life. Now you hear comments like if it weren't for her, it's her fault, if it hadn't been for her, she causes all the trouble between us.

I simply can't identify with any of this kind of idle talk. I was truly blessed with the most generous, kind and loving human being you could find on the face of the earth to be my mother-in-law. As I said in the beginning of my story, she and Mama went to grade school together back in 1896. As little girls, they were good friends.

I met Stella Pearle (Young) Rhodes in 1941. I never heard her say anything bad about anyone at any time during the time I knew her. She was a second mother to me, and she loved me like one of her own daughters. She told me so.

Stella was so sweet to Gayle, my sister number eight. I guess they had been very close for over thirty years. At Christmas time, Gayle would send her a box of goodies. Stella looked forward to getting the box. Usually there was a wrapped gift inside the box with the candy and cookies. When Stella Perle had to go the rest home, Gayle's boxes didn't stop. She still sent Stella gifts. Gayle sent her flowers from time to time also.

I was visiting Stella at the rest home one day, and she said she had something she wanted to show me. She knelt down and pulled out a box from under the bed. Gayle had sent her a music box shaped like a tiny piano. She kept it hidden because her belongings had disappeared at different times. Isn't that a disgrace for these lovely little old ladies and men to have things stolen at the rest home? I certainly think so. Anyway, she wanted me to have the little music box. I took it, thanked her and told her I would see that it was taken care of.

Another time we were visiting Stella in the rest home, she gave me some old coins, nickels, dimes and quarters. She told me the nickels had been used to close Dad Rhodes' eyes after he passed away. They did it that way back years ago.

I lost my second mama on January 3, 1993. I gave Sherri the music box Stella had given to me, because I knew she would also see that it was taken care of. The mantel clock that had belonged to Stella's mother, Grandma Nancy Young, she had given to me and I let Gary have it. She had given me dishes, and I have given them to Gary and Sherri.

Years earlier I was invited to Stella's house one Sunday for lunch after I met and had started dating her son, Hubert Rhodes. I can't remember what she had, but she was a good cook and I know she knew how to cook beans. She had me come to her house to eat beans every Wednesday when I was working in town. She always had a good dinner fixed for me and we had time to visit. (This was before I married her boy with a good car, with good brakes and a big heart.)

She had turkeys and geese in a pen between the house and the "outside throne." You had to go through the flock to get to your destination. Now this was often a problem, don't you know? She told me old Tom was one mean turkey and that he was one to flog at the drop of a hat. I would have worn that hat, too, had it been dropped in my path. I went prepared. I found a stick that wouldn't bend. Well, I started through the pen where he was. Old Tom, his feathers strutting all over the place, started gobbling at me. My first thought was to protect myself. After all, I was taller than he was, but that turkey started after me. Well, when I swung at that bird, I didn't think I hit him that hard. I really didn't, but I must have hit him just in the right place because he went down, flat as he could get on the ground. He was out cold! I didn't kill him, but that last strike broke that turkey from attacking anyone again. He came out of it, and I guess he lived happily ever after or until butchering time. He had several hens out there, so he probably forgot all about "this old hen." Can you imagine eating a turkey with that kind of behavior? That mean old turkey wouldn't have even tasted good, don't you know?

Stella became my second mama a short time after that. Dad Rhodes told my Mama that Helen and Hubert's wedding was the nicest place he had ever been. I guess he told several people that day that same thing.

While Al and Stella Rhodes still lived at Pawnee Station, Kansas, we visited them often. They made me feel welcome, even after I clubbed old Tom Turkey out cold. They were both very special people in my life.

One precious memory I have of Al Rhodes, and will forever, is standing out of sight, of course, listening to him sing from an old hymnal. Dad Rhodes was getting up in years and loved to sing. He had a beautiful voice and was a handsome old fellow. I so vividly can remember him standing there, leaning on the buffet, singing without an accompanist. *"The Old Rugged Cross"* and *"What A Friend We Have In Jesus"* seemed to be his favorites. If I live to be a hundred years old, this memory will still be with me. Thank you, Dad Rhodes, for leaving such an imprint in my mind and on my heart. May God bless you both, Al and Stella. You are both two sweet people in my memories.

Stella never learned to drive a car. My mama didn't drive a car either. I suppose they saw no need to learn, since they were both busy doing the things most mamas do. Besides, there were plenty of youngins' around anxious to get behind the wheel and drive them where they needed to go. Lot of the wives back in those days never learned to drive a car.

Al Rhodes had a pet name for his wife, Stella. He called her "Queenie." My Papa called my Mama "Bunt." Where in the world he came up with "Bunt" for a pet name, I'll never know.

Hubert had a younger brother named Wayne. I believe he was the age of my sister number eight, Gayle. Wayne had a pet goat that I truly believe could have climbed Mt. Everest without a rope or any kind of pushing. He would try to eat everything not tied down or underground.

After Stella entered the rest home, several years later, I took her out on her birthday. She had been my second mama for quite awhile by now. She looked at the menu. I told her she could order anything she wanted because I was buying. She said, "Do you know what I'd like to have?" I said, "What?" She said, "I would like to have a wiener on a bun. That's all I want." I said, "Then, by George, that's what you may have!"

I asked the waitress if by any chance they would have wieners and could they put it on a bun. She said they could. You can bet your bottom dollar she got it. She didn't want any mustard or ketchup on it. She just wanted it plain with a cup of coffee. She didn't even want any dessert. She ate it and enjoyed every bit.

I can imagine how one of these little old men and women might crave a wiener, pizza or foods they shouldn't have or don't get in the rest home. One time I went to a rest home to give a friend of mine a permanent. She had been coming to my salon, so I needed to go there to do the service. I asked her if they were good to her, if she had everything she needed, was the food good, etc. She told me she would love to have some bacon for breakfast. Now, since the owners of the home didn't believe in eating pork, they didn't serve it. I called her son about the situation. Guess what! She was given some bacon with some of her meals, don't you know?

There are so many precious memories I have kept in my mind of my second mom, Stella Rhodes. She was always doing something for someone. When Stella would speak of someone being small, she would say, "She was about as big as a cake of soap after a full day of washing." Cute, huh?

She wore her hair long, but kept it rolled into a single roll around the back of her head. I wanted to cut it one time, but at that time she wouldn't hear of it. A few years later, when she went into the rest home, the girls talked her into having it cut short. She looked very pretty with it cut short.

Mama taught me how to make monkey dolls out of men's work socks. They are so ugly they are cute! One year, I made twenty of those little beauties. A minister from Kansas City bought seven of them, and I've wondered why he wanted so many of them. Do you think he might have been getting them for his grandchildren? I never thought of that.

I just loved to do my craft shows. I've met so many nice people and I love to sew. It's a good way to take in pocket change and sell all of the things I love to make. I had a show once in Parsons, Kansas. A young couple came by my table carrying a little child about eight months old. He was crying and wouldn't take his bottle. They couldn't get him to hush, so I took a small stuffed horse from my table and gave it to the baby. I don't put buttons or snaps on my toys, because it makes them safer for the children. The mother thanked me and went on her way. They came back by a little later, and the baby had gone to sleep sucking on the leg of the horse. The mother said he put the horse in his mouth and it was like giving him a bottle.

Dana and I would get together and work on ideas that we thought might be good sellers for craft shows. There is a buyer for all the projects you exhibit. I've been told that my work is very neat and that I had good taste in choosing the correct fabrics for all my designs.

I've never had one craft show where I didn't give an elderly man or woman or a child, after asking mommy, a plate of cookies, candy or a loaf of mini-bread. The elderly folks and the wee ones paid with a big smile and thank you. It made me happy to share. Believe me! One time, I gave a friend a pound of pecan meats. That's true love. I hope Mary enjoyed them.

When we used to come back to Kansas from Idaho Falls and our visit was over, we would try to leave, but it got harder each time. We would start to pull out and Papa and Mama watched until we got out of sight. Papa would give me a dollar for gas. (It was eighteen cents a gallon then.)

Both of our children, "little gems," were born in Idaho Falls, Idaho. My son, Gary Allen Rhodes, was born July 22, 1948, in the Mormon hospital there. I believe his hospital bill was seventy-six dollars. When he was born, I had to share a ward with three other mothers. They said the first question I asked was if he had ten fingers and ten toes. He did. He was perfect.

My daughter, Sherri Ann, was born in the Catholic hospital January 10, 1950, and her bill was seventy-five dollars. The doctors charged about the same with both babies. Now it is surely more than that. When Sherri was born, Hubert came in and said, "You've always wanted a dishwasher. Now you have one." My little dishwasher turned out to be a very good cook and did dishes, too.

When Sherri got to the age of two, I started her potty training. She was excited and very seldom had an accident in her little ruffled panties. She and Gary would love to dress up in the clothes I made for them. (I don't know if children wear homemade clothes now. They like the name-brand things. I could have sewn a "Rhodes Original" label in theirs, but I didn't.)

This little story just came to my mind, so I must tell you about it now. In 1962 I had to have major surgery. Sister Wilma offered to come to my house, help take care of me and help in the kitchen, too. She was amazed to see my little cook doing everything I would have had to do. Sherri always liked to help me cut out biscuits, cookies and noodles. By the time she was nine years old, she could cook a complete meal of fried chicken, potatoes, gravy, vegetable and dessert with no help from me.

Now Gary was a different story. He didn't like being in the kitchen, but liked the outdoors. I think I mentioned before he liked to pick flowers and bring them to me. He still brings me flowers for Mother's Day and birthdays, plus dinner out at my favorite "eating trough."

Gary was just four months old, and we had just gotten home from a fishing trip on the Snake River. When we got in the door, our landlord came to tell us that Hubert's father, Allen Rhodes, had passed away unexpectedly. We were all just worn out, but we had to make plans to start back to Kansas. I got busy and did laundry, packed clothes and tried to sleep an hour or two. I prepared bottles for the "wee one."

We left about 2 a.m. for Bourbon County in Kansas. We drove without sleep until we got home. Gary was so tired and exhausted. He kept crying and crying; his bottle didn't help. He just wouldn't hush. We finally got home and Papa took him on his lap and started looking at a magazine. Now remember, Gary was four months old. I guess the crackling of the paper was soothing his little ears. It sounds unbelievable, but this is true. He went to sleep, slept all night and wasn't fussy the next day.

Mama Clark got started early the next morning and gave him his bath. She dressed him up cute. This was the first time they had seen him. When Stella saw Gary, she broke down and cried also. This was also the first time she had seen him. I don't know why Papa and Mama never told any of us kids they loved us, because I know they did. They wouldn't have kept us all together and kept food and clothes for us if they didn't. Papa kissed me at the cemetery the day of Dad Rhodes' funeral. He may have kissed me when I was a little girl, but I don't remember ever being kissed by either of them before that day. Just think of all the years we missed!

When Gary was little, he liked to carry fish worms and little knives in his overall pockets. Sherri would store and carry her treasures in the pockets on her little dresses. You may think it silly for me to remember such little things about my children when they were growing up, but they are such sweet memories.

We bought Gary a tricycle when he was about eighteen months old. He loved his new wheels, but had a hard time learning to ride it. Hubert tied his little feet to the pedals and would push him along. Gary would think he was doing all the work. He learned right away after that and was so proud. When Sherri came along and big enough to ride, she stood behind Gary on the "stand-up" section. She held onto to Gary so she wouldn't fall off. They had so much fun.

One day when Gary was through riding his tricycle, he left it outside the fence in the way of the farm tractor. Well, his daddy was moving the tractor and not looking where he was backing, backed over it and mashed it flat. I was so thankful Gary was in the house.

Well, this little son grew up, got married and has two sons, Marcus and Trenton. When Marcus was around two, he got a tricycle and Gary taught him how to ride it. Marc left his wheels where they weren't supposed to be, and Gary backed over it, just like Hubert had done!

When Sherri was about five years old, Gary seven, Hubert took them fishing late one afternoon. They went to a small creek close to home. It was getting late, and naturally it kept getting darker. I got so worried and angry that they would stay so long. They finally came up the driveway. Headlights never looked so good.

Sherri had caught a channel cat about eighteen inches long. After that, they were "hooked," and none of them wanted to come home just yet. They kept fishing and Sherri caught another one about the same size. Sherri had caught the two fish on a cane pole with a grasshopper for bait. Hubert had to help Sherri land the two fish, as they were too big for a five and seven-year-old to lift out, don't you know? There's another story where the big ones did not get away.

When they showed me their catch, I understood. They didn't know I shed a few tears when they got home. I had been imagining all kinds of things, so the tears were tears of joy that they were safe. We mothers tend to worry when our loved ones are late, don't we?

One time, Hubert, Gary, Sherri, Mama and I went to Diamond, Missouri, to pick strawberries. I certainly remember this trip. I think we picked between two and three crates of berries that day. Mama hung right in there to the clock-out time. Gary and Sherri helped, too. We still had work to do the next day preparing the strawberries for the freezer.

In this picture Gary and Sherri are taking their bath in a galvanized tub in the kitchen of our old farmhouse house near Redfield, Kansas. In 1953 there was no indoor plumbing so this was the only way.

Mama just loved to get outside and harvest. After she moved to town, she made a garden in her back yard. She loved to pick berries and pick up pecans, too. Oscar and Wilma always had a lot of nuts and would let family come in and pick for half.

This one time when we were there, Mama was kind of off by herself and started to walk up the embankment where we were all preparing lunch. A huge German Shepherd dog was there. I think he belonged to Wilma's daughter. Anyway, he saw Mama walking toward us and started growling and barking at her, as if he were going to attack her. I was scared to death and yelled for someone to get that crazy dog away from her. They did and tied him up after that.

Oscar and Wilma were at our house to eat one time. I had made macaroni salad, and Oscar said it was the one dish I made that wasn't fit to eat. Even though he didn't like the salad, I had plenty of other dishes he chowed down on. I always enjoyed having them come to eat with us. None of my family is particular about what they eat or how it is cooked. We eat and enjoy the food set before us and are so thankful for it.

CHAPTER 9

HUBERT QUALIFIED to enroll in the GI program, so he decided he would train in agriculture. His time was running out, and if he didn't go then he would lose out on the program. We decided to go back to Kansas, from where we started. We headed back there in the spring of 1950.

Well, my mother-in-law had a herd of cattle and a farm, so she wanted us to use it while Hubert was in school. When we left Idaho Falls for Kansas, it really was a big decision. We had furniture, two children and a bushel or two of memories.

Hubert bought a good-size truck and also made a two-wheel trailer to move our belongings. I drove the 1937 Pontiac (wish I had it now) loaded with my two babies, Gary and Sherri, all our luggage and everything you needed for traveling, like snacks, diapers and water. (I was always taught to take fresh water.) Hubert drove the big truck and pulled the loaded two-wheel trailer.

We were somewhere in Colorado going through a city, and as we were crossing about four rough railroad tracks the two-wheel trailer broke loose and swerved over to the right side of the street. Of course, I was right behind Hubert and when I saw what happened, I shoved my car into a high gear and took out after him, driving too fast and honking the horn.

I finally got him stopped a mile down the highway. We went back and got our wheels. The gentleman at the depot saw the accident and pulled the trailer off the tracks for safety. We were coupling the trailer to the hitch, and all this time Hubert kept saying, "When you saw what happened, why this, why that?" The gentleman came to my rescue and said, "Sir, the minute she saw that trailer break loose, she took out lickity-split to catch you. She did exactly what she should have done." Sometimes it's easy to lash out at someone. Just think, we three could have been in the truck with Hubert and we wouldn't have missed the trailer until we stopped for gas, to eat, rent a motel or maybe even getting home and start to unload. Anyway, we all lived through it.

Sherri was about ten months old when we came back to Kansas from Idaho. She was just starting to walk and was so pretty and cute. She was a darlin'. Sister number one, Dana, loved children and wanted to hold Sherri on her lap. My precious daughter wouldn't have anything to do with anyone. She just wanted to sit on her "mudder's" lap. Yes, that's what she called me. After all, my baby had never seen any of my family, so she was frightened. Dana asked me if it made me feel good to know she wanted just me, and it did!

We got back to the farm, and I had never been so depressed in my life. There were weeds as tall as the house, and there certainly was a lot of cleaning up to do inside the house, too. We had nothing to work with, for the floors, windows and walls were all bare, but with a little money and hard work we got the place livable. It wasn't much, but we were clean, dry and had food.

Hubert got enrolled in classes in the Agriculture College. He and a neighbor man took turns driving. It was one night a week, about thirty miles one way. Lorraine would stay with me one week, then the next week I'd stay with her until the men came home from school. We eventually started staying in our own homes.

I would always wait up for Hubert to get home. One night I was reading while I was waiting and fell asleep. It was about 10:30 at night and the children were sleeping. I heard something scratching on the window screen. I was so afraid! I thought if it was him get-ting home, he would have knocked. I kept quiet. There was another scratch, then another. I became absolutely petrified. I was so afraid, I honestly believe if there had been a gun in the house, I would have used it. I thought it had to be a stranger. I had no phone to call for help, so I waited a little longer and finally there was a knock on the door and Hubert called out my name. You can bet your bottom dollar we had an understanding on a few things after that night, a very clear understanding. I was so angry he put me through this frightful experience, don't you know?

A little while later at this same place we had an auction and sold everything except our home furnishings, clothing and our "Tippy" dog. I'll tell you more about the auction later, but please let me tell you a couple of things about Tippy. Our neighbor gave us this little black and white dog. He was just an alley dog, but he needed a home, too. We named him Tippy, for he had four white paws and a white tip on his tail. Tippy seemed to be just right for him.

Tippy started to grow up and was glad to see us when we got home from work or anywhere. As I said, Tippy was growing and that meant he was getting interested in other black, yellow, brown or white canines. It didn't matter what color. Tippy came home one day and had been beaten so badly that one of his eyeballs was protruding. It was just disgusting. I couldn't imagine anyone treating an animal like that. Right then, I didn't know who the guilty one was. Well, our neighbor, Bill, the dog-beater had a female, and Tippy had, like any dog would do, made a visit to her place. Bill told our best friend, Ray Hartman, what had happened. Naturally, Ray told us. Bill certainly dissolved our friendship that day.

Little Tippy got mean after that. If we didn't speak to him when we came in after dark, he would try to bite. After we moved to town, we had to keep him tied up. One day he disappeared, chain and all. We never found Tippy, and we were all very sad. This puppy wasn't pedigree material, but to us he was solid "black" gold. He loved us and we loved him. I just hope he found a second home.

While the children were still small, my brother gave me a "runt" pig out of the litter. He was going to destroy the little pig because he really didn't look too promising. I begged for him and told Herman I would feed and care for Porky. With the help of Gary, Sherri and God in Heaven, Porky soon became a full-grown hog.

We mentioned butchering him. That idea sailed out the window. The children wanted no part of it, so we decided to sell Porky and get another one to butcher. I called Ray Smith and sold Porky. He wanted to give me thirty dollars for that great big hunk, the handsome king of pigs. I told him I would have to have fifty dollars for him and wouldn't load him out of the pen for less. Guess which one got her way! When they loaded the porker and started to leave, little tears started from four eyes.

Things got better, and soon Porky was put behind us. He had been a real joy to the children. He was such a pet, and we loved him, too. Can you imagine what might have happened had Porky been, you know? Probably gone out the back door with Ray's turnips. We certainly couldn't have eaten him.

While we were still living in the same house, without Porky, we had failure after failure. We tried crops and garden, plus our hogs and dairy cattle. I suppose you could say we did all right with the cattle, but that's about all.

We joined the artificial breeding association. The first year we had one brown Swiss cow that had twin heifer calves. She had one baby before we went to work. When we got home from work and went to the barn, I drew to Hubert's attention that the little heifer had grown quite a bit in eight hours. We started looking and, sure enough, there were two little babies.

We had a beautiful stand of soybeans. Well, you have probably guessed. The beans were ready to harvest, and we hired a man for the job. It started raining, and it kept raining until he couldn't get into the field. Ray Turner told us if we could get them closer to the house, he could finish them. There was only one thing to do. Hubert and I put on the rubber boots and gloves, got the two-wheel trailer and tractor and headed for the soybean field. We pulled them out of the ground and hauled every one of them to the house. After we finished, we felt like we had a full day's work, each day. You talk about a big job, but we did it.

On top of all that, we all came down with the flu or light colds that winter. I didn't feel like cooking or eating after the food was cooked, but we were trying to get by. We should have done the onion poultice cure, but I didn't even feel like peeling the onions.

One afternoon one of our neighbors, Alice Coyan, brought a big bowl of chocolate cookies to us. She was like a walking angel. My little ones soon found the bottom of the plate. If you are fortunate to have friends like the Dan Coyan family, you have it made, big-time. We sort of expected our church to lend us a hand. Since we didn't see anything of them, do you suppose they were afraid of catching something?

When Sherri was getting ready to have her third birthday, there was no money for a gift. I had a card, so I dropped a stick of gum in the card. I guess you could say we were having hard times, too. Those were the days. I believe Sherri may still have the card and stick of gum. I know she stored them in my cedar chest to keep them safe.

I gave Sherri that first piece of furniture I ever owned. It was a gift for my seventeenth birthday from Hubert, her father. Being my little pack rat, she probably has saved many treasures in that cedar chest for her children, Rusty and Kristi, just as I did for her and Gary.

While we were living at that old farm, it certainly seemed like a second depression. Everything went against us. One morning a real bad windstorm came over our place and did a lot of damage to our crops and house.

There wasn't much of a foundation under the house. When the wind hit, all four of us were so scared and we just knew our house was going to blow away. That old house shook so bad that we were expecting it to go any minute. Hubert and I were thinking the same. We got the children, put them between us and sat down on the divan. We held them close and thought our time had come. Naturally, we started to pray for help. We had no shelter and not much time to get to one. I don't know what Hubert's prayer was, but I asked God to take care of us, keep us safe and spare our old house. Our milk truck had stopped to pick up our cans of milk. The driver told us he was afraid the house was going to go, so he pulled his big truck out of the path in case the house blew down and away. Guess what! HE (God) was with us all the way through this storm and all the way since then! He has certainly answered many of our prayers. Sometimes the answer isn't what we want to hear, but He always answers, don't you know?

Along about then, we were seeing some very lean times and tried to save in every way we could. Hubert needed a haircut, and I knew I could do it. After all, I had been cutting hair since "heck was a pup." I hadn't gone to cosmetology school yet, but I knew I could do it. Well, I did give him his hair cut. That was on Saturday. I can't remember what the reason was for missing church the following Sunday morning, but he didn't go. I really didn't think it looked too botched. Anyway, in a short time his hair had grown back like it was before and he needed another cut. He lost my number to call for an appointment, if you know what I mean. That first time I cut a man's hair was quite an experience. I'm not sure if I got a thank you from him, but it didn't cost him a dime.

Papa and Dana, sister number one, competed against each other in the competition for the tallest stalk of corn at the county fair in 1955. Papa won the blue ribbon, but I'm not sure that he had found out he had won. Mama and Papa were planning on going to the fair in the afternoon to check it out and see who had won the contest. Unfortunately, while pulling a small trailer with barrels to get water for his hogs, Papa was involved in a two-car accident just a mile from home. He was killed instantly. I can't imagine causing an accident and having to live with it for the rest of my life.

This was the worst shock I have ever experienced. I thought my whole life had ended. Papa was close to all of us, but I not only lost Papa, I lost my good friend. I was working at Key Work Clothes at that time, so the employees took up a collection of money for Mama, brought a big ham already cooked and sliced, a big bunch of groceries, coffee, bread, sugar, canned goods, etc. Mama was next to tears again. She said she didn't know there were people like that out there.

Ed was a hard-working, trustworthy man who loved us all. As far as I know, everyone loved him. I bought him a new white shirt, so he would look nice on his final day with us. At his funeral, the chapel was full of friends and neighbors. They lined the yard and into the street. The funeral director told me Papa's funeral was, if not the largest, one of the largest he had ever been a part of at the Konantz Chapel.

But we still had Mama. She was strong and she would hold the family together. Mama told me several years later that when Papa was killed in the car accident, the sheriff called her on the phone and gave her the bad news. I believe Mama was about sixty-seven years old and lived several miles out in the country with no close neighbors. That sheriff should have called our brother or a sister to meet him at the home to give Mama this terrible news. Agree? It certainly was a good thing Mama was the strong lady that she was to do what she had to do during that horrible time.

Mama told me later when she got the news and hung up the phone, she went over to Papa's chair, picked up his pipe and slippers and dropped them in the stove. I don't know why she did it and she probably didn't either.

My brother, Herman, told me when our dear Papa was killed that some thief came and stole the tools he carried in his car before the car was towed away from the scene of the accident. Now this as bad as someone stealing flowers from a grave. Herman also told me that while he was in the hospital one time that someone went to his farm and stole tools from him. Maybe these thieves thought Herman and Papa didn't need them anymore, but it was still stealing.

All the time I lived in the country and worked at Key Work Clothes, I rode to work with another man and his wife. One morning he told me someone got his sack lunch, and the one that was left for him was an egg salad sandwich. He said he ate it even though it wasn't good. I told him a similar incident happened to me. I opened the brown bag and pulled out my sandwich. I found a bologna sandwich. I never could stand that meat. (I still can't.) We still laugh about that one. You see, I rode in the front seat, and when we got to work, we got out of the car and we each picked up a bag. They were identical brown bags. He got mine and I had gotten his lunch. We have lived a long time after trading lunches, which was in the middle fifties. Both of us are still going ninety miles an hour. He is my age, and I think he is also an Aquarius. We didn't hold hard feelings over him not liking my egg salad.

I remember a good laugh I must jot down here. We had several young people in our neighborhood and church. They were just kids, boys and girls just like yours and mine. As I mentioned, we had a "two-seater" outdoor throne on the farm. About the same time each night after dinner, Hubert would take the lantern and make his usual trip to the outdoor palace. This particular night was Halloween, and several came to trick or treat us. When he got to the palace and opened the door, about four or five of our geese flapped out at him. Someone had locked the geese inside. I guess they were as anxious to get out as Hubert was to get in. The neighbor kids all denied doing this prank, but we knew someone was guilty. It's funny now, but it wasn't that night. You can bet your bottom dollar that made Hubert's trip a little more necessary.

As I wrote previously, we had returned to Kansas planning to make a lot of money like every other farmer, but it seemed like this wasn't in God's plan. If we didn't drown out, we burned up. If it wasn't one problem, there would be another to cause crop failure. We had hail one year that shredded our corn and demolished my garden. We were already struggling to get along.

Both of us were working at Key Work Clothes in Ft. Scott. We came in one evening after work and walked into a mess. We were heating with coal in a Warm Morning heater. Hubert had "banked" the stove for the day to make it easier to start a fire. The stove had blown up and scattered soot all over everything! I had taken about all I could take. I sat down and cried. What's the use? We were working so very hard and falling backward every step. I said, "This is it. We are moving to town to a warm house, good water and closer to work!"

So again we sold our stock, cattle, hogs, chickens and the belongings we didn't need any longer at a public auction. We had a big sale. Crowds of people came. While they were selling the cattle, the auctioneer asked Hubert about each cow, how much milk she gave, if she was sound, etc. They came to this one and asked about her being productive. Hubert told the auctioneer the cow had one quarter that was bad. I was standing out in the crowd and heard a man tell another man that Hubert was too honest for his own good. Well, please let me say right here, honesty never hurt anyone. That old cow brought as much as the rest of them. Oh, yes, they all sold well. Honesty really paid off that day, just like it always does, don't you know?

We had a lot of good times and certainly some sad times at that old farm. Some memories I would like to forget, but those times are part of my life, so I can't and would not want to erase them completely. You can bet your bottom dollar I was glad to get away from that place.

We were moved within two weeks. We didn't have our animals and chickens, but we had a garden in town. That's all you need if you are working forty hours a week. We also had running water and a bathroom in the house.

Have you ever had a tramp at your door? We did, just a week before Christmas in 1956. We had eaten early that evening and planning to wrap gifts. Someone knocked at the door. I thought, oh boy, someone is coming to drink coffee and enjoy some of my famous cookies. I always had some baked. I opened the door, and there stood a man dressed poorly, thin and looked mighty hungry. He said, "Do you have some work I could do for something to eat?" If he had come around a year or so earlier, he could have helped us pull our soybeans or clean up all of that soot I left out there in the country, but he wasn't there then; he was here now.

I called my husband to the door, and we talked to him a bit more. In the olden days I wasn't afraid of strangers, as we are today. After all, he looked hungry. You can bet your bottom dollars, I get hungry now and then and when I do, I eat. We let him come in and told him we had finished eating, but I would reheat some food. He asked if he could wash his hands. We went into the bathroom with him to show him where everything was. He refused to dry on our towel and insisted on drying his hands on his handkerchief.

He sat down and ate like it was going to be his last meal. He was starving. When I saw him standing there at the door, I thought to myself, what if it were my Papa standing there hungry and homeless and no one would help him? We always had a roof and four walls, food and a lot of company. I guess you could say we were rich, don't you know?

I've never been a person with a lot of pets around, but I have been known to make exceptions. If they belong to someone else, I can take them or leave them. I love baby geese, chickens, calves and colts, but you see, they are all kept outside.

One morning, when Hubert and I got to work, there was the cutest, adorable little black puppy you could ever imagine. He looked mighty lonesome running around outside the building. He was still there at noon and also at four o'clock when we got off work. Everyone ignored him, even though he was trying to find someone who cared. He was trying to get some attention. He was coal black with the exception of two brown paws and one brown ear. He was just an alley dog, and you wouldn't place him in a pedigree category.

Guess who turned into a dogcatcher? This is one of the exceptions I mentioned before. We took the little mutt home, built a place with a light to keep him warm. You can bet your bottom dollar he was warm and full that night. I watched the newspaper in the lost and found section to see if someone was looking for him, but I think he was just dumped there. It is sad, but there are people who do that. We couldn't find the owner, so we decided he had found a home with us. Sylvester was the name we picked, naming him after a television entertainer who was popular that year. We had him only a short time, and one night his heat light burned out. Sylvester got too cold that night and he got sick. He didn't last long. His little grave is in the back yard of where we were living. While we lived there, Gary and Sherri put flowers on his little grave.

I believe I mentioned before that Gary liked to pick flowers for me. When he was three, he would be outside and come in with a bouquet. There were more dandelions than orchids in our yard, so he picked dandelions. He cut them all off the same length and tied a string around them to hold them and brought them in to me. His little hands were soiled with yellow and green stains. He handed them up to me and said, "Here, Mom." This is true love. Orchids or roses would not have been any more special to me than the dandelion weeds he brought me, because they were given in love.

While Hubert, Gary, Sherri and I were living on Cleveland Street in Ft. Scott, Sherri became very ill with a severe headache and high temperature. We didn't know what was going on, so we took her to the emergency room at the hospital, where she was admitted.

After running several tests, the doctor told us they had found she had a disease called encephalitis. The common name for this disease is sleeping sickness and is carried and spread by mosquitoes, which were really bad at that time in 1957. I didn't know it then, but we should have taken her to a specialist in that field. She was very sick for several days. It is a serious disease and can cause death or leave a person with permanent physical handicaps. With prayers and our care, she got well.

A daughter of one of the local doctors contracted it a week or so later. He took her to a hospital in Kansas City for care. That should tell you something, shouldn't it? That is exactly what we should have done.

My sister, Dana, was working as an aide at that time for our hospital in Ft. Scott. The word got around there was a patient coming in who was in bad shape and to prepare a room for this patient. Dana told me later she had almost fainted when she came to my room and saw it was me. You see, the ninth of twelve from the Usta Place had contracted the same disease. Sherri, who had a much more severe case of encephalitis, had just recovered from it, and now I had come down with it, too. I'll tell you one thing, there was one sick "mudder" and daughter. With care and blessing from our Heavenly Father, we both got well and had no permanent damage from it.

Hubert and I got our first television in 1957. Yes, it was black and white, but it was just as much a sleep robber as the colored screens we watch now. Sherri must have been around seven years old when we got the television. She was watching a show where a little baby lamb drowned in some flooding waters. I guess she thought the story was real because she got so upset and was crying so hard, I had to splash water in her face to get her to stop crying and settle down. Television programs have changed over the years, but the impact it has on adults and children has not.

CHAPTER 10

WHEN I FIRST WENT TO TOWN to work, I found an apartment in the home of a beauty operator. She lived downstairs, and all of the upstairs was made into about five apartments, as I remember. I had a one-room apartment at the head of the stairs, where I cooked, ate and slept. It was big enough for me. I had an antique ice box (it wasn't an antique then) that held about a fifteen-pound block of ice. Once in a while I'd forget to empty the drain pan. That sucker would run over and make such a mess.

Can you believe I paid a whole twelve dollars a month for that place? It didn't have air conditioning either. I used a fan until I went to sleep, with my head stuck out of the window. I shared the upstairs bathroom with the other girls and had laundry privileges in the owner's utility room. Oh yes! We got all of our utilities paid, too.

My landlady was a very dear, sensitive person. She loved all of us girls and treated us like we were her daughters. I can't say the same for her husband, if you can call him that. I never cared for him at all.

Irene loved to make chili and really knew how to make it. She would make a big pot of chili on Friday afternoon and invite all of the girls to come eat with her. She had crackers, but also made toast, because she liked toast with hers.

I saved a little money along, and when I was married the first time, I had some in the bank. In the olden days my take-home pay was around $14 or so a week. Once a month, $1.25 was held out for Blue Cross and Blue Shield. Social Security was twenty-five to thirty cents a week. Isn't this hard to believe? Expenses for an apartment, health insurance, utilities and Social Security are lots of bucks now. This seems like a hundred years ago, but I guess it's been about sixty.

Irene, my landlady, wanted me to give her a machine permanent one time. I was about seventeen, I guess, but I knew I could do it. (Mrs. Fowler said she knew I'd be back the first time I talked to her about cosmetology school and that I was a born cosmetologist.) That first machine permanent I gave to Irene turned out just dandy. After living at this apartment with the beauty salon downstairs, I knew that someday I wanted to have my own salon.

Irene used to speak of a couple being out parked somewhere and she would say, "They were just out there funning." Now days, it's called "sleeping with him or her" or "making out."

A few years after all of this, Irene found out she had diabetes and died a while later. We all lost a good friend. Irene was a real joy. I have many good memories of her and will never forget her.

I was working at Key Work Clothes, but I had enrolled in cosmetology school in 1958 at Pittsburg, Kansas. I was really counting on getting into the spring class. Sure enough! They called on Thursday and wanted me to come on the following Monday. I went to my floor lady at work and told her I had the opportunity to start school the following Monday, but I felt I should give her a two-week notice. I explained to her that I would probably have to wait six months for the next class to start. Her answer: "Oh my, no. If you have this chance, go ahead and go. If you ever need a job, your work record is great. You have a job here anytime." Isn't that just swell?

I called my sister number seven, Margie, who was an operator already and told her I was starting. She told me her husband, Bob, was waiting to get in a class also. This was the first I had heard about him waiting to get into class. I called the school, and somehow he started the same day with me. So that I wouldn't have to drive, I paid Bob and rode with him.

Let me say right now, it wasn't easy. Mama got sick with diabetes. My nephew, Paul, had a bad accident, was burned very bad and was in the hospital six weeks. Margie and Bob's basement flooded one night after a big rain. We had a lot of things to deal with. On top of all of this, Hubert and I had bought another house and had to get moved.

This man, who was a real estate agent, had advertised his house for sale. He had his business office right in the front part of this house. We went over to this house at 1023 S. Main, went through the house and bought it right then. You see, his office was the ideal place for my future salon. I started making plans right away, don't you know?

One morning in class my instructor chose me to demonstrate hair cutting. Now this little lady had quite a bit of hair, so I thought this is going to be fun. Mrs. Fowler, my instructor, didn't even know I had been cutting hair since I was twelve years old. I felt so honored for her to ask me to do this cut. You see, if I made a mistake, I would be in trouble big-time! A mannequin's hair does not grow back.

Our class gave a demonstration in tinting and bleaching at the college one evening. Can you guess who was elected to do the demonstration? That's right. I called a friend in Ft. Scott to be my model. She was thrilled and started celebrating early. When I went to pick her up, she was as drunk as a skunk. At least she could walk by the time we got to class. She talked a lot, but kept us all in stitches. Oh yes! I did a real good number on her and passed the test.

I had a classmate in beauty school named Thelma, and we became good friends. This lady looked, walked, talked and smiled so much like a lady I knew and had worked with at Key Work Clothes in Ft. Scott. One day I asked Thelma if she happened to know a lady in Ft. Scott by the name of Pearl. Before I could say her last name, Thelma said, "That's my mother!" As it turned out, we had a mutual friend, her mama!

One morning, I believe it was the first or second day of school, Mrs. Fowler informed us that she didn't want to see any of us lay our comb or brush down while working on a patron. She definitely didn't want to see any of us open a bobby pin with our teeth. "Use your fingers" was the command. She said, "You are training to be professionals, and professionals don't open bobby pins with their teeth." I already knew that. You must remember I lived at a beauty operator's apartment, where I learned a lot.

We were in class one morning, and the air conditioning wasn't working. It was hot as blazes in there. I was too warm and said, "Gee, I'm sweating!" Mrs. Fowler heard me and said, "Mrs. Rhodes, humans perspire, horses sweat." I said, "Well, just call me a jackass. I'm sweating." I have never in my life seen anyone laugh so hard. Her being a cosmetologist, she was wearing plenty of eye make-up. The mascara was running down to her chin. After that morning, we became very good friends. Maybe that's the reason I was chosen out of three classes to demonstrate hair cutting, tinting and bleaching. You don't suppose it was because she thought I was the best at it?

In cosmetology, three classes were going at the same time (freshman, junior, and senior). We took all kinds of training answering the phone, making appointments, etc. We booked a caller with whoever was available to do the service requested. On this particular day when I was a freshman, this lady called for an appointment and was booked with me. I guess you could say she didn't make my day. When she came in, I took one look and decided I didn't want to work on her. You see, I didn't mind soiled hair or clothes, but this lady had sores on her arms, neck, face and legs. I'll tell you right here and now that I went into cosmetology with perfect health, examined by their doctors. I planned to conclude my training in the same condition, don't you know? After I refused to work with this lady, my instructor told me she couldn't expect me to do something she would not do. Finally, one of the juniors, wearing rubber gloves, took the appointment. What a nightmare!

While we were in beauty school, as I mentioned before, we all worked on each other to get experience and have the hours to turn in on our worksheets. We had to turn in so many cuts, colors, manicures and scalp treatments each week for class. For instance, one day I gave Bob, my brother-in-law, a facial. He fell asleep because he was so relaxed. We had to wake him up so he could give someone a facial for his worksheet.

One morning they thought they would do a henna pack (color) on me. Not! I had enough natural red. Please don't get me wrong, I adore red, a lot of it, but not orange red on me. I finally agreed to a strand test. I cut a small strand where I wouldn't miss it and let the class try the test. My strand of hair was beautiful before we started the party. The color certainly didn't do a thing for my hair strand. After the party, it wasn't pretty at all. I was certainly glad I didn't let them have my whole head on the block.I guess I've always been too fussy about letting just anyone work on me. To this day, I love to have my hair brushed, because it's like twenty minutes of therapy, but I prefer to do the work on my hair myself.

We finally ended our training in cosmetology, and before we left for Topeka State Board, Mrs. Fowler had what she called "mock" State Board, which consisted of twenty or thirty questions on each subject. We had started our exams, and I couldn't remember how to spell formaldehyde. I'm pretty good in spelling, but that day I was trying too hard. I told Mrs. Fowler I knew the answer, but my mind was blank. She told me to just make a stab at it and she would know what I mean. Wasn't that cool? Well, I passed it just dandy. I didn't even misspell formaldehyde, like I thought I had. We also had to make and keep a daily notebook that was to be turned in at the end of our cosmetology course. I kept mine just the way I was supposed to, plus I put extra things in it, too. After I turned it in, it was graded, and she gave it back to me to keep. I was floating on cloud number nine thousand, I suppose. I never dreamed I would have a note that would read, "Very neat and complete," with an A++ written on it.

Since Bob and I started school the same day, we finished the same day, and that meant off to Topeka, Kansas, for State Board. We couldn't leave without giving every one a hug and, oh yes, we had a lovely banquet for the graduates at Hotel Besse in Pittsburg. It was really a nice evening and was worth the wait.

Now, Topeka is a good-sized place for someone like me who hasn't been around that much. I was sure thankful we could all go together. We, the whole class, had reservations at Hotel Jayhawk, with Mrs. Fowler right with us. When we arrived at the hotel, we had to park three blocks away. We took out with our luggage, supply kit and started walking. It seemed like we would never get there. Now keep in mind, we had carried our stuff three blocks.

We finally got to the hotel lounge and checked in. Keep in mind also that I was from a small town of ten thousand. I thought I had the right to do and say what came naturally. I usually do. That's the Clark Clan seeping out. Whoever came up with the saying "you can take the girl out of the country but you can't take the country out of the girl" must have known me in another life. As I said, we entered the hotel. There was the bellboy, red hat and all. (I loved his red hat.) He was waiting for someone just like me. It showed all over, I suppose. He reached out to take my luggage up to my room, by way of the elevator, no less. I imagine he was expecting a good piece of pocket paper. I had a shocking news flash for that young man. I said, "Thank you, but I'll ride it upstairs. I've carried it halfway across Topeka. I believe I can throw it on the elevator!" I did just that and did fine. I bet he thought, "That poor country girl didn't know she is supposed to pay me to help her." I surprised him. You see, I'd been around a few of those educational bushes myself, and it didn't include paying someone for nothing. You could bet your bottom dollar, I was the first country girl and maybe the last who was a couple of steps ahead of him. What do you think? I suppose I embarrassed a few, but I didn't go up there to try to impress a bellboy or anyone else for that matter. I just wanted to take my State Board test and get back to my children.

The next morning we appeared in our crisp white uniforms and white shoes, with kit in hand, ready for action! We could use anyone in our class for a model. My scissors and comb were ready! I did everything like I was supposed to do and I didn't get scolded for anything. I was assigned to block and permanent wave (no lotion) a section of hair. I didn't know the inspector was watching. Guess what? She was! She stepped up beside me, unrolled one rod and said, "Mrs. Rhodes, this is a perfect job of rolling a perm." I knew something she didn't know. I had been cutting hair and rolling perms for a few years.

We finally finished the day and started back to Ft. Scott. I was sure I had passed exams, but I wanted that license in my hand and my shop and operator's license, too. They told us it would be a month or so before we could expect our salon license. We would get our operator's license right away, which would permit us to work in a licensed salon, but I wanted my own salon. I had it all ready to go, but I had to wait on someone who didn't seem as anxious as I was.

I waited and waited and waited. I wondered what was taking so long. My salon had new floor covering, walls and ceiling, done in beige and aqua, pink telephone, vanity bench, pink and aqua furniture. All was so pretty, and to think it was me starting my own business. But it was like everything else, hurry up and wait. It seemed like I could hear better on my pink telephone. I was getting anxious to see if all those new handles, combs and scissors fit my hands as well in my own shop as they did in school. You can bet your bottom dollar they would. Maybe they would fit even better, because I was working for myself and getting paid. While I was in school, I didn't make too much in tips, but to know I had all of those people asking for "Mrs. Rhodes" when they made their appointment was pay enough. (I received several gifts from these people when I graduated.)

I had to either wait on my license or go to work for someone else in a licensed salon. Well, hard-headed Helen wanted to work now. As I mentioned before, Margie, my sister number seven already had her shop, so Bob was all set up, ready to hit the shampoo bowl. Margie's shop had two units, but not enough room for a third operator. She knew I was waiting on the license and couldn't open until I got it.

I don't know where the idea came from, but she asked if I wanted to work at her shop. Bob was already working in her "licensed" shop, but Margie said they had been wanting to take a trip to California. This would work out well, because they wouldn't have to close their shop. It sounded pretty good to me. Margie had been an operator for twenty years or so, and she had a good-size clientele built up. It scared me a little, but I'm a hard-headed, hard-working Helen, so I said I would give it a whirl.

I set my own prices, and this did not seem to be too much of a problem. There was an exception. One nice lady came in my first week in the shop. Now remember, a shampoo and set was $1.25 back in the fifties and was a good price. It was quite a bit for some to rake up, so I could somewhat understand. I finished my service, and she asked me what she owed me. I told her the shampoo, set and color would be $1.75. She got sort of huffy and asked me how I could charge that much more than Margie, just getting out of school. My answer to her was, "Do you mean to tell me you have been coming to Margie all these years and Margie still just charges you $1.25?" Needless to say, she didn't book with me again. This was no problem at my end. I had her spot filled immediately. At the end of the day, I took half of the earnings and put Margie's half in her sugar bowl, cleaned the shop and went over to 1023 S. Main, my home.

Margie and Bob finally got home. We talked awhile, and I handed Margie her "loot." She said, "Now, wait and let me count out your half." I told her I took my share first, in case the second share was short! Margie could not believe I had done so well my first month as a business lady. I knew I could. They were pleased. I told them there is just one thing that might be a problem. I may have lost a patron because this woman didn't rebook for an appointment. Bob asked who it was, and I guess Margie was pleased the second time. Bob said they had wanted to get rid of her for a long time. I did it for them. They should have given me a little extra for taking care of that little task for them. Do you suppose Margie thought this might happen while she was gone? Beats me.

When I was working at Margie's shop one day, Gary, who was about ten years old at the time, called and was crying. He told me his baby squirrels ran away and up a tree. It was really a blessing to me, but his little heart was broken. We tried to comfort him by telling him that the babies belonged up in the trees, not in a pen where they weren't happy. We got food for the squirrels so he could put it out for them to eat. That helped heal his pain and it made us both feel better.

At last, I finally got my salon license. I sat down and cried. My grand opening was October 13, 1958. The florist brought 24 large chrysanthemums. I thought they were from Hubert. Not! The card read, "Good Luck, Helen," and was signed from Mary Reber, who was my boss at my old job at Key Work Clothes. Wasn't that a thoughtful thing for her to do? She was such a nice person and a pretty lady with real black hair.

Some women who came to my salon sometimes had to go to the hospital for a while. One or two had to go to a rest home. If I had someone who had died, I would have to go to the funeral home to fix her hair for the services. My first experience with having to go to the funeral home was a lady who had come to my salon for a long time. Her husband called me to do her hair, and I told him I would be glad to do it. I did not charge for this service, of course. When I got to the funeral home, the director came in and said, "Helen, if you have any questions, I'll be in the outer office." I said to him, "I have news for you. If I have any questions, you will be right here beside me!" The trips to the funeral home got easier each time, but it was quite an experience for me, don't you know?

When I was still working in my salon, I had clientele of all ages. The youngest was a beautiful child only three years old. I believe she had only one kidney and somewhere along her little life got cancer in this kidney. Her mother would bring her in and I would do her hair. I gave her permanents and hair cuts. She always loved my earrings, so I would take them off and give them to her.

Well, the cancer eventually took her life, and the family asked me to do her hair one last time for the funeral service. I wouldn't have wanted anyone else to do it but, believe me, it was the hardest thing I ever had to do in my life. It was like a big doll lying there. She was so beautiful. After this was all over, her mother brought back all of the earrings I had given the little girl. She had them all tucked away in a nice little box.

I worked about six weeks at the Ben Franklin store in Ft. Scott a few years earlier and was stationed behind the candy counter. I liked the work but decided to go back to Key Work Clothes, and as you have read, later quit there and went to cosmetology school. Some years after I had opened my shop, someone decided they needed to audit my beauty salon business. Now you can bet your bottom dollar I didn't do this on purpose, but I had forgotten to file income tax on the six weeks' employment at the dime store. Talk about a shock! I could just see me in those striped shirts. I was even thinking I might get a short term for good behavior. Several friends promised to bring me cookies while behind bars. As it turned out, the Internal Revenue Service took my "pocket change" and never bothered me again. I guess they took a second look at this honest face.

I had another dear friend who was a registered nurse in the maternity ward at the hospital. She came to my shop each week and we had coffee every time. Lelia was of Catholic belief, but fell for one of our neighbor boys who was a Baptist. That didn't make him a bad person. Anyway, they got married, and I understand her church wasn't too happy about the marriage. Lelia had a cute way of turning her head when she talked. She was so pretty and had a personality that wouldn't quit.

On the days Lelia came to my shop, I saved plenty of time on my appointment book because we liked to visit and talk. After all, we had a lot in common. George! She was unloading on me one day, and she couldn't understand why their relationship had to be so complicated. She looked up at me, tears in her eyes, and said, "I'm Catholic and George is Baptist, but I love him." I could understand.

She and George adopted a little girl and they had grandchildren. George died later and Leila became ill, having to be on a dialysis machine three times a week in Kansas City. I lost my dear friend to cancer. I'm lucky to have known her all those years.

I believe Lelia was on duty at the hospital when all of my grandchildren were born. She was head nurse the night Rusty was born. Seven babies were born at the hospital at about the same time that night. Lelia and Dr. Henry Aldis were very busy, so between Sherri's contractions they sent me out to tell the waiting husbands the sex and condition of both wife and baby. I guess you could have called me a "nurse's aide" that night.

Russ, my son-in-law, and I stayed with Sherri while she was in labor. About eight minutes after they took her to the delivery, I had my first grandson. I got to see him before he was cleaned up and got snapshots of him right there. How many are able to experience this? It pays to know the right people in high places. (The maternity ward was on the top floor of the hospital.) I got to do the same with my second grandson, Marcus Allen. I got pictures of him when he was five minutes old.

I'll tell you the story about those pictures I took of Marcus. I sent the film through one of our stores, and can you believe it? They lost my film. Oh, they tried to make it up with a free roll of film, plus developing. I told them "they better wake up and smell the roses." I would never send a film through them again. They did it once and it could happen again. I nearly lost my temper that day. I don't lose it often, but that day was a time when I came the closest I had in a long time.

I just happened to think about a very sweet lady who used to come to my salon. She had a little daughter with hair almost to the floor. I don't think it had ever been cut. She came with her mama to the shop and just wanted to be a big girl, I guess. Well, she decided she wanted to get her hair cut and wouldn't let anyone but me cut it. Since she was too short for my big chair, I let her sit on a board stretched across the arms of the chair. When I finished her hair, she looked so cute with it short. I couldn't charge her mom. Instead I gave the little girl a silver dollar. You can bet your bottom dollar I was thrilled when she chose me to do the honors of giving her first cut.

I truly bet you would all agree you should keep all receipts for items you buy. I do. When I was married, I bought a pretty going-away dress. I paid for it, honest! I had my receipt, but I got a statement from them showing a balance due. It made me so angry, because I knew it was paid. I looked everywhere, but couldn't find my receipt. The store argued I still owed some. Well, I finally found the receipt in an old white purse, tucked away in a dresser drawer. I went to the store and demanded to talk to the manager. He said, "Our books don't show it's paid." I said my receipt shows it is and told him to get my account marked "paid in full." He did. I was never in the store again. They later went out of business. It was probably due to poor bookkeeping.

I was trying to lay away a few dollars to put down on a new car and, believe me, it took awhile. Sometime after moving to Main

Street, I took in ironing to help pay for a 1957 Ford. Now, to most of you, that sounds like a lot of work. You are right, it was. It was almost as much work as picking up spuds in Idaho, but I did what I had to do.

My close friend hired me to watch her three little children, with the youngest being three years old. When their mama dropped them off, the youngest had long stringy hair, and it was in her eyes and food when she tried to eat. I took her into my salon, seated her on the same booster board and gave her a pixie cut. (It was popular then.) When Daddy and Mama came to pick them up, her mother said, "What did you do to Susan?" I said "You hired me to take care of them, and the first thing she needed was a haircut." After I finished cutting that long stringy hair, I found a beautiful face like an angel. She was so pretty and still is. I'm surprised they let me off that easy. I didn't charge for the pixie cut.

While I was working in the salon, right on Main Street, my brother had the habit of driving by coming back from the sale barn. He spent certain days of the week there watching cattle sell, sometimes buying. He had a red cab truck, so when he went by my shop, he would start "tooting" his horn about a half of a block away. Naturally, the ladies in the salon would see me wave to him. I believe they thought I was flirting with someone. That's funny. I never told them any different.

Another precious memory in my salon is of one of my regulars. She came every week for several years. Hazel was helping her husband in the hay field, loading the truck, I believe. She had fallen and broken her back. Anyway, she was in a cast and couldn't bend over. I did her hair, and that was nice for her. One day I asked her if I could do anything else for her. She told me she had a hard time washing her feet and shaving her legs. I said, "Hazel, just stay put. I'll be back in a minute." I got my razor and did the job. She insisted on paying me. I said, "No. I might fall off of a load of hay sometime, and if I break a bone, you may shave me." That was the deal of the day.

Hazel and her husband always had a nice garden. One time Hazel needed a permanent wave. She wanted to trade a bushel of sweet corn to pay for the perm. I said, "Why not?" Her hair looked so nice, and I slept so well that night and the next and the next. Neat, huh? The corn was good, too!

One day Harley and I were talking about a lot of subjects, and death was mentioned. I absolutely do not want to be cremated, but at the same time, there would be no danger of being buried alive if that method was chosen. As a matter of fact, I told Harley to make sure I am embalmed, don't you know?

Speaking of being somewhere without air, when I was in my teens, I thought it was smart to play tricks on people. I would call a grocery store and ask if they had Prince Albert in a can. When they would say yes, I would ask them if they thought it would be a good idea to let him out for air. This is another trick we would do as kids. We all loved to talk on the old telephone, but we weren't allowed to play around on the phone. We would call Central and ask for the correct time. We did this when Papa and Mama were outside, so they never knew that we talked on the phone, even if it was just for a little bit.

One time while driving through Colorado on her way back to Missouri, Pansy, sister number five, noticed in the middle of the night she was running low on gas. She found a station that was closed, but after noticing a dim light inside she knocked on the door. A man came and told her he was closed. Pansy told him she was on her way to Missouri and needed to fill the tank. He opened up the station just for her.

They started talking and he asked who she was and where she was headed. Pansy told him her maiden name was Clark. He said, "You don't happen to be Ed Clark's daughter, do you?" Surprised at the question, she told him she was. To her surprise, this nice man was Papa's brother, John Kelley Clark, the same uncle who stayed all night with us when we lived east of Nevada, Missouri! Uncle John was on his way somewhere to pick up a prisoner to take to jail and stopped by to stay with us. This was the only time we had met him. He was a sheriff then, and Pansy said he was still a sheriff in Colorado, besides running the station. Sounds to me like he was a busy man. It does run in the family, you know.

It seems like Pansy hit some really exciting times during her traveling from Missouri to Washington and back. Another time, I believe in 1968, Pansy and Tony had been back to Missouri and were returning with a load of furniture and belongings to Spokane, Washington.

They stopped in Mountain Home, Idaho, to have lunch and then started on up the highway. They again stopped at Pasco, Washington, for gas and food. Pansy started to pay the cashier and found she had no money. Somewhere along the way, she had lost her wallet with $300 inside. They phoned back to the truck stop where they had eaten. The manager told them the wallet had been found by a truck driver, who had turned it in to a waitress, and offered to mail it to her.

As it turned out, they were grounded in Pasco because Mount St. Helen had erupted and the highways were closed. Pansy had packed some food and water for the trip, so they lucked out there. A beautiful lady, a total stranger, gave Pansy $20 for food until the wallet arrived. She told Pansy there was no need to pay it back. Wasn't that a fabulous thing for those people to have done? God bless the truck driver who turned the wallet in, the waitress who mailed it to Pansy, and the woman who gave her money!

CHAPTER 11

Hubert AND I ATTENDED a Youth for Christ Banquet in Overland Park one weekend when the kids were in their early teens. I got all dolled up with a new dress, etc. Lillian, a customer from my beauty salon, said she had a mink stole that would look great with the dress I was going to wear. I told her I was afraid I might lose it, but she told me it was insured and insisted that I wear it and have fun. (Lillian was the same lady I told you about earlier in my story who accepted my request to be my model for demonstrating tinting and bleaching in beauty college, the friend who was drunk as a skunk when I went to pick her up.) Well, I took the mink stole and had fun, but I held that mink stole on my chair all evening. I must say I did look magnificent, but then I always do. You can tell there is no conceit left in my family because I took it all.

I don't remember ever going anywhere that we didn't have our children with us. The Youth for Christ banquet was for teachers and instructors only, or they would have been with us then. I missed them so much. We stopped and brought each of them a little gift, since they had to stay home. Sherri was a big fan of Ricky Nelson, so we brought her one of his records. That would have been in the sixties, but Sherri still has that record. We made it up to the kids for not getting to go with us and treated them to a nice dinner out.

When Gary was about eight years old, he decided he wanted to run away because he was very unhappy about something. I guess kids get that feeling now and then. Hubert and I told him we didn't want him out there cold and hungry, so we got him a coat and made him some sandwiches. I put the sandwiches in a hankie and tied it to a stick, to make them easy to carry. Of course, we were right behind him when he went to the door. He opened the door, stepped outside and looked around. I guess the world looked pretty big to a little boy about then. He changed his mind when he thought there wasn't an argument about him leaving. To this day, I don't know what made him want to run away. Do you suppose it was because I was a mean old mama? I don't think so. Every step he took towards the door, I whispered, "Please, God." He was listening.

We never experienced any wanting to run away with Sherri unless, well, maybe in her teens. She would have rather spent her time bandaging her arm and putting it in a sling to pretend she had a bad injury. She would wear these bandages for two or three hours. I was thankful it was just playtime. We always figured she would be a nurse when she grew up because of all the bandaging she liked to do when she was young, but she didn't go into any kind of medical field. She was so precious and cute and still is. I was truly blessed with two precious children and four precious grandchildren, but then they think I'm a precious granny, too.

When Gary and Sherri were little and we would have a communion service at church, they wondered why they couldn't have a "snack" when the rest of us did. Our little children would look up with tears in their eyes. They never did say anything, but with the look in their eyes they were asking, "Where is mine?" It was a precious moment.

We were still going to Mt. Orum, a little country neighborhood church, where we had made a lot of very close friends. We lived across the road from the Ray Hartman farm, so we visited with them through the week and on Sundays. Their daughter-in-law, Arla Hartman, was the babysitter for Gary and Sherri when I had to work away from home. I was already working, but this job gave me a paycheck to help buy groceries to go on the bottom slice of bread for sandwiches. You can bet your bottom dollar it wasn't easy to leave my little ones every morning. It made it a little easier when they wanted to stay with Arla when I went to pick them up after work. Does that tell you something? It does to me.

I don't know who thought of it, but the two Hartman families and our family planned a visit to Swope Park in Kansas City one weekend. I wasn't overly excited about getting on the roller coaster, but someone called me a chicken. That did it! This old hen didn't want to be called a chicken, so I agreed to try it. Now it seemed like this roller coaster at the park was going ninety miles an hour, up and down, in and around, and once in awhile upside down. Maybe not, but it seemed like it. I was sitting in the seat with Leo (Pervey), Arla's husband, and I told him if I ever got off that ride alive, I'd never get on another one. I haven't.

Later, we were all walking around looking at treasures we hadn't seen before. Naturally, we had the children with us. I suppose Sherri was about two and a half years old and Gary was about four. When we stopped at a display to look around, Sherri just kept on walking. Before I knew it, she wasn't anywhere in sight. I absolutely went berserk! I couldn't imagine how she could have gotten out of sight so quickly. I just knew she had been abducted. We were all scared to death.

The workers at the park asked me what Sherri was wearing. I was so upset, I could hardly remember the dress, much less the color. Even strangers stopped to help us look for our little girl. Ray Hartman found Sherri walking along with several other people, and since she hadn't looked up, thought she was still with us.

I bet you can't guess what I did. No, we didn't leave the park. First I picked her up and hugged her, then held her by the hand. We didn't let the wee ones out of our sight the rest of the day. We were so frightened. There wasn't any excuse for her wandering away. I just wasn't watching her close enough. It was my responsibility to watch her, and it was my negligence that caused her to be lost, don't you know? In a place like that or anywhere, moms and dads should hold on to that precious little hand. In crowds, across the street or in big stores, it's a good idea.

When Sherri had the measles in 1956, she was so sick. I had to run to the grocery store, so Hubert stayed with her. I thought she needed a treat, so I got her and Gary a Hostess Snowball. I thought it might help to make her feel better. Money wasn't quite as scarce as it had been just a few years before.

Who in the world would forget anything like your children being sick or special little treats that meant so much? Not this old mom! I can also remember how the light hurt her eyes. She couldn't stand the shade open through the day and didn't want the light on at night.

Sherri didn't want much to eat, and when she ate she preferred eating in the dark.

Gary didn't have as much trouble when he had the measles, but they were both very sick when they had chicken pox. I kept both of the children in my bedroom because it was easier to keep it dark for them and make them comfortable.

Sherri had to have a tonsillectomy when she was six. I knew as well as I know God makes green apples, she was too young to be left alone in the hospital. Again, Hubert took care of Gary and I stayed with our little daughter. The hospital furnished me a cot and I slept in her room.

Sherri's surgery took place early in the morning. Guess what they brought her for her first meal that afternoon. They brought half-cooked broccoli. I couldn't cut it with a fork. I don't know to this day how they expected someone just going through a tonsillectomy to chew and swallow that stuff. I ordered another tray for my little girl and asked for foods she could swallow.

When we got ready to check out, the hospital presented me with a bill for a dollar. The hospital charged me a dollar for the cot I slept on, but our insurance had paid all of the rest of her bill. Believe me, that cot was worth more than that to me.

This reminds me of when Sherri started to grow up and wanted to look mature, like all the other little girls growing up and filling out. She was always so petite and slender. When she and Gary had the mumps, the doctor came to the house to check on them. She asked Dr. Cooper what she could do to gain weight. Dr. Cooper told her she could drink a malt every day and stay in bed. Can you imagine that? She decided to wait and give time a chance to do the chore. It worked. Even though she didn't get too tall, she developed into a beautiful young lady with a nice figure. She could wear whatever her little heart desired.

You can bet your bottom dollar it was fun to sew for her and Gary when they were little. I still sew for Sherri, but as little ones I dressed them in identical sun clothes. I made most all of their clothing when they were small.

As you have read my story so far, can you see I've had my share of good times and bad times? It all boils down to this. The good times make up for the times when life was tough.

Hubert had a cousin, Mac, on the police force years ago in Ft. Scott, Kansas. He was such a beautiful person. If he saw our car parked somewhere and the meter was out, he would put a coin in it. I don't know if it was legal for him to do it or not, but I suppose that it was. For those of you who don't know what a parking meter is, I'll tell you. They used to have a meter at each parking stall, and you would have to put money in it to park there. You got so many minutes for a penny. If your time ran out before you got back to your car and a policeman came by, he would give you a ticket. Some towns still use parking meters now, but as years pass by I'm sure they will all disappear. By the time my great-grandchildren get to read my story, there will probably not be any of those meters left.

Gary was learning to drive and had a car that needed a new muffler. Cousin Mac told Gary he wouldn't give him a ticket if he would get it fixed now. If not, he would have to write him up. I thought that was neighborly of him. (He was our neighbor and cousin.)

I asked Gary recently if he could remember something special, like when he was a child. He said, "You mean like when you swatted me and broke the yardstick?" I said, "I guess so. Why did I swat you?" He couldn't remember why or what for, just the swat. Now this creates a question. Why, with the memory I have, can't I remember that?

I remember when disciplining, setting them on a chair for awhile. With active children, that hurts more than a switchin' does. I always got switched, not the chair. I don't know if he had dreams that this happened or this mean old mom just forgot. He loves me, so why question this in my golden years.

I feel like it is necessary to enter this news flash. Once when Gary and Sherri were in their early teens, they competed against each other in a tennis tournament the city of Ft. Scott sponsored. I don't know the final score, but Sherri won the competition. Gary didn't speak to her for a few days. He told her he thought she should let him win, because he had a better chance of going on and beating some of the others. Even though she didn't win a trophy in that tournament, Sherri felt she should do her best and that's what she did.

Then when Gary was in football, I closed my beauty salon one afternoon, grabbed my eight-millimeter movie camera and headed for the football field. Know what? Number 17 made a touchdown that day. I had my camera going, and the man next to me said, "Number 17 just made touchdown! I almost dropped my camera. You see, that player number 17 who had just made the touchdown was Gary.

How often do you get a chance like that? It was his only touchdown, and I got it on film!

I remember this one time when Ft. Scott was playing football against Chanute, Kansas. How could I ever forget this story! We always went with the team to the out-of-town games. In this particular game I had a very strong feeling I wanted to follow the bus home. There were about fifteen seconds left to play, so we got up and started to leave the stadium. I kept saying, "I want to follow the bus." I wanted to wait, but Hubert said, "We could start and the bus would catch up with us."

We started home and had gone several miles, but there was no sign of a bus. We stopped once for about fifteen minutes, thinking they might have stopped for a burger, but still no sign of them. We drove on home and got home around midnight. Still there was no bus. I knew something was wrong. I felt so strongly about it. I saw a car coming toward our home about 2 a.m. It stopped. I ran to the porch, and by then the school nurse and coach were bringing Gary up the sidewalk.

Gary had been injured during the last fifteen seconds of the game. He got up from the ground and, of course, since the game was over, he left the field and went to the locker room with his teammates. It wasn't until then that they knew he was hurt.

He had been at the hospital in Chanute for observation and didn't remember it happening or anything about the hospital. He had suffered a concussion, and the coach told us the doctor in Chanute had advised having our own doctor see him again. I called and Dr. Basham came to our house, checked Gary and told us to try to keep him awake, not to let him go to sleep for awhile. Gary turned out fine, and I never heard about playing football again. Thank God! The coach told me at the house all Gary kept saying was, "Don't tell my mom. Don't tell my mom!" I suppose he was afraid I would insist on him quitting.

Key Work Clothes had a Christmas party every year. One year I won a meritorious award. Also, I sang *"White Christmas"* one year at a Key party with Nellie Schuman accompanying me on the piano. Another year at the Key Christmas Party, I got brave and wore a short, sexy pink lace party dress, pink shoes and sprayed my high hair "pink." I walked in with Hubert, and I guess everyone there thought he had brought another woman. I certainly looked different. I had them wondering for quite awhile. My friends later told me they didn't know me!

Gary and Sherri used to spend a lot of time at the Ft. Scott pool in the summer. One year Gary got an ear infection and I took him to Dr. Cooper. The doctor flushed his ear and this made him a little dizzy. On the way to our car, Gary felt like he was going to faint, so I got him to the shade for awhile. Since the car was about a block away, I was in a bind. Sherri was with us but was just learning to drive. I had her go get the car. While she was gone, a neighbor lady walked by, and I expected her to offer to help us. She looked ahead and didn't stop. I couldn't believe it. I've never been that busy! Little Sherri, bless her heart, came back with the car, a 1967 Ford Customline, picked us up, and we went home. Gary made it okay.

A few years after that I read in the news that Louise's son was killed instantly in a motorcycle accident. If I had been there, I would have tried to help in any way I could. We need to be there for each other, don't you know?

Mama was helping us move to South Main Street from Cleveland Street in the spring of 1958. At our new home, boysenberries were growing in our backyard. Mama just loved them and ate two small bowls with sugar in a very short time. She became very ill. I got Dr. Basham to come to the house, and he sat with her for about an hour. We put her in the hospital, and after tests they found she had diabetes. She lived until August 5, 1970.

Have you noticed now days how so many kids get bored? Boy, in the "Usta Place" days there wasn't any time for boredom. If we didn't have anything to do, Mama would find something. She was bad about that, but it got the job done before it became too large.

Many years ago in my teens, I lived in a town that remodeled their jail, built new cells, etc. At the grand opening, sister number one, Dana, a friend of mine and I attended the opening. After visiting with the matron awhile, she asked if we would like to step inside this one cell. Being like we are, wanting our money's worth, stepped inside. She closed the door and locked it. The matron said, "You can't say now you've never been in jail." She did unlock the door and let us go free. She thought it was funny, and it was, but scary, too. After this little episode, you can bet your bottom dollar I made up my mind right then I never wanted to go behind bars, jail or any kind. Since then I've tried to stay away from trouble and behind closed doors. It's too hard to breathe in there.

Quite some time ago we attended a little old country church, where everyone knew everyone, and we would bend over backward to help anyone in need. It's hard to find churches anymore with this kind of fellowship, but Mt. Orum is still going strong.

As I mentioned before in my story, I used to sing a lot and sang at our church in the choir and duets, etc. Our minister at this particular time, Rev. D. A. McGuire, was a very sweet man with a wife and five children. He asked me if Ruth and I could sing a duet sometime. Well, you know me. I'm always able and ready to show off. We practiced several hymns, but they all sounded pretty good. It was hard to decide, but we finally picked *"Sunrise Tomorrow."* The following Sunday morning we sang our duet. There were two elderly ladies sitting in the third pew from the front who cried all the way through our song. It must have touched their hearts very much. What do you think? Anything worth doing is worth doing well, don't you know?

Several years ago when we were still going to this same church at Redfield, Kansas, I was not only the song leader and secretary and treasurer of Sunday School, but I also found time to sing duets with a friend. I had another friend, Margie Horn, who was the pianist at the Grace Baptist Tabernacle in Ft. Scott. With her great help and the help of the ministers, Ruth and I made an album of hymns. Our songs were used as the theme song for a radio program on K.M.D.O. The program was broadcast from Grace Baptist Tabernacle in Ft. Scott. It was so much fun. We tried, all of us, to find any mistakes, but we just couldn't find any. We really sounded pretty good then, and still do.

We sang at Mt. Orum just a couple of years ago at their Homecoming Celebration. Several of the families at the homecoming used to go to church back when we did. Some of their children, who have obviously grown up and married, were also able to come. It was good to get to see them after so many years.

Please let me add a little note here. My three grandsons all call me Grandma Helen, but my granddaughter, Kristi, calls me Granny. I love all four of them, and I love both of the names.

Gary and Sherri played together a lot and had loads of fun playing with the children in the neighborhood. One year we got them a sled for Christmas and planned on their sharing it like the Clark clan did at the Usta Place. The neighborhood kids had a favorite hill on the street close to us perfect for sledding. The city blocked the street off for the children, and naturally they had a bonfire to warm the cold feet and fingers between runs down the hill. This was really a fun place during snow season.

Sherri came home and told us Gary wouldn't share the sled with her. Of course, we told Gary he had to share the sled. He agreed to share it with her, so Hubert and I thought all was okay. Well, she came home again and claimed Gary wasn't sharing the sled. We confronted Gary, and he claimed he did share it with his little sister. The confusion came with the meaning of sharing. It boiled down to this: Gary had it going down the hill, Sherri had it going up. She didn't think this was quite fair, and somehow I didn't either. It would have been better for each to have his own sled and he or she could pull it to the top.

When Gary wanted to tease Sherri, he would sing "Baby face, you've got the cutest little baby face." She didn't like to be called baby. NOT AT ALL! Gary is eighteen months older than Sherri, and sometimes they did not get along very well. Their squabbles were typical between brother and sister.

When Gary was in junior high school, the time came for the parent-teacher conference. I'd had one encounter with this teacher before, but this visit was for my son. As usual, I was very busy doing my duties, but you can bet your bottom dollar I wouldn't miss a chance like this. After all, he was the teacher who let students grade each other's spelling papers. We didn't have much in common, but I wasn't about to turn this visit aside. His wife was one of my standing appointments at my salon.

I put on my nice dress (not red this time), black heels, plenty of jewelry, perfume, hair done to the tilt, and went to junior high. Gary told me after school that afternoon he was so proud of me and I looked really nice. (Gary, you made my day that day! Thank you!)

At the time this next story takes place, we were living on South Main in Ft. Scott. As our home was across the alley from the high school tennis courts, the children could play tennis anytime they wanted. Our children's friends would come to our home to play, grab a racket and head for the courts.

Gary had one friend who came often for tennis. It was very warm one day, and I guess they got pretty thirsty, but didn't come in for a drink. I was usually in the salon, so I didn't know until Gary told me that they had been thirsty. He told me he wanted to bring his little friend inside, but he (Gary) didn't think we had nice enough furnishings and was afraid his friend would make fun of us. Not! This little guy came from a well-to-do family. We're talking plenty well-to-do! I told my son if he ever had friends at his home, he should never, never, never worry about us not having nice enough furniture. Shoot, our kitchen was very clean and beautiful. I designed it when we remodeled our home. Besides, our dishes and glasses were always spotless and, oh yes, paid for. I told Gary and Sherri their friends were always welcome in our home.

There are so many precious memories that don't take too long to write down, but have lasted a lifetime. I've kept valentines the children have made for me from the time they could write and use scissors. I was never all that great when it came to poetry, but the children would sometimes make up their own verse for these homemade cards. Some of these beauties really tug at my heart when I get them out to look at them. Gary made one that read: "Roses are red, violets are blue, Sherri loves you, and I do too." Sherri made a valentine one time that had a drawstring through four paper hearts. In each heart she had written a precious message. When you pulled the string, the hearts would open and the messages could be read. It was so artistic.

Gary had a very close friend, Forrest Farmer, who lived just across the tennis court, so it was very handy for them to get together. In a nearby stream they caught crawdads and any other critters they could find around the water.

Little Forrest spent about as much time in our kitchen and yard as he did at home. He was a beautiful little boy and could chow down homemade chocolate chip cookies in my kitchen like they were going out of style. We loved him like one of our own children.

One day he came over and was carrying a quart jar. I'll bet your bottom dollar you can't guess what was inside, so I'll tell you. He had three baby snakes in that jar and wanted to show them to me. He took the lid off the jar, and one slithered out and took off across the street and one took off under our house. He was really proud of his catch, even if he only had one left. (I've wondered many times why God put all of those beautiful creatures here on Earth. I've decided His reason was to make an angel out of me. Get it?)

This is a sad story, but has a precious ending. One Saturday about a week before Christmas in 1963 the boys, along with two other friends, decided they would go to the country and cut Christmas trees. Hubert and I had given Gary and Sherri money to buy our gifts for Christmas, so Gary decided he wanted to go with Sherri

Christmas shopping instead of cutting trees. They jumped on the city bus and off they went to town.

Later I was working in my beauty salon and the phone rang. It was Hubert, and he asked me if Gary was home. I told him no, that he and Sherri had gone Christmas shopping. He asked me if I was sure, and I told him I was because I had seen them get on the bus and leave. I asked him why he was asking. You see, Forrest's mother worked with Hubert at Key Work Clothes. He told me that Forrest's mother had just gotten the bad news that Forrest, on the way out to cut the trees, had been killed in a car accident. As they were ready to top a hill, the driver lost control on loose rock and the car turned over several times.

When I finished my shampoo and set, I locked my door and went over to Ruth's house. You see, we felt like Forrest was one of us. His father came to the door, but told me Ruth wasn't able to see anyone. I told him she was my friend and that I must see her. I went in and didn't have to say a word. I just held her. She knew how I felt, too.

The whole town was shocked beyond reason. Naturally, we were so thankful Gary had changed his mind. I don't know what changed his mind, but I believe God had a hand in it. Forrest wrote a poem one time titled, "Where Is God, God Is Everywhere!"

Now don't you believe God was watching over our precious child? I truly do and believe this is love all the way to town and back. Our children had also suffered a great loss, and it was really hard for them to cope with the loss of their close friend. They had spent so much time together, and they missed him very much.

This is the precious ending to the sad story. When Christmas morning came and we unwrapped our gifts, you wouldn't guess in a million years what the children bought for us with the money we gave them to shop. I can hardly wait to tell you. I got a stuffed skunk, and Hubert got a stuffed teddy bear. They bought what they liked and gave what we loved. We still have those little stuffed animals.

Another sad event took place in this famous beauty salon on November 22, 1963. I was in my salon doing a cut, shampoo and set when the phone rang. Thinking it was a call for an appointment, I answered. Instead it was my sister number six, Margie, and she asked if I had the news on. When I told her I was in my salon working, she told me President Kennedy had been assassinated. He along with his wife, Jackie, and then Vice President Lyndon Johnson, had been in a parade when it happened.

I was just stunned. My patron, Ester Weeks, wanted to watch the news, so I took rollers, clippies, comb and styling lotion into the living room and finished the set. She wasn't in a big hurry to dry her hair, so we had a cup of coffee (and cried) while we watched the breaking news. Ester and I became close friends after that day. Neither of us mentioned being a Republican or Democrat.

When Sherri was about six years old, she and Linda Seaver were going to make some toast. I was gone at the time, but Hubert was out in the yard working. Well, they got the toast made, but the butter was hard. They decided they would put it in the oven and melt it. In doing this, the butter somehow caught on fire. They called Hubert inside, and he took care of putting the fire out. He didn't give her a spanking for it, because I think he knew it wasn't done intentionally. I'm sure they learned a lesson. Great-grandchildren, when you read my story, I'm sure you will wonder why Sherri didn't just put the butter in the microwave. Well, there was not such thing as a microwave back then. Times have changed a lot since your parents and grandparents were little.

Sherri, only a few years ago, told me about this happening. Another time when I was away from the house, Gary and Sherri wouldn't eat what Hubert had prepared for their supper, probably spinach. He got his belt, the one with Yellowstone National Park spelled out with beads. (I remember when we bought that one.) Anyway, he was going through the motions of spanking them with the belt, but was hitting the back of the chairs. He never touched them, but Sherri pretended to cry to make him think he had hit her. I guess it worked, because he quit swatting.

Somehow, I have a feeling Hubert knew exactly what he was doing. He would never be mean to them, including making them eat a food they didn't like. I think he was just threatening and then went along with her little joke.

I had this one particular lady, a standing appointment each Thursday at my beauty shop. She was a dear lady, but had one hang-up. She wanted a lot of hair spray. Since I don't use spray, it seemed like a lot, but I sprayed it stiff. She said, "Here, let me!" She would use it seven or eight minutes. So help me, I believe her hair could have walked off alone.

Another lady used spray and with the same words she said, "Let me." She sprayed so much I stepped back away from the mist. I sure didn't need to breathe that stuff. She said, "This will hold all week."

That's right! She didn't touch it until she came for her appointment the next week.

Like I said, I don't use spray, and I'll bet you are wondering why I keep a can in my bathroom. I use it to oil my squeaky hinges on the doors. (Too bad it doesn't work on hips, knees, ankles, elbows and necks.)

It seems like it was this mean old mama that had to do all the correcting. In 1967, when Sherri started dating her husband, Russ, we were living in Ft. Scott. She came in after her first date with him, which was a blind date, and told me she couldn't remember his last name, but she was going to marry him. (He didn't know it yet.) Well, I told her she wasn't, and then the next day I told her she couldn't go out with him anymore. That went over like a lead balloon, and she asked if she could at least get a Coke and tell him she couldn't see him anymore. I told her yes, thinking she would go to a drive-in some place in town and explain that her parents wouldn't allow her to see him again. This was not the plan. They drove to Pittsburg, which was thirty miles away, to get this Coke. Of course, I was fit to be tied when she finally got home and confronted her with the length of time she had been gone. She informed me that she didn't say where she was going and that I hadn't said how long she could be gone. This was the first time Sherri had ever done anything against my wishes, so I knew that this was apparently important to her.

I consented to letting her date Russ, and about a month later she came in and told me she and Russ were talking about getting married. I told her no she wasn't, she was going to finish school and go to college. She told me she intended to finish high school, but she was getting married after that.

I realized I was fighting a losing battle when they set the date for June 15, 1968. They will celebrate their thirtieth wedding anniversary next year. (There really is this thing they call love at first sight.)

I have had very nice neighbors in places where I've lived. Down at the Usta Place we had neighbors you could trust with anything you owned plus the house key. A handshake was as good as a contract. Now when you shake a hand, you better watch your wallet or your back. There are still good honest people out there.

One example of a good neighbor is one who lived down the street from us in Ft. Scott when we lived at 323 N. Cleveland. This fine neighbor had a good basement where we were welcome to go in case of a tornado. Dorothy said we were welcome anytime.

Once I was clear across town visiting a friend in the hospital when the tornado sirens went off. It's a long way from this famous basement, but I didn't waste any time getting over to Cleveland Street. (Come to think of it, I believe I may have run a stop sign or two. I didn't see any officers or cars coming. Do you suppose everyone was already in a shelter somewhere? I don't think so.) Anyway, I wasn't stopped for speeding, so I was just lucky. When I got to the Salsbury house, about twenty people were already there in the basement. I called their basement "The Salsbury Safe House." I certainly appreciated their hospitality. Dorothy and I still talk about the basement and all the other good times we shared.

Merle and Dorothy live in Pittsburg now and own a fresh doughnut shop. I stop in there from time to time for coffee and I, of course, bring some doughnuts home. I think he makes the best doughnuts in town. If you get a chance stop in for a delicious doughnut, tell Merle and Dorothy that Helen sent you!

I must tell you another cute happening. It was a rule at the Rhodes house that when the children got off the school bus, they were to come right home and stay until Hubert or I got home from work. No other children were to come to play inside. We lived just a small walk from the bus stop, and they weren't alone for more than a half to three-quarters of an hour.

This particular winter afternoon they started home, and somehow Sherri got her snow suite a little muddy and wet. I guess Gary thought she would get in big trouble with mean old mom, so he rinsed the mud out and laid the suit flat on the floor furnace to dry. He was thinking it would be dry before Mom got home. Needless to say, it shouldn't have been laid flat on the furnace. Perhaps on a hanger two feet above would have done the trick. That was the last of that little snowsuit. The heat scorched holes all over it. It was ruined.

Things can always be worse. It could have caused a fire. After all, Gary was just trying to protect his little sister, don't you know? No, they didn't get into trouble. I remember when I played in mud and water. As I mentioned before, my teacher would dry my socks and shoes if they were wet when I got to school.

Papa and Mama taught us at a very early age old-fashioned values. We all accepted those values. Being honest, accepting responsibility and doing for each other were some of what we were taught. I suppose to a certain extent, Hubert and I taught Gary and Sherri the same old-fashioned values. They would just follow in our footsteps, living their lives as they saw us do.

After I grew up, went through the "college of hard knocks," got married and had my two little "gems," Hubert made a five-inch step stool for them to stand on to reach the sink to brush their teeth. I taught them at an early age to take care of their teeth, and to this day they both have beautiful teeth. Gary at the age of forty-nine has never had a cavity, and I believe Sherri has only had two. I care for my teeth the F.B.I. method, floss, brush and irrigate.

I can't count the times I kissed all those little "owies" to make them all better. First Gary came along, and I always kissed them to make them better, then Sherri also needed her "owies" kissed. Wouldn't it be fun to have our children little again? If that were true, I wouldn't have all my beautiful grandchildren, Rusty, Marc, Kristi and Trenton.

When Kristi was born, I went to Russ and Sherri's house to help care for Rusty. He was in kindergarten then, so I would see that he got to school and then picked him up when he got out. I slept in Rusty's bed, so I would hear him if he needed me for anything. When we got in bed the first night, Rusty asked me if I wanted to wind. He slept with wind-up stuffed animals and wanted to share with me the opportunity to wind some of his musical friends. I wasn't used to having a toy chest in bed, but they stayed until the sandman came. I still have a letter from him saying, "Thank you, Grandma, for staying with me and taking me to school."

Rusty is twenty-six years old now and has been married to Stacy for almost five years. They own the *Star Journal* newspaper in Hillsboro, Kansas. It seems like only a couple of years ago he was learning to ride a bicycle and write his name.

Here I go, jumping around in time again. When Sherri was little and went shopping, she and Gary would ride the city bus to town. Sherri usually bought me a beautiful handkerchief. I don't know how many she has bought for me over the years, but I still have all of them. This is true love. She knew I loved handkerchiefs.

I can be at my very lowest and guess what. The florist will deliver a beautiful arrangement of pink and white carnations. She seems to know the time I need it most, and it works every time.

When Sherri and Tina Schafer, another neighbor, were little girls, they would go around to yards in the neighborhood and pick wildflowers. They would fix up little bouquets, tie them with a ribbon and try to sell them to the little old ladies in our neighborhood for a nickel. One time they picked some wildflowers in the yard of Maude Hemingway and then sold them to her. She was really a nice lady and just couldn't tell the girls no. Of course, when I found out about the little business they had started, I put a halt to it.

When Gary was about two years old and if we happened to be out at night, he would look up at the moon and say "moo moo." One could imagine we had a cow in the car. Children say the cutest things.

When Sherri was a little older, she liked to brush my hair. She charged me fifty cents then, and it was worth every penny. Besides, it gave her a chance to earn spending money. You could bet your bottom dollar it would still be appreciated and be so relaxing.

One time we raised a lot of tomatoes and had way more than we could use. I had given to the neighbors and still had lots of them. I told the children we would make a stand for them and they could sell slicing tomatoes. I happen to know some children love to do things like this. I believe kids need to learn responsibility and re-spect as soon as 1-2-3 and A-B-C. Don't you agree? It also gives them a chance to earn spending money.

We got the stand ready for them, and they got it all set up. Sherri had a nice tomato, but it had a crack in it. She didn't want to sell a bad one, so she laid it back away from the rest of them. A customer came to the stand wanting to buy tomatoes and asked for that one. She told him it had a crack in it and that she didn't want to sell it to him. He insisted that he wanted that one. She told him she would just give it to him, and he still insisted on buying it. I'm not sure just how it came out, but Sherri is a "chip from you know where," so I doubt she sold it to him.

Sherri is grown up now, with children of her own. She, of course, doesn't sit on my lap anymore, but we have a beautiful relationship. That suits me just dandy. We both love to shop and eat out. When she visits me, she brushes my hair and rubs my back and feet. (She doesn't charge for this service anymore.)

I must tell you this. Gary admitted to me just recently that when he and Sherri were little, he would unwrap his gifts from under the Christmas tree and then rewrap them. He was too anxious to wait. He must have been a good wrapper, because this was a surprise to me. He had me fooled and never let on that he already knew what he had in his packages.

When the children were probably six and eight years old, we

took our lunch after church, along with the Glen Banwart family, and went to Farlington Lake for a picnic and good time. We found a place that looked good for swimming and playing. We checked the water and it was about a foot deep. Well, that's what we thought anyway. We were all having a good time wading and playing when Glen noticed Gary struggling to get to shallower water. He got out there and pulled him out of danger. Glen waded out a little further, close to where Gary was, and there was a drop-off. Glen is over six feet tall and the water was over his head. He said, "Let's get out of here. This place is unsafe for children to be playing." Needless to say, we found another picnic and swimming area.

We certainly spent a lot of hours with this young man and his family. They were both a lot of fun and would eat whatever I put on the table. Sherri said she can remember me getting up early on Sunday mornings to fry chicken to take on picnics with them. Ruth was also a good cook, and we would sometimes eat at their house after church. We never knew what she would come up with, but we knew it would be good.

I was doing the breakfast dishes one morning, hurrying as usual and maybe getting a little careless. I started washing the juice glasses. I suppose everyone else uses a brush to get inside glasses, but I always put my hand inside the glass with the dishcloth and wipe it that way. I have this habit of doing things as easily and quickly as I can, so I can do something else. Well, the glass broke, cutting my right hand across the first knuckle on my little finger. It was cut open and bleeding like crazy. I called Gary in to my rescue, and he said, "Now, Mom, don't worry. You'll be all right." He got a white bath towel and wrapped my hand tightly to try to keep it from bleeding. You see, it cut across a small vein. We started for the hospital, and Gary said, "Mom, be brave." How famous these words are! By the time Gary, Sherri and I got to the emergency room, the white towel was solid red. (If anybody up to that day might have questioned me not having red blood, I proved I did that day.) The doctor took eight stitches to sew me back together, but it didn't leave much of a scar. I was glad I had Gary there to chauffeur me. He kept saying, "Mom, be brave." It was so funny.

My precious little daughter helped me that evening with everything. She took over all the cooking and washing dishes, until I could have my hand in water. She was such a help to me, but then she always was a big help to me with anything and everything.

You know the old saying, "If the shoe fits, wear it"? If my shoe doesn't fit, I put it back on the shelf with all the rest of the others in the store that don't fit. I have a hard foot to fit and very seldom find a pair that really feels good.

I would always get up early on Sunday morning and prepare our lunch, so it would be partly ready when we got home from church. This one Sunday, I thought I had really outdone myself. I don't know right off-hand what I made, but it was probably roast beef. Anyway, we were eating and I said, "Is this lunch fit for a king or what?" Gary said, "Mom, it's really fit for a king. Here, king." Then he whistled for the dog. I really wasn't expecting that kind of an answer and I didn't appreciate it either. I thought I had made an exceptionally good meal that day.

One afternoon Sherri and Gary were at their Aunt Margie's house. They were playing cowboys and I suppose indians with my nephew, Bobby, in the back yard. I believe they ranged in age from five to seven. Gary and Bobby decided they would be the bad guys and hang Sherri. Isn't that just absolutely terrible? They had her in a wagon, with a rope around her neck, hands tied behind her back, ready to pull the wagon out from under her. About the time for the grand finale, Margie saw what was about to happen and stopped the playtime for the day. Anyway, she broke it up. I just thank God Margie saw them in time. It could have been a terrible tragedy. Kids will be kids, but they can all do some dangerous things sometimes.

We were talking one day about storms, tornadoes and hurricanes. Now I understand that hurricanes are named after a person or persons that have the same characteristics behind their name as do the hurricanes. I said to Hubert, "I wonder why they haven't named one Helen." He chuckled, "I don't suppose there has been one that treacherous yet." Now I think that was tacky. Years ago I had a little book called *"What's In A Name."* Too bad I didn't hang on to that one. I could have settled that remark. Those were the days. (Since this conversation took place, there has been a hurricane named "Helen." It was like all the rest of them: "windy"!)

Someone told me one time, "Helen, I don't think you ever met a stranger." She was probably right at the time. I have met a few people since then who have had a few strange ways.

Going back to our Usta Place for awhile, when we were all little ones, I don't remember having any store-bought toys. I had never seen a bicycle, but you must remember we didn't get out too much.

There could have been a factory of them stored away on a side road and I wouldn't have known about it. There was always talking and singing going on, but nothing about bikes.

Early in the forties, Papa bought Gayle and Meryl Darlene each a bicycle, and I learned to ride one then. I could take off pretty well, but had a hard time finding the brakes. I didn't do any fancy tricks. I guess if you can get on, hold it up and peddle to your destination, you pretty well had

I was 15 years old when this picture was taken. This was the first time I had tried riding a bicycle.

it conquered. You could always find a tree, ditch, or a building to get stopped, don't you know?

When my children grew up and were ready for a bike in the early fifties, naturally the money was still too scarce for anything like a new bicycle, but there wasn't anything wrong with finding a good used one. Their dad, Hubert, found two used ones. There are used bikes and there are used, used ones, so we visited the pig! To make the pocket change go far enough, he bought the used, used ones needing new tires, peddles, seats and chains, plus pink and blue paint. He probably could have bought new ones for all he had in them. I don't know yet where these bikes were stored during the operations and convalescence. Anyway, they were finished and waiting for the two deliriously happy children Christmas morning. I don't know which of the three were the most proud. The children rode them until it was time for a used car. The bikes were probably put in a garage sale to make room in our garage for the 1956 Chevy Gary had found. He mowed yards, cut hedge, set out rose bushes and saved his money for his first set of transportation.

When we were attending Mt. Orum Baptist Church, we were active in the church and had perfect attendance for a long time. We all loved our church and working in it. The children and their father were baptized there. After we moved in to Ft. Scott, we still drove

This picture of Gary and Sherri was taken in 1960 on our way to Idaho to visit our friends. We had stopped just outside of Gunnison, Colorado to rest for a while.

back to services at Mt. Orum, but eventually we decided to find a church in town to save so much driving and bring our membership into the church there. The one church we considered was close to our home, and so we talked to the minister. It was going pretty well, but there was one drawback. The rule in the church was that we all had to be re-baptized. I didn't really think that the second baptism was that necessary. As I said before, I was saved and baptized in the forties. To me, it was the real thing, and I felt it was the same for my little family. This minister said, "Mt. Orum doesn't have much of a doctrine." Now that dumb remark made me huffy again. (I get real huffy now and then.) There were several churches in Ft. Scott, so the following Sunday we attended the First Baptist. We were welcomed with open arms. They accepted us with love and without all of us being baptized again.

Hubert started teaching Sunday school and is still very active in the church. I joined and sang in the choir all the years I was in Ft. Scott. We were all so happy to find a new church home. Rev. Craven couldn't realize how much the church lost by turning us away. Don't you agree? A rule like this in a church is something to really study over. Our Heavenly Father knows best, don't you know?

CHAPTER 12

I WAS THINKING of changing jobs from my salon to doing something else. I decided to apply in the ammunition plant at Parsons, Kansas. I applied and was hired September 5th, 1967. I've never had trouble finding work, but my problem is finding time to do what I want to do and have to do. I worked there almost ten years, and I kept my salon open on Saturdays and did my appointments then.

One time I was working the first shift, 12 midnight to 8 a.m. and had a shampoo and set booked in the morning. I was hurrying (speeding) to get home to do the set, and I didn't think about the Kansas Highway Patrol being out on the prowl that early. They could have been drinking coffee or something. I had never seen such a bright red light in my life. I looked in my rear view mirror and I saw that pretty red flashing light coming up as fast as me. I figured he had me in mind, because there weren't any other cars around. When I realized this, naturally I pulled over. Now he didn't have his siren on, but somehow I knew the time had come. I had been driving for years and had never had either a parking ticket or a speeding ticket. Anyway, he got out his book, and I presented my driver's license to him. I said, "I don't suppose you could give me a warning ticket?" He said, "Helen, we don't have those in Crawford County." He charged me $24.10 for this little episode, and I still have the receipt as a reminder to keep my speed down. I'm glad he clocked me when he did because had he clocked me twenty minutes earlier, he probably wouldn't have caught me, don't you know? I sure didn't like getting that ticket, but I did manage to talk him into keeping it quiet! (Keep it out of the newspaper).

Thirty-five people were hired for the first crew. They chose four to train for the safety squad team. We took training in how to handle disasters. I asked my foreman why he chose me with all these other qualified people. He said that I seemed to be more level-headed and under control than the rest. My early training at the Usta Place probably played a big part.

When we would have a blow (explosion), the rule was to leave the area and get to the change house to safety. I was near the two largest blows they had while I was there. This one time it was a bad one and the alert sounded. Everyone took out to the change house. I looked over to this older woman, and her hands looked like hamburger. She started screaming and was scared to death. I could not leave that poor lady alone. The ambulance was on the way. I stayed with Addie until they took her to the hospital, then I went to the change house.

As my inspection foreman saw me come in, he thought I was the injured one. He came over and said, "Are you all right?" I told him I was fine, but I couldn't leave Addie up there alone. He put his arms around me, and we both cried. I was really uncomfortable for him to put his arms around me.

Now when I was first hired at this plant, we weren't too busy, and being on the first shift, 12 a.m. to 8 a.m., we would sit and tell stories. One would get pretty sleepy in a place like this. There were no chairs, so we sat on the floor and tried to pass the time. I found the conversation wasn't too exciting, and it's hard to stay awake when there is no work. I got sleepier by the minute, and I did finally fall asleep on this blessed shift. While I was napping, an army surveillance gentleman, Mr. Coleman, walked by our station. Another inspector started to wake me up. Mr. Coleman said, "Let her sleep. We aren't doing anything anyway!" I have never been so embarrassed in all my life. If he had been looking for an easy way to can an inspector, he certainly had the bucket of proof. He was such a nice person and we had several nice chats after that. His smile and personality had no brakes; it wouldn't stop!

One of the millwrights at the plant surprised us all one night with what he called "chicken bites." We all shared and enjoyed the feast. When we had chowed down the last one, that joker told us they were turkey mountain oysters. To this day I question just what he brought for our treat? Whatever it was, it tasted great.

While I was still working at this plant, we were all searched every morning going in and sometimes leaving. One morning as we went through the guard gate and were stopped for routine check, the guard had a drug-sniffing dog to help him in the search. The guard told me to open my lunch pail for the hound to sniff. It made me very upset. I don't do cigarettes, alcohol or drugs. I did not want that dog sniffing my apple and sandwiches. I let the guard know right away he could turn my pail inside out and taste the contents of my thermos, but I refused to let that pooch sniff my food. He said, "You may go." What do you suppose he really thought of a lady talking to a guard like this?

Sometime later we were eating our lunch at this plant. You wouldn't believe what I found in the bottom of my lunch pail? A book of matches! Matches, cigarette lighters or guns inside the change house or on the grounds was prohibited, so when I found the book of matches, I knew someone was trying to get me into trouble. I didn't (and don't) smoke, so I had no reason to have them. I was in inspection at the time, and I'm sure there were a few who didn't like my looks. I was paid to inspect and I did just that.

One morning I was doing my job when I found a critical, which is loose powder on unsealed detonator. Well, I stopped the machine and put production on 100% inspection. I had to call my foreman and show him what I had found in my inspection. He said, "If we don't get our quota out by this afternoon, it will be my neck!" You see he wanted me to let that critical pass and get out production. I said, "It's a critical. I can see where this is not crimped tightly. If I don't write it up, it could be my neck and badge. I was hired in to inspect and that's what I'm doing." I always believe he tested me just to see if I would back down. Not this old girl!

Oh yes, I suppose you want to know what happened to the matches? I took them upstairs to the throne and flushed them down yonder. I had no use for them, so that's that. (I might give one-third of my bottom dollar to know who wanted me out of there so badly.)

I drove from Ft. Scott, Kansas to Parsons, Kansas for awhile while working at the ammunition plant, which was about 64 miles one way. I always had riders who helped on expenses. I was only late one time, and it was only one minute! This particular day I rode with another lady. She stopped to pick up another rider, and we waited at this corner where they were all supposed to meet. The woman never showed up, and waiting made us run behind the only time in all the years I worked there. She broke my time for "not tardy" record. I didn't like that too much. Had I been driving that day this would never have happened, but there wasn't much I could do. I wasn't absent too much either.

Now if there was a death in the family, we were allowed three days off. Other than that I had a good work record. I definitely had to be at the hospital when my four precious grandchildren arrived, don't you know? Since I had a good record, it wasn't a problem for me to take off.

We were sitting at lunch one day (Harley and I had just been married a little while) and were all talking about Christmas gifts. I asked some of the young sprouts there what in the world do you get a man who has everything? This one little noisy mouth said "penicillin." Now wasn't that just out of this world?

We had a very nice black lady working in inspection. I noticed she ate at a table by herself. I asked the other inspectors if they knew why and they said they didn't know. Well, Carrie was a good worker and a very nice person, so I went over and asked her to eat with us. After that, we inspectors all sat together. One day Carrie brought a barbecued chicken for lunch. We all helped her eat it. It sure was good.

As I mentioned before, when I drove to the plant I had riders to help with expenses. At one time, I had a young couple riding with me who were very nice. He had been married before and I believe had two children. We started to work the same day and were on the same shift for several months. One day he said, "The day I met you, I thought you were the most cantankerous woman I had ever met." I said, "Gale, keep looking. They are out there." He quickly spoke up and said, "No, I meant you aren't like that at all." We were good friends.

One weekend he was in the woods to hunt and fish. He always carried a pistol to shoot snakes. This one day he was several yards from his car and somehow tripped. His gun fired, hitting him in the lower part of his stomach. It was very serious. He always had a citizen's band radio in his car, but he couldn't walk after the shot, so he told us he crawled to his car and tried to flag a passing motorist. They wouldn't stop. He managed to get to his car, unlocked it and got on his citizen's band to call for help. He told his location and condition. Well, as it happened, the car that had just passed heard his call for help and they got him to the hospital.

When I heard about the accident, I called his room, thinking someone else would be there to answer his phone. Instead Gale answered. I said, "I don't want you to talk long, but how are you?" He said, " Helen, I hurt. I just got back from a walk in the hall." I couldn't believe he was out of bed so soon! He said, "They got me up the next day." Gail died the day after I talked to him. He was really shot up on the inside. It was sure too bad, as he left a lovely wife and two small children at home, plus the two older children. He was a beautiful person.

One day we were running lickity-split there on the line to make the daily quota. Well, there comes a time when one needs to be relieved for restroom needs. This day I was that one. I asked the bay man to cover for me. (We had conveyor work so someone must fill in for you). He told me, "You can't go now. There is no one to fill in for you." I told him, "Just watch me." I left for the restroom and he took over for me. After all, I was running a special errand. When I got back and took over my position, he picked up a hammer and pretended he was going to knock my brains out. I told him to go ahead, but he didn't.

A lot of women would not leave the line, I suppose being afraid of losing their job. Not this lady! I think you are allowed time for this type of errand. Anyway, I was looking for a job when I found this one. If you want to work, you don't have to look too long or hard.

While I was working in production at the plant, you had to change shifts and work with different people. We were doing our daily routine one morning, and out of the blue this very nice lady said, "Do you know when you cook bacon, you cook it on one side till it's done, then turn it to cook on the other side? Don't turn it over and over." I said, "Who cares?" I'm really a good fast cook. I throw it in the microwave and it's done all at once. You see, you don't have to turn it at all. She didn't care for me very much after that. She wanted to start an argument.

Speaking of microwaves, when I got my first one I was thrilled beyond reason. I decided to make hot rolls for dinner, so I put a dozen brown and serve rolls in that precious little time saver and set the timer. I took them out but they weren't done, so in they went the second time. Same thing happened. They still weren't brown. I was ready to take it back, because I didn't think it was working. It was working all right. I believe on the third try, I realized this one didn't brown food! If you could have torn the rolls apart, you could have killed a good-size bull with one of them. You certainly can learn the "hard" way sometimes. (No pun intended) I've always heard that experience is the best teacher. We still laugh over this one.

There was another nice person, Jim, who rode with me from Ft. Scott. After a little while, he and his wife moved here to Pittsburg, so I picked him up down here. One time we were returning home from work and an old man pulled out in front of me. I thought he was going to stop before pulling on to the highway. Not! Well to keep from hitting him in the side, I hit the shoulder and gave him more time to get out of my way. When we were driving to work the next day, Jim said, "You sure made an angel out of me, Helen." I said, "How's that? He said, "You scared the hell out of me yesterday." (If that is the case, Heaven must be full of my former riders.)

When I was still living in Ft. Scott, one night Jim and I were working the 4 p.m. to 12 p.m. shift. We were going north on Highway 69, and about twenty miles south of Ft. Scott we met a young girl who looked about sixteen or eighteen years old. She was running towards Pittsburg. As we drove on down the road, I said, "Jim, do you suppose she will be all right? If you are with me, we will turn back and help her!" He was willing to go back and see what was going on. We pulled up beside her, and she was so scared. She said her boyfriend was drunk and tried to rape her. I said, "Young lady, we will help you, but first you must empty your purse and we'll check your pockets for weapons." She was anxious to cooperate. We took her all the way back to Pittsburg, Kansas, to her friend's place. We both felt better going back and helping the little girl. Jim and I didn't get back to Ft. Scott that morning till 3 a.m. My husband, Hubert, was concerned at that time. After all, I usually made it home about 1:30 a.m. I'm not too sure he ever believed this story, but Jim and I knew. It took a while for Jim and me to believe what we had gone through. I've thanked God many times since that night that we came by when we did.

As Jim and I were driving to work another morning, it had rained all night the night before. There was flooding everywhere with water over the highway in one place. Our driver, Lynn, was almost afraid to drive through it, but managed to get his yellow Gremlin through the water without getting our feet wet. As he was delivering us to safe dry highway, he said, "I'm going through here, but don't any of you ladies ever try to do it. When we get through the high water, forget today!"

We were all sitting around on break one day talking about everything and everyone. Ralph, a minister in our group, was a very nice person to work with and talk to. I said something about having a cold beer when I got home that night. You see, it was very hot and we had no air conditioning. The reverend said, "Helen are you really going to drink a beer?" I told him, "Yes, if I get thirsty." He politely said, "Helen, you are far out!" I don't think Ralph had a clue just how far out I would be if I had that cold one or two, since I didn't drink beer and was just kidding him, don't you know? It was so funny. I heard some time later that he had passed away, but I hope not. He was so nice and had a lot to offer to society.

Many of you reading my story probably won't believe what I am about to tell you, but here goes. When both of my children were born, I wanted very much to breast-feed them. The situation just wasn't in my favor. I asked both of my doctors what I could do to help my wish along. They both told me to drink beer. Now I thought that was really far out. In those days, one or two beers each day would have been too many. I really needed to be able to stand on two feet and keep a clear head, so we decided Gary and Sherri would be drinking their milk from a bottle. They did just fine on condensed milk and water, with a little sugar added.

One year I entered a quilt in the Bourbon County Fair. The pattern for the quilt was called Cathedral Window and used 2,480 different fabric prints. Of course, I won the blue ribbon. It is really a beautiful quilt. I put several hours of work into making it, but it was worth the many stitches it took to put together such a beautiful quilt.

Dana got me started in craft shows. I already knew how to sew and do some crafts, but I bought liquid embroidery paints and supplies from her. We went to the same shows and set up side by side. When one needed to take a break to eat or go to the restroom, the other could watch both tables. Dana had been doing arts and crafts for about thirty-five years, and we did a lot of shows together. In the later years, it got to the place where it was hard for her to get her car loaded and unloaded. Harley would help her get her crafts to the car after the shows were over. That was the biggest job. Eventually, she couldn't drive out of town, so she started exhibiting her designs in a craft window and did quite well selling from there.

I had painted a set of tea towels with cows on them. Dana hadn't seen the pattern before and asked if she could use mine to trace them. Since Dana had just been released from the hospital and I didn't want her to overdo, I gave her a new one to stamp so she wouldn't have to trace them. Also, I surprised her with a set of new stamped towels, ready to paint. She was one pleased sister.

I buy cracked pecans and pick them out for my baking and also to sell during the holidays. Dana asked me to order twenty-five pounds for her. When I got them, I shifted into another gear so I could go faster, and picked hers out, too.

When I was exhibiting at a craft show in Parsons, Kansas, a Japanese lady bought some of my patterns to take back to Japan for gifts. I thought that was cool and was pleased she had picked some of my crafts to take back with her.

I still make good cookies. My youngest grandson says, "Grandma, you make the best chocolate chip cookies." I think so, too. Thank you, Trenton! I love to bake and take cookies to friends and family. As a matter of fact, I'm kind of known as the "cookie lady" at home and the shows I go to.

I was going to set up a booth at the Good Old Days show in Ft. Scott. I was about halfway to Ft. Scott when I had truck trouble. A lady came by and asked if I needed help. I asked her to call Gary Rhodes, my son, and tell him to come help me. She asked if he was Marc and Trenton's dad, and I told her he was. She said her daughter used to babysit with Marc and Trenton. We talked awhile and she said she was headed for Ft. Scott, so I asked her if she would call my son Gary and tell him I needed help. It was the first part of June and hotter than blazes. She said she would be glad to. About thirty minutes later I looked up and there came Gary, Mary and my two grandsons. Mary figured I'd be thirsty, so she brought a jug of ice tea. That tasted mighty good. Mary was a giving and thoughtful person.

I want to mention here that it was in 1968 when Hubert and I divorced. I will not go into detail about the divorce, but only wanted to briefly mention the fact that after our divorce, I moved to Pittsburg from our house in Ft. Scott. Unlike many couples who divorce, Hubert and I are still friends, even though we have both remarried. As a matter of fact, when Gary or Sherri have a family gathering at their houses to celebrate a birthday or holiday, they invite both couples to come to the party. Some people think this is strange, but it has made it much easier on our children for us to remain civil to each other, and there will always be a special place in my heart for him.

Dana and I had talked about writing our story about the Clark family to pass down to future family members. She planned on doing what I'm doing right now, but wanted to do a Clark Family Cookbook first. I want to tell you a little about that cookbook. First of all, the name of the cookbook is "Five Generations Cookbook from the Usta Place." Many of the family members contributed our good old favorite recipes. We have everything from Mama's famous fruitcake to the horse colic remedy. Some of the information I mentioned at the beginning of my story about my ancestors came from information she had in the Clark Family Cookbook.

Second sister Wilma (Clark) Woody contributed the following Recipe for Happiness: Two heaping cups of patience, two handfuls of generosity, a big heart of love, one handful of understanding, a dash of laughter, plenty of faith and a sprinkle of kindness. Combine patience, love and generosity with understanding. Add a dash of laughter, sprinkle generously with kindness, add plenty of faith and mix well. Spread over a period of time and serve a big helping to everyone you meet.

We had a friend who died a few years ago, and this friend always put out a great garden. He grew the most common plants you'd plant in a vegetable garden. We were visiting him one afternoon, and he pulled a green bean and insisted I take a bite. Well, I have this idea that vegetables right out of the garden should be washed. He didn't use a lot of sprays on his plants, and his garden was as clean as the blue sky, so I ate his raw green bean. It didn't lack too much as far as flavor is concerned, except maybe a little bacon fat. That bean was so tender and sweet and he was very proud of his home-grown vegetables. Oh, yes! Our friend never threw away peelings or table scraps. Everything went into making a compost, to be used the next year. This friend was like most of my family. He truly loved the soil.

After this good friend died, the family had an auction to get rid of his belongings. He had a huge key collection. Well, guess who was the highest bidder? Me! He had keys to cars built from 1920 to 1960. I certainly treasure them.

CHAPTER 13

WHEN HARLEY AND I decided to tie that tangled knot, there was a lot of planning. First I had to get my vacation squared away. We weren't planning a trip, but I received a letter telling me I had won a nice free gift, if I would view some real estate at a resort in Oklahoma. (If you live long enough and get on this popular mailing list, you will probably get one, too.) Well, you know what curiosity does, besides kill the cat. We weren't expecting much, so we weren't disappointed and we got just that. Two baking dishes were what we received, which were in my very next garage sale.

We decided to drive on down to Arkansas to visit my sister, Ruby, and her husband, John, and then on down to Ava, Missouri, to visit Harley's only living brother and family. He wanted me to meet his Aunt Belle and Aunt Gertie. Harley warned me before we got there to be careful what I say around Aunt Gertie, because she is really religious and straight-laced. I worried needlessly. We had dinner that evening and stayed all night. We had told her we had just gotten "hitched." I haven't met a Sexton yet that I haven't liked. I hope the feeling is mutual.

When we woke up the next morning, there was a big doll between us. Some night! I never did find out where he got the doll. I started wondering what kind of a fish I had caught here. He definitely is a keeper. It's been 27 years already.

One day, back in the eighties, I walked out to pick up the mail. I got a letter from a gentleman specializing in tracing missing persons. He said he had reason to believe that I, Helen, might be the person he was seeking in the unclaimed properties. Well, like all other junk mail, I was skeptical. (I remembered our trip to Oklahoma for baking dishes.) He hadn't asked for any money, so I decided to pursue it a little further. I took the letter to a couple of attorneys here in Pittsburg, and they both seemed to think it was sound. They both recommended I send the information he was asking for and see what happened. He had mentioned my grandparents in the letter, so I really thought he was on the level.

He wanted me to send a list of full names and address of my parents, brothers and sisters, alive or deceased. Well, that sounded easy enough, so I got it all typed up, and after about four or five letters of information, everything was legal.

My Papa's brother's unmarried daughter had died, and her estate was being divided. Each uncle received one share. Since Papa was deceased, his share was split ten ways. By this time each share was sliced pretty thin. Sure, each of us didn't get much money, but the experience of finding out I was an heir was fabulous. It was a first for me and probably the last. I was the only one of the clan who got a letter. We tried to find out how he knew about this old girl, but he told me they don't make it a policy to give out that kind of information.

For several years I had a good friend who had worked as a nurse's aide in a hospital for over twenty-five years. She was a lovely person, very neat, clean and conscientious in everything she did. This lady always wanted to give, but never wanted to take anything that people wanted to give her. She was very good in her work.

When she got off work one evening, everything seemed to be all right. Her patients were all doing fine and resting comfortably. After she returned the next morning and started making her rounds, she stepped into the room of one of her patients and found her lying there with a sheet over her head. They were waiting for the funeral home people to come. This lady couldn't believe what she was seeing, because her patient was not near death when she left her the night before. She pulled the sheet back and started looking for some sign of life. There was a faint pulse. She checked again. Sure enough! The lady was breathing. This aide rang for the head nurse to come check, and she confirmed what the aide had found. A resuscitator was rolled in and the patient was placed on it, enabling her to start breathing easier. This patient lived for about six months after that.

Things like this make you realize how valuable and important you are in your work. This is really a true experience. You see, I knew this nurse's aide very well. This incident, plus all of the other nice things and good bedside manner, was the reason she was voted the "nurse's aide of the year." She told me this at our family reunion one year. Oh, yes, I suppose you are wondering who this lady was. She was my sister number three, Vena.

A little while after she retired, Vena got a good-sized check from social security office. They told her they had not figured her earnings correctly, and the back money was to bring it up to her correct earnings. She was telling me when she got the check that there were different ones in the family who told her they needed this, that or something else. She told them she wasn't spending that money on any of them and that she was going to save it. She had been giving and giving all her life and she deserved to save it for herself. May God bless you, Vena, sister number three.

About six or seven years ago, Ray Sexton, Harley's brother, was mowing in his hay field and noticed a small tan bundle with dark spots lying quietly in the weeds at the side of his lespedeza field. I've heard if a doe has twins and one is puny, she will abandon the weakest of the two and raise only the strong one. In this case, this baby definitely needed a mama or papa (Ray) to take him to food and shelter. Ray said it was the cutest little fawn you ever did see.

We heard so much about this little critter, we could hardly wait to see him. I thought they were blowing the whole story out of proportion, but they weren't. It was about nine or ten months before we got to see "Rudolph." He was so cute. He would raise up on his hind legs and look in the window. He had a field day in Ray and Mable's garden, nipping at the green beans and green leaves. I believe green beans were his favorite. Rudolph sure wasn't Mable's favorite though.

Ray had a black dog that slept with Rudolph. The two animals hit it off right away. We had been outside one afternoon when it started to rain. We hurried inside and took off our raincoats. I threw mine across the porch swing. When we went back outside later, Rudolph was lying under my coat out of the rain. He was dry and happy. Ray raised him on cow's milk and when he was old enough, Rudolph got the best grain a deer ever had. Now Rudolph wasn't penned up. He came and went in the yard as he wanted, living like a king. He had it made with plenty of playtime and no work time.

Boy, did that little darlin' start to grow! I took some homemade candy down there one time and found out I wasn't the only one who liked peanut butter balls. I took about two dozen for him, and he got a little huffy when they were all gone. He would eat anything out of your hand.

By now, Rudolph was getting to be a little more than Ray could handle. Ray was around eighty-four, and since the family was afraid Rudolph would push him down, Ray took him about thirty miles away and turned him loose. When Ray got home, he thought all was well, but he got a big surprise. Rudolph was there in time for supper. This is really true. The "red-nosed reindeer" traveled fast, but they didn't expect this one traveling above the speed limit. He was so tame, he might walk up to any hunter, so Ray thought it would be wise to take him to a wildlife reservation. Since he was like a pet, they didn't want him shot. The whole family had become very attached to him. The last place they took him had a fenced pasture. He hasn't been seen at the Sexton ranch, so he must be there to stay. You can bet your bottom dollar there are some little Rudolphs out there running and jumping.

If old Ruff knew you, he wouldn't bite you. If he didn't know you, you better stay out of his way. We were all on the front porch talking one afternoon, and Ruff came up and lay down between us, right on my feet. I couldn't move. I told Ray to get that dog off of me. Ray told me that he wouldn't bite me but I wasn't convinced, so I told Ray I was afraid Ruff would change his mind and to get him off.

As I mentioned before, I haven't met a Sexton yet I didn't like and, believe me, there are a lot of them. If there is a Sexton who doesn't care for me, they have certainly put up a big front, because they all treat me with nothing but kindness. I think you call it love. The feeling is mutual, don't you know? There are so many precious memories from the Sexton home. I'll treasure them forever.

In past years, we went deer hunting when we went to visit Ray and his family. When Harley and Ray weren't able to climb through the woods anymore, they let the younger Sextons carry the big heavy guns and hunt the deer, while the rest of us stayed at the house to catch up on our visiting. When we first started going to Ray's during deer season, all of his grandchildren were just babies. We watched them grow up, get married and have children of their own. They are the ones who do the hunting now.

It was fun to take homemade cookies and other homemade goodies for the children. You can win a little child over quickly with a chocolate chip cookie. Somehow, I doubt very much if I would have needed the goodies to win the hearts of any of these little guys, since they are "chips off of the old main block." Because they were Ray's grandchildren, they couldn't lose.

I would take casseroles and desserts when we would go to visit Ray's family. One time, when I took a dessert called Dream Pie Squares, Tim, one of Ray's grandchildren, told me he had one serving, but would like to have another. Of course, I told him he could have another and was glad he liked it. Tim was always so sweet to me when we were there visiting. Lots of times children don't have time for older folks, don't you know? (By the way, just like it was at the Usta Place, I didn't have to worry about what to do with the leftovers.)

Another time I took French Chicken Casserole for lunch. One of the young men asked me if I would make another one when I got home and mail it back to him. I told him if I could find a refrigerated mail truck, I would do it. I guess he liked the casserole. I still haven't found that special refrigerated mail truck.

When we would visit Ray, Cora Ann and Dale would walk over to their father's house to visit, since they lived across the road. Dale would pick up Janet and Rick, one on each arm, and carry both sleeping children home. It was so precious to see a daddy do this. (It reminded me of the loving care my Papa and Mama gave us at the Usta Place.) Now Janet is married and has a son, Dalton, who is such a darling child.

Ray had two grandchildren, Rodney and Carla, who visited them often while we were down there. They were so precious and I loved both of them. One time, I gave each of them a silver dollar. When I gave it to them, I said, "Put these in a safe place, don't ever spend them, and you will never be broke." Do you suppose they still have them? I'll bet "their" silver dollar they do!

I'll treasure this memory for years, and I want to share it with you. We were on our way to Ray's for a visit in September 1973. We had just finished breakfast and were leaving the cafe. Harley pulled out and stopped before crossing the highway. We started to cross, headed for the Sexton home. This was the first time (and last) that I didn't look both ways, helping Harley drive. You see, I was busy refreshing my lipstick. He hadn't seen the van coming and we got hit on the left front fender, doing a great deal of damage to the truck and frame. (A witness told us later that the van was traveling at a high rate of speed.) Thank God, there were no injuries in either vehicle. I don't know to this day what kept the van from turning over. He was weaving back and forth, rocking side to side.

I was so frightened. We were stopped in the middle of the highway and couldn't move until a police officer got there. We waited for someone, anyone, to stop and assist us. Finally, a lady and her daughter pulled up. It was Ray's daughter and granddaughter. Wanda told us they were driving by and Carla said, "That's Uncle Harley and Aunt Helen!" I suppose Carla was five or six years old at the time. Wanda said she noticed two vehicles had stopped, but didn't pay any attention because she never thought about it being anyone she knew. When Carla recognized us, they went around the block and came back.

After we hugged and cried a little, Wanda and Carla followed us to a garage, where we had to leave our pick-up a few days for repairs. We loaded up in Wanda's car and headed on out to Ray's house. If Wanda hadn't come by when she did, it would have been much harder on Harley and me. I'm sure thankful Carla recognized our truck.

Ray's oldest son, Harlen, and his family brought us back to Pittsburg. This was fun, even if the circumstances were not the best. We drove back down there a few days later to get our pick-up. I drove the 1975 Scamp home and Harley followed in the pick-up. Maybe I should have followed him home. After all, he was driving when all this happened. If the other driver hadn't been speeding, it wouldn't have happened.

By the way, since we were out of state, we got a ticket. The other driver wasn't ticketed for speeding. After our accident at that intersection, a four-way stop and speed limit was added. Thank God everything turned out all right! Thanks again, Harlen, Wanda, Rodney and Carla for all of the help that day. May God bless you!

For the last several years, Wilma, sister number two, and her son, Paul, would go to the cemeteries on Memorial Day. I would take something already cooked and with mine and hers, we had a nice lunch. This way, we sisters get to visit and get the decorating done, too.

A few years ago, Paul told us we could go pick all the strawberries we wanted. We got down to the patch, white slacks and all, and before we knew it, we had picked almost sixty boxes. We didn't take that many, but we were like Mama in the blackberry patch. I didn't want to leave one berry out there. It was fun for me because I love to get out and harvest a crop of anything needing to be harvested. You know, like the peas, potatoes, soybeans mentioned earlier in my story? I guess you might call me "hard-working." The berries were free to us, so we picked extra for Paul. When we went to the garden, the berries were lying there red as could be. They were just waiting for Harley and me. You could pick two boxes without moving. We thought eight boxes would be plenty, but by now you know "me and my ways." I must pick on. We just kept pickin' and grinnin'. I think Harley enjoyed it, too. That day I was fine. It was the next day that the muscles appeared we didn't know we had. Good grief! I didn't have one place that didn't hurt. Harley was hurting, too.

One time I was at Wilma's and she said, " Why don't you take a bucket and go dig you some potatoes?" I grabbed a fork and bucket and headed down to the garden again. That day I ended up digging the rest of the potatoes. I mean all of them. It helped her and I enjoyed the potatoes, too. It was so hot, I didn't think I was going to hold out, but kept on diggin'. They seem to taste better right out of the garden, don't you know?

It just seems like I find work when I'm not in the market. Jobs just seem to pop up when they see me coming. I heard about a black-berry patch on a farm that belonged to Harley's friend. Mr. Reed knew I was a workaholic, so he told me about the nice berries and to go over and pick all I wanted. When we got to the bushes, they reached several feet towards Heaven. Along the edge of the patch, we had to pull them down to pick them. Now when you got in the middle, that was a different story. They were so thick you could hardly get through or see each other.

I imagine you have all heard of chiggers. There must have been forty-three million to one quart of berries. Now I've been around those little critters all my life, but not so many at one time. They were bad! We picked all we wanted and left the patch early. You see, you don't need or want that many under these conditions. We took our hot showers when we got home and talked about that little venture for a long while, because that's how long the bites itched.

A few years back, Mr. Reed said Marc and Trenton could come out there and fish in his famous pond. It is a pretty setting with a bridge over one end of the lake. They didn't catch real big ones, but they were biting. Mr. Reed said, "Keep them." In my book they wouldn't be keepers, but then what do I know about fishing?

Mr. Reed brought me a chair to sit in while the boys got their limit. I thanked him and said, "I'll be too busy baiting hooks." Shoot, these little darlins' knew more about baiting hooks than granny.

When we were helping the little guys clean the "minnows," our good neighbor, Joe Steele, came in from fishing and had several "keepers" on his stringer. Being the kind of person he is, Joe brought Marc and Trenton some big ones. Joe also gave the boys a bunch of fishing lures, so Marc and Trenton went back to Ft. Scott two happy grandchildren. Granny was very happy to see them so excited. Down deep it doesn't take too much to make a child happy. Try giving him or her some of your time.

I suppose most everyone can use some extra pocket change. I've always been one looking for an easy way to get it, but I haven't found that way yet. I go around with my head lowered always looking for coins. I've seen customers actually walk over coins in the parking lot or in the stores, or if they drop a penny, they are in too much of a hurry to pick it up. Not me, "heads up or tails up," I still bend over. While walking to our mail box, I found three quarters. I always find coins on the ground, sometimes paper. One time I found a ten-dollar bill and another time a five-dollar bill. I have had to work hard for what I have earned and learned, and I am so thankful for being able to do just that.

About two years ago I started bending over and picking up aluminum cans. When Harley and I go for a walk, I pick them up on the way out and back. Gary has a full-time job, but can't stand to see a can laying anywhere. Yes, he picks them up, too. I can't let one stay on the parking lot at the Supercenter. I know they appreciate me cleaning up the parking lot. It helps them and me, too. I am going to turn my cans in one of these days. You see, I'm saving them to buy a newer car. By the time I get enough to buy this car, I'll either be too old or they won't issue me a license. Until I get enough to buy another, I'll just hang out in my little 1975 Plymouth Scamp. It doesn't look too whoopee, but that little darlin' starts in zero weather. That counts for a lot.

I hear something new every time you turn around. I was talking to a friend a while back and was telling her I was writing my story. We were talking about when her grandmother died. She was a sweet old lady of 101 when she died. Donna said she remembered coming to our house and ringing our bell. Hearing a bell ring, you imagine an angel getting its wings. She said she thought of grandma getting hers.

Every time our doorbell rings or during the holidays when our little bells would jingle, I would think of Grandma Phillips. When the line of cars were moving down the street headed for the cemetery after her funeral, I can't remember one car not stopping, out of respect. Donna told me the next day that Grandma Phillips would be so happy if she knew she had actually stopped traffic the day of her funeral!

Have you ever been to a garage sale? I'll call them garage sales because it's stuff you store in the garage, so the car sits outside. I wish we could have had them way back when I was at the Usta Place. I might have found a good pair of used shoes or a red hat. Suppose? I went to a garage sale a while back and found an old 1847 Rogers serving spoon. It matches one I have that belonged to Mama. This one I found at the sale took a lot of polishing.

The first thing I bought for myself after I grew up and started working was a pair of red high heels. You can bet your bottom dollar I did some high steppin'. I'm surprised, but I don't remember how much they cost. I suppose I could have spent my money on something a little more useful, but I'm sure at the time those high-heeled shoes seemed like the most important thing on which I could spend my money.

I remember in the "olden days" I could buy a five-cent hamburger with everything, even cheese. They were good hamburgers made with real meat and cheese. Hubert and I would sometimes stop for one on our way home after seeing a movie.

In 1981, when we were set up at the street fair, Good Old Days in Ft. Scott, my only granddaughter, Kristi Ann Stenseng, was entered in a beauty contest. Of course, she won. She is beautiful and in several generations down of the Clark clan. A gift certificate was the prize she won.

Here is another unbelievable story. Baby sister, Meryl Darlene, was back from the coast visiting us a while back. She wanted to cook dinner for us and let me sit back and enjoy. I didn't argue with this brave idea. She made steaks, baked potato and salad. After we cleared the table, she went outside to have a cigarette.

While sitting there on the steps, she asked me to come outside. She told me hot tea was the strongest drink she had consumed, but she thought she saw some dirt moving. We all took notice, and sure as God made little green apples, a mole was digging his way to somewhere. Harley dashed out the back door and around to the storage shed and got the tools to help that critter get out. Harley got him all right, and his digging days ended quickly.

I really don't suppose this would happen again in a million years, unless I planned it. At the Clark reunion in 1979 I baked a chocolate horseshoe cake for my contribution of dessert. Please keep in mind there were twelve of us Usta Place kids, plus Papa and Mama. Count the roses on the cake. It never entered my mind until a niece at the reunion said to me, "Aunt Helen, there is a rose for each one." I counted them. Sure enough, there were fourteen roses on the cake, one for each of us twelve kids and one for Papa and Mama. I had made all of the flowers for the cake, but never realized what I had done. Neat, huh?

Mama used to plant castor beans around in her vegetable garden to keep the moles out. I suppose I should have scattered some of those beans around here. I'm not sure if you can even buy castor bean seed. I'll see if I can find some for the garden next year.

A few months ago, my husband was scheduled for some nasal surgery, to be done in a hospital in Kansas City. We had all the plans made, such as date, time and place. Now when either one of us has to stay overnight in the hospital, the other would roll in a cot and sleep there, too.

This is the good part. The surgery was completed and the doctor came in and was talking to me about what he had to do. He assured me Harley did fine and was going to be all right, but he wanted him to stay two or three days. The doctor asked me if I was going home and a number where he could reach me. I told the doctor that I was staying with Harley. That was just fine, but the doctor told me he didn't want me to leave the hospital after dark, because it wasn't safe for me in the part of town where we were. He told me that they didn't have any cots, but he would get me a folding chair bed. Guess what! They were all occupied the first night, but patients were leaving so the doctor had the nurse bring one to me the next day. I suppose you are wondering where I slept that first night. Well, they brought me a pillow and blankets. I slept on the floor by Harley's bed.

When we got ready to go home, the doctor said, "I don't do this often, but I'm going to give you my home phone number in case you need to call for any reason. Call me day or night." Now I had never seen this doctor before, but he took care of Harley and me. This beautiful man had also told me there was traffic in and out of the rooms all night and that if we had any money, rings, watches, or valuables of any kind, we should put them in a safe in our hospital room. (Do you suppose he had anyone in mind?) We could make up our own combination. We had a little of the above, so we whispered to each other (just in case) and used a combination of our social security numbers. We experimented with the safe before we played for keeps. It worked, so we felt better about everything. Isn't this doctor just wonderful?

I've known several doctors in my lifetime, and right now we have the kindest, most loving and generous doctor. He gives us time, listens to what we have to say, makes suggestions, and refers us to specialists if we need one. This doctor is absolutely the best one you could ask for, and he likes to grow tomatoes, too.

Dr. H. Sisk (my doctor)

CHAPTER 14

I KEEP REMEMBERING so many of beautiful memories that I really want to add to my story. Mama told me years ago that a short while after she and Papa were married, they were down at the creek fishing one time and decided to go swimming. While playing in the water, somehow she lost her wedding band. It was pure luck for them that the water wasn't very deep. After searching for awhile, they found the band. Mama was a very lucky young lady. The band was made smaller, not taking a chance it would happen again.

After remembering this story, it reminded me of another valuable item lost and a lucky find. We were at Sherri's house several years ago. It was Sunday morning and we were getting dressed to start home. My fingers were swollen and I couldn't get two of my rings on. They were my mother's ring and grandmother's ring. I wrapped them neatly in a tissue and I thought I put them in a safe place. NOT! We most always had breakfast later, because we aren't hungry that early. We started home and drove for an hour, then stopped to eat in Fredonia, Kansas. After we ate and were paying for our breakfast, I noticed some homemade raspberry jelly for sale. Since I don't have raspberries, I bought some jelly. (I made lots of jelly and would sell it at my arts and craft shows. I really miss not doing crafts anymore.) When I started to pay for my jelly, I needed some small change. I opened my coin purse, paid for the jelly, and we resumed our drive home. We got home safely and I started to sort through packages, put things away, dirty clothes in the hamper, unload suitcases, and naturally put my jewelry away. You can't imagine my surprise when I couldn't find my rings!

I thought back and remembered the only time I had my little purse open was at the jelly counter at the restaurant. I didn't know the name of the place, but I could find out. (Fredonia is a small place.) I called the telephone operator and asked for a listing of a restaurant in Fredonia that was in the north edge of town. This operator was so nice and very helpful in finding the business number. She had a number fitting that location.

Well, I dialed the number and the manager answered. I told him about my loss and I described the rings to him. He said, "We have them. One of my employees found them and turned them in!" These rings are not valuable to anyone else, but they are to me, don't you know? The manager said he would have this young lady mail them to me. I was so afraid they would get lost in the mail. (I sure didn't need two losses.) This young lady was going to high school and working, too. She packaged the rings (carefully) and mailed them by registered mail. I never was so glad to get a piece of mail in my life. I'll tell you one thing for sure. I haven't and will never be that careless again. This proves there are still honest young people. Thanks, Tara! I know you will be blessed a second time someday for your honesty.

We just celebrated Mother's Day again by having dinner out and money gifts. Do you want to know something? Gary and Sherri make every day seem like Mother's Day. Isn't that just absolutely fabulous? I think so.

Our precious Mama not only knew how to sew, cook and harvest a garden, but she liked to crochet, too. I had a beautiful china cabinet which Hubert had given me for a gift once, but have now given it to Sherri. Anyway, while Mama was in the hospital one time, she crocheted six matching doilies to show off my new treasure. They are so pretty and to know she sat up in her hospital bed and made them just for me makes them even more special. Mama told me later she had told Margie they were for me, and if anything happened to her she wanted Margie to make sure I got them.

Mama told me several years ago, I think it was when I lived in Idaho, that she was crocheting and accidentally jabbed her crochet hook into her left hand between her thumb and forefinger. I bet you could almost guess who took it out? I imagine Papa held the area tightly to help ease the pain and extracted the hook just as it went in. He pulled straight out, and I know this hurt so badly. In the olden days one didn't go to the doctor for tiny accidents that happened. We all think we have to now.

We went down to the Usta Place awhile ago, and we always stop at our cemetery first. (It's a quarter of a mile from the old Usta Place.) Now, just for fun, I took my metal detector to go hunting. We played around in the yard and driveway for a half hour or so, and bingo, we got a message. Oh, yes! We took a tool to dig. We dug down about four inches. I bet you couldn't guess in six months what we found. Well, we found window weights out of the Usta Place windows. The house has been gone for years, and the farmer who bought the place farms almost to the foundation of the house and barn, too. There is nothing left there but the storm shelter. In plowing and harrowing in all these years, this dirt covered the goodies.

I've raised those windows a time or two. One of these days I'm going back down there with my detector, in my spare time, and find all that money that we all lost in those yesterdays. I don't suppose I'll need a truck. In the first place, there wasn't any extra to lose, and what they could scrape up was used to feed and clothe us. I'm so thankful for Papa and Mama staying side by side and keeping us all together. It surely took a lot of faith and hard work to make this happen.

Dana had told me several years ago that when she was younger she had made up her mind if anything happened to our parents, she would stay with us and keep us all together. I know she would have done just that. She knew how important it was to keep all of us together.

Harley and I were talking recently how kids are raised now compared to the Usta Place days or the olden days. There is no comparison. It seems like these days children want all name-brand shoes and clothing. Most all of them who are old enough to drive think they need a car. I understand a lot of these little "guys" work and need some transportation. I've noticed also that when our young couples marry, they want all new stuff. They don't seem to want to start out with used furniture, like some of us. Maybe they can handle the bills for furniture, cars, rent, utilities, insurance and medicine. It never was hard for me, because I didn't need all of the above.

I told Harley it was sure a good thing I didn't need much to get

I snapped this precious picture of Gary and Sherri when they were saying their prayers one night in 1955. Gary was seven and Sherri was five years old.

by. I tried not to buy beyond my means, don't you know? I suppose it has to do with not missing what you don't have, just like it was at the Usta Place.

Let me mention a little about talking back or sassing parents. We didn't do it! We didn't do it twice anyway. Harley told me that if any of his siblings talked back to their dad like kids do today, his dad would have knocked them into the Christmas holiday, even if it was the middle of July! Now that's quite a knock. It sounds to me like Dad Sexton may have been a tad strict. You can bet your bottom dollar I can identify with that "strict" stuff.

I'm sure most of you saw the movie or read the book called *"The Learning Tree."* While I was living in Ft. Scott, this movie was being made and several scenes were filmed in front of and close by my home. Oh, yes! One of my sisters served on the jury in the movie. It was quite exciting to have this movie being filmed right there is my home town.

When Sherri was about five and a half years old, we bought her an accordion and she took lessons. Her teacher told me that up to that time, Sherri was the youngest student to whom she had given lessons. This teacher had a daughter of her own and had started her out younger than Sherri. I understand her daughter taught accordion when she grew up. I've lost contact with them now and don't know if she still teaches.

Gary loved the drums. When he was about three years old, he would take anything he could lift and beat on anything that was his height and pretend he was a drummer. I guess you could have called him "the little drummer boy." He had good rhythm then and still does. In later years, Gary bought a seven-piece set of drums. I was at Gary's house once when he turned his stereo on, so I could try out the new drum set. I sat down and started that noise. He said, "Mom, where did you learn to play drums?" I told him I learned from him. That was funny? He was so surprised his mother would know how to play them. I believe if anyone is musically inclined, he has the natural rhythm for drums. (He didn't know that before he was ever thought of, I played the drums a time or two.)

Sherri now has a piano and can play it, too. I get to play Sherri's piano when I go there, which isn't often enough. Both of the children sing very well. How could they miss? Actually, I have several nieces and nephews who sing quite well also.

Our dear sister, Vena Ales (Clark) Smith left us July 4, 1989. She had written a poem in October 1988. Her granddaughter read this poem at Vena's funeral service. I would like to share it with you.

OUR OLD HOME PLACE

> Our old home place has long been gone.
> A place where we loved to play and call home.
> Mama and Papa and all of us kids
> Lived in this house, like we "usta " did.
> We didn't have money but lots of love,
> The only thing Mama and Papa had plenty of.
> They worked very hard to feed us kids.

You can bet your life they did.
We made a garden and canned the "stuff,"
Mama made sure she canned enough.
We picked strawberries and blackberries, too.
Mama canned several jars and thought that would do.
Times were hard and we didn't have money.
Papa cut down a tree to get wild honey.
We had a cow that Papa milked every day.
He made sure she had plenty of hay.
We had an old organ we all learned to play,
Someone was playing it most every day.
At Christmas we all got at least one toy.
That made our hearts full of joy.
We never went hungry; we were always fed.
At night when they put us to bed,
Some had to sleep three in a bed,
Some at the foot and some at the head.
We had to walk two miles to school.
There we learned the "golden rule."
There were eleven of us kids, Mom and Dad,
The best parents any kids ever had.

by Vena Ales Smith

This is exactly the way it was. We give you an A+, Vena! Thank you!

CHAPTER 15

ONE EVENING a short time ago, I was looking for some snap-shots in my album. I ran across a gift that was given to me for Christmas by one of my teachers in 1937. Do you remember the little hard-back autograph books that were so popular way back then? I was looking through it, and would you believe each of my loving sisters wrote a short verse and signed her name? I treasure this. As I write my story, we still have six sisters out of nine girls still living.

I want to mention something else that is really neat. When I was about fourteen, I had this bright idea of putting my name in a bottle and throwing it in Big Drywood Creek west of Nevada, Missouri. I put my name and address in the bottle, sealed it securely and threw it in the water. I had almost given up the idea that anyone find it, when one day I got a letter (I still have the letter because I never throw anything away) from a young man who worked in Nevada, Missouri. Just about as soon as I finished reading the letter from him, I got a warning in person from dear Mama that I wasn't to answer his letter. I guess I understand now, but I didn't then. After all, I was just a little "snot." I didn't have any business writing to a stranger, but I really didn't have a lot of business tossing my name in the Big Drywood Creek, don't you know?

When I went to work at Key Work Clothes, I was sixteen years young. (You had to be sixteen to work there.) I put my name and address under the paper label on the back pocket of a pair of over-alls. I waited and waited and finally got a letter from a man in South Dakota. He told me all about himself. He was a farmer and owned a chicken ranch. He didn't mention if it was fighting chickens, laying hens or frying chickens. I never found out a thing. Want to know why? Mama put the brakes on this idea, too. She gave me orders not to answer his letter. I didn't have a chance for anything exciting. Mama was there and put a halt on everything. Just think, if I could have lassoed this dude and this was a frying chicken ranch, I could have had "Clark's Chicken Buffet." Neat, huh? I wouldn't have had to go too far to enjoy a dinner. I like chicken any way you cook it. Then again, he may have been a married old man with a coop full of screaming little chicks. Again, I will never know. You can bet your bottom dollar I'd have enjoyed that chicken farm. I told you all about the chicken and the eggs away back at the start of my story.

I love to bake cookies and make all kinds of candy around the holidays. I take plates of this stuff around to different places, like certain floors at the hospital, emergency room, doctor's office, our optometrist in Ft. Scott and Kansas City, and I don't forget the neighbors either. (They are starting to call me the cookie lady. Meryl Darlene calls me the cookie monster or maker, one or the other.) I suppose I could be called worse.

One time when I was on my way up to the second floor at the hospital with a plate of chocolate chip cookies, I met my doctor and two other doctors in the hall. We talked for a minute and he said, "What do you have there?" After I told him, he took the plate, opened it, took three cookies and gave the plate back. He ate them all right there, so I know they all didn't get dumped. I just bet the ones I took to the second floor were enjoyed, too.

Sherri told me not long ago that when she was fourteen years old she wrote a poem about the Kennedy assassination. She told me a sad story. Her teacher, if you can call her a teacher, wouldn't accept it to be admitted to the book of poems from the class. I couldn't believe something like that could happen to us, and I don't know why Sherri didn't mention it. If I had known about this at the time, this old girl would have gone to that class and straightened the situation out. I don't even have a word for that teacher. She claimed Sherri had copied the poem from somewhere else. Nonsense! I am sorry now that my precious daughter was denied that opportunity. I asked Sherri if she still had the poem. She said she thought, because she was so hurt that the teacher, Miss Hughes, didn't believe she had written it, that she told her teacher to just throw it away. She looked in the cedar chest for a copy, since she couldn't remember for sure, but could not find it. Sherri, if you would have told me about the poem and Miss Hughes refusing to print it because she didn't think you wrote it, I would have made a little visit to her room. You can believe that, even bet your bottom dollar.

Sherri proved she is capable of writing beautiful poetry. She has since then written several poems, one being for her dad and me. I have included that poem on a page later in my book. I know you will agree with me that she doesn't have to copy the words of someone else.

One time, probably the fifth or sixth grade, Sherri's music teacher gave her an "F" in music because she wouldn't dance in class. I had to go to school again. I told the teacher we didn't believe in and take our children to dances. At that time we went to a church that didn't believe in dancing. Anyway, she brought Sherri's grade up to an "A." Gary had just started to school, and this one evening he said, "I got so cold this morning, I was freezing." I said, "Why didn't you go inside the school?" (He had to ride the first bus, and until the second bus got there the school was locked.) I didn't know about this dumb idea. I called the principal, asked him why the poor little kids were having to stand in the cold. Know what? He claimed he didn't know they were outside. I said, "Where are you that time of the morning?" I got that taken care of also. The next morning when Gary's bus got to school, the schoolhouse door was unlocked.

Gary was still in school and was going to have a spelling test. The night before I stayed up until about eleven o'clock helping him study. The next day he took the test and got a "B," because there were three words spelled incorrectly. I looked the test over and didn't think it was right. I think I am pretty good in spelling, but I got the dictionary out and double-checked the three words. He had only spelled one word wrong. Gary told me the students graded each other's tests. To think that his teacher had let the students grade the tests made me very unhappy, so I went to school again.

In all the years the children were in school, I made three trips to get disagreements straightened out. (By the way, I didn't take apples on any of these trips. These were business trips.) The only pay I got for all the times I had to go or call the school was the satisfaction of knowing our children's rights were acknowledged.

When I had my beauty salon, the children had to walk about

four blocks to school. One afternoon when the children got home, I was in my beauty salon with a lady and they peeked in to let me know they were home. This lady said, "Helen, are these your children"? I said, "They sure are." She told me they were the nicest children and that if she was out in the yard when they came by her house, they would stop to visit with her for a little while.

Speaking of school, while I was in my salon, one came every week and her sister came now and then. I noticed Mable had the same name as a man I used to go to Totten School with when we lived at the "Usta Place." I asked her if by any chance she knew him. She was married to him! When he came after her, I told him who I was, and we had a nice visit, threshing over old times. He remembered all of us Clarks, too. When we had our school reunion, we didn't have to look for him to let him know about it. I had already found him!

We have a friend here in town who grows lots of fresh vegetables, and he sells his produce. He told me once he had so many green beans going to waste. He offered them free to anyone who would pick them. He couldn't find anyone who wanted to spare the elbow grease. You can bet your bottom dollar I'd have been there if I'd known in time. I would have picked them, but I would have paid him. They are such nice people. He loves the soil and gardening. I suppose if he had picked and delivered the vegetables, there would have plenty of takers.

My granddaughter is getting married this summer. The time is going by so fast. Harley said, "Maybe I should get a new suit." I told him I could get it and let it be a Christmas gift. My, how the time flies. Where did the winter and spring go? I just got my wrappings pressed and the ribbons put away from last year!

Do you ever stop to think if everyone washes their hands before preparing or serving our food? Do you wonder if employees wash their hands before packaging meat in the supermarket? Well, I can't honestly name the guilty one, but this gross experience happened to me.

I was starting to make hamburgers for dinner one evening. After I had made the first patty and began to form the second, you would never guess in a million hours what I saw there in that meat. I certainly got sick in my stomach. I put it all back in the carton and took the ground chuck back to the store. I went straight to the manager. I informed him that I had found hair in the meat and it didn't come from anyone's head. Want to know his response? He told me to go get another package and it wouldn't cost anything. I gave him a look, which was probably the look of the century, and told him he couldn't be serious. I gave him the meat and told him I didn't care what he did with it, but to just get it out of my sight. I went to the restroom and washed my hands. Do you suppose they removed the hair and repacked the meat? I'll never know, because that was my last trip to that place.

I'm always finding things where they don't belong. Shortly after that nightmare, Harley and I stopped in Louisburg, Kansas, for breakfast. We were drinking our coffee, and eventually our breakfast was served. Guess what again? Across the top of my gravy and biscuits was a black hair four or five inches long. It didn't take long at all to get the waitress. When I told her to get it out of my sight, she wanted to know why. She must have had poor eyesight to miss that long thing. She told me she would bring me another serving, and I told her I didn't want another one. The cook would have probably whisked the hair off and served it again. After this episode, the breakfast that I didn't eat was on the house. We never ate there again.

Speaking of hair in food, in your eyes and mouth, and everywhere else, it really "grosses" me out for someone with long hair to walk past me and brush that long shaggy hair against me. At one time, we had a dentist here in Pittsburg whose assistant had long stringy hair that didn't look well-dressed. When she bent over me (the patient), her hair was all over me. Mind you, she wore the rubber gloves so she wouldn't get my diseases and then brushed her hair back with the gloves on and would then have her hands close to or in my mouth. This is so unsanitary. It should have been tied up short or in a net.

I decided even before she finished with me, this was the last trip to this dentist for me. I started searching for a new dentist right away. Had the doctor asked why I didn't come back, I would have said, "Things were getting too hairy around there."

DEAR MOM AND DAD

I've never really told you how I feel in my heart.
I've never been too good with words; maybe this will be a start.
Writing these words to say thank you, seems so little, I guess.
You deserve so much more 'cause you are the best of the best.

You are both very special, is one thing I want to say
Each have your own special talents; you use them in your own special way.
I love you both for all you've done, for me and for many others.
You are exactly who I would have chosen to be my dad and mother.

Caring, hard work, love and sharing; these are just a sample
Of the many things you've taught me, shown me by example.
Thanks for all you've done, for the example you set for me.
For the guidance, hard work, and home; you're the best there could ever be.

I have always been proud of you, happy to walk by your side.
You have a special place in my heart and it's filled with nothing but pride.
I have always been proud to say, "This is my mom and dad."
Not everyone is this lucky or blessed; to me this is very sad.

I could never repay you for all you've given me.
For no dollar amount can be placed on what you cannot see.
Along with all the material things you both have provided.
The spiritual side of my life you have also guided.

There is something special about me, but it's something that can't be seen.
It's only because I'm your child. That's what is special about me.
You both make me feel I'm somebody; just how I cannot say.
All I know is that you do it, in your own little special ways.

I've never felt that I deserved the wonderful parents I had.
I have yet to understand, but be assured, I am certainly glad.
My life has truly been blessed, because you were there for me.
I am who I am because of you; it's so plain to see.

I thank God for parents like you. I thank Him 'most every day.
I ask Him to bless your lives, bless you in every way.
I have yet to understand why God made me for just you.
I hope that I have made you proud and hope you feel that way, too.

I always wanted, when I grew up, to be just like you.
But as I did I realized, it wouldn't be easy to do.
You are both one of kind, it's not easy to fill your shoes.
For no one, my wonderful parents, could ever be like you.

By Sherri A. Stenseng   (September 12, 1998)

CHAPTER 16

WHEN WE WENT THROUGH the 1993 flood in Pittsburg, where
we live now, the local television station and the local newspaper
reporters came to interview all of us. One of the men close to us here
told me I was the best talker out here, so I should do all of the talking and answer all the questions, too. Well, he didn't have an inkling
how much experience I have along this side of the tracks, so I did
just that. I told them all what happened, what we went through,
and how some of us had to live in a motel for quite some time. Some
of the residents had family close by and some didn't. Anyway, we
made the front page once or twice.

We went to bed about 10:30 p.m. on September 22, 1993. It was
misting, but we never dreamed of what we would be facing the next
morning with flooding. When we woke up about 7:30 a.m. the next
morning, it was raining quite hard. My first thought was to check
the creek. We had lived right there, same place, for twenty years,
but we never had been run out of there. I looked down to see if the
water was coming out. Sure enough! I put my boots on, grabbed my
umbrella and went down to check it out. Our good neighbors, who
lived at the first place next to the water, were already there watching. Bob said it had risen twelve inches in thirty minutes. What we
all didn't know right then was that they had around seventeen inches
between Arma and Pittsburg. That should have been enough warn-

ing right then, but like I said, we didn't know about it yet. We just waited. With that much rain, the river really came up fast. Now we are speaking fast! You could take your eyes away for twenty to twenty-five minutes and you can imagine how quickly it was rising. There was water, water everywhere, and not a drop to drink. We had never seen rain like this.

I wanted to leave at this time, but Harley kept saying, "It won't get any higher." Harley was ill at that time and had to have oxygen plus medicine, so he just didn't want to pack up and leave. The water kept getting higher and higher. Everyone else living in the park had left. By then, there was about two feet of water around our house. You absolutely can't believe water could rise so quickly, and this water was just filthy.

The friend I mentioned before waded up to our steps and said, "Harley, get your stuff together. I've got Dale's boat and we'll get you and Helen out of here! The water is still coming up and fast." To this day, I have a deep feeling down inside for this man who cared enough to wade back to help Harley and me. Well, he had the boat, but the oars had floated away.

Now here is another blessing. Another dear friend was standing there in two and a half feet of water ready to pull the boat. Barbara, another good friend, stood there crying. You see, she lived next to the creek and was losing a good part of her belongings. She had gone to work early that morning, before the flooding started. By the time she was called and told about the high water, there wasn't time for her to load up her valuables. Some of us were at least able to get some necessities ready. I got our medicine, oxygen concentrator, flashlight, water, umbrella and our suitcase packed and headed for higher ground. Barbara pulled and Bob pushed the boat over past our storage barn, unloaded stuff into our pick-up and got to the west end of the park. The ground was higher there. When they were helping us to the pick-up, I saw our other neighbor standing there watching the water. I asked him, "Ken, do you think it will get any higher?" It did, don't you know? Ken said he would never forget how cute Harley and I looked in that boat. I didn't feel very cute.

We live one-half mile from the city but couldn't cross the water, as it was too high and swift. We were stranded, as was everyone else. It was about 5 p. m. We couldn't get out in any direction to go to a motel. We all went to a building where they keep county equipment. It was so oily and smelly in there. I knew Harley couldn't sleep in a place like that. (I also have a little trouble breathing.) About 5:30 p.m., here came Bob again. He said, "Let's see if we can find a way out of here." He said, "Harley, follow right behind me and I'll see if I can get you and Helen out of here and into town." Bless his heart. We started out, and in one place about eight miles north of where we were the water was over the road, but we got through it all right.

I thought once we got to US 69 highway and into Pittsburg, we would get a motel and be fine. Wrong! All the motels were already filled. You see, a lot of Pittsburg was flooded, plus there were tourists, too. I thought when we get to town, I'm staying at the Super 8. Wrong again! She said they were full at 11 a. m. Finding a motel was harder than packing our boat. Keep in mind, we hadn't eaten any food since lunch. The gas and water lines were all affected by the water, as were the electricity and phone lines. We finally remembered another motel and we went there. He said, "We have a room that is being cleaned right now. You can have it." We were wet and dirty from the floodwater, and we were getting so cold. I asked Harley if he wanted the shower or should I be greedy and go first. We were hungry and Harley needed to go on his oxygen, so I called a restaurant in Pittsburg that has a buffet to see if they could deliver some food. He told me half of his crew couldn't get in to work because of the flood, so he didn't have anyone who could bring it. He suggested that I call a fast food restaurant that delivers. I did and had food and coffee brought to the motel.

We were out of our home for thirteen days. Our house had two to three inches of water. I never, ever want to go through that again! I had my freezer in my storage shed beside the house and didn't worry about it. When we came back to the house, I had never seen such a mess in my entire life. My freezer had washed away from the wall, flipped over backward, the lid fell back and you guessed it. The food was exposed to that filthy water. I obviously lost everything in the freezer, including fifty pounds of pecans and twenty pounds of walnuts I had shelled. The freezer was full of meat, too. I cried.

Members of the Buddhist T.Z. Uz Chi Charity Enterprise Foundation came to our park on Saturday to help ease the financial burden of flood victims. This was the first monetary aid we had received. The foundation is based in Taiwan, with headquarters in Kansas City. Members of the foundation contacted a student from Pittsburg State University, Chein Liang Lin, who is a member of the Chinese association. I was the resident Lin called and told about the aid.

This young man was like a breath of fresh air, don't you know? While we were standing around talking with these young people from the college, crying on each other's shoulders, Tracy brought us lots of coffee. I want to say thanks again to Tracy for the many cups of coffee brought to all of us. You were a good neighbor.

We had signed up with Federal Emergency Management Agency (F.E.M.A.) but had no idea when to expect help and how much help it would be. The help from the Chinese organization was on the spot. There was no waiting for the money to come to help with expenses. They wrote each of us a check right on the spot.

My beautiful sisters, Dana and Wilma, wanted to send us financial help. I really was touched by their generosity, but I told them we were getting help. We were finally able to move back home. I never realized a mobile home could look so good. Remember, I cleaned and cleaned again before we moved back, using gallons of Lysol.

We were sitting in the kitchen some time later when we saw a car drive in. I didn't recognize the driver or the car, but she came to our door. Remember our good friend who pushed us out of the flood in a canoe? It was his oldest daughter. She came in and told us she wanted to tell us something before we read it in the newspaper. She told us her dad, Bob, had a heart attack the night before and died. It was really a shock to both of us, because the last time he was here to visit he looked and acted as though he felt better than he had for a long time. Bob was a diabetic and had heart problems, too. Of course, we attended his services. Had they asked me, I would loved to have said a few words at the funeral about what he meant to Harley and me and all the good deeds he did for everyone he knew.

I may have told you earlier in my story that Bob loved his Harley Davidson motorcycle. When my grandsons, Marc and Trenton, were small, they would see Bob ride in on that beautiful set of wheels. Being dressed and looking like he did, they thought he was a mean man. Bob wore his hair long, had whiskers to match and wore dark glasses and black leather. If you didn't know him, I guess you might think he did look mean. Bob surprised us and came by our craft table at the Good Old Days celebration in Ft. Scott one time. When Mark asked me if I knew that man, I told him Bob was our good neighbor. Marc told me he and Trenton had seen Bob drive by our house on his motorcycle and figured he was mean. I told Bob later about the boys seeing him and thinking he was probably mean. He said, "I am."

He liked to use his tiller to till the ground for my garden. He used to say he always got the first ripe one of the year. I was never sure if he got the first one or not, but if he didn't, he should have. It meant a lot to me to get that ground tilled.

Please let me enter this precious memory here. At Christmas time Bob would fill a large plastic bowl with apples, oranges, wrapped candy and several kinds of nuts. He would deliver one of these bowls to each of his friends. It was his way of showing how much he cared. I asked him why he didn't crack and pick out the nuts in my bowl. Bob knew that I was not a lover of cats and dogs, so to get my goat he was always trying to give me one that no one wanted.

This good neighbor loved to talk and visit with his friends. He was such a good listener. In all conversations, however, you really need a good listener. We were standing outside late one afternoon and I'm not sure how it started, but we got on the subject of the poem, *"Footprints in the Sand."* Somewhere in the conversation I must have said I would like to have the poem. I never thought any more about it. Well, Bob went to Florida on his "bike" to see his children one summer. When he came home, he came up the walk and handed me a present. He said, "I saw this in a store and I thought of you." It was a plaque with *"Footprints in the Sand"* on it. I treasure this gift he brought me. Thanks, Bob. It was really good to have you as neighbor and friend. God bless you.

We had another good friend here in the park who lost her husband a while ago. The night he died, his nurse called me and asked if Harley and I would look after her and see if she was all right when she got home. Bea was about seventy-two years old. I told her it was no problem and that I would watch for her to come home. I asked her to come stay with us in our extra bedroom. She was just tickled pink to get to stay, since she had no family close by. She had dinner and breakfast with us.

I may have mentioned this before. If so, you might read it again. When Harley decided to take his retirement, I thought it would be just fabulous to throw a surprise party. I started making plans early. After all, it takes a lot of planning and sneaking around to get something like this together. I started with the invitations, then made the reservations at one of the famous chicken restaurants here close to home. After all, most everyone likes chicken.

Along about that time, I was in the fancy cake business, so I needed to do something special for this special occasion. I made a cake in the shape of a pill bottle, plus two small cakes for the lid. Naturally, I wrote out the prescription on the cake and added the doctor's name. It turned out really neat. This occasion was in one of the warmer months, so I had a time keeping the cake standing upright.

With the help of my children and the employees at the restaurant, it was a total surprise to Harley, with a capital "S." I asked all the guests to be there at a certain time before Harley and me. Then I had the hostess usher Harley and me to the "party." When we walked in, cameras were flashing and happy wishes shouted. Harley's two eyes were as wide as could be and he was speechless.

I had gone out in the afternoon and decorated the tables, arranged napkins, plates, nut cups and the cake. All we had to do was sit down, eat our supper and serve the beautiful cake. It certainly was a fun night.

Not too many years later another surprise retirement party was held, but I was the guest of honor. Sherri made a money tree, and the guests brought or sent "green leaves" for the tree. It was a lot of fun to "pick" the leaves from the tree and go shopping, don't you know?

Our family tries to eat at this chicken restaurant whenever Sherri's family is back here to visit. When all the families, children, grandchildren and spouses were in Ft. Scott to help my ex-husband, Hubert, celebrate his eightieth birthday, again several of us met at Chicken Anne's to eat.

Papa took time out from his work to have his picture taken with me.

CHAPTER 17

I HAD BEEN having a very severe pain in my right ankle, so I went to my doctor, and after he took an X-ray and examination he sent me to an orthopedic surgeon. The surgeon wanted to try some physical therapy before surgery. I went though this procedure, and when I went back I had no pain at all. I was surprised my agony had disappeared. I sat up on his table and I said, "How do you explain my pain leaving so quickly?" He glanced over to Harley and back to me and said, "I touched you." So just to seal the comedy, I sang, "He touched Me, Oh, He Touched Me"! He said, "You can sing, too?" It was so funny. You all should have been there, not for therapy, just for the entertainment.

When Harley and I first started dating, it was a usual ritual that before we went out to dinner we would have a root beer float. (I don't like it now.) We went to a fast food place here in Pittsburg and sat outside on a picnic bench and drank our float. Now you all may wonder what is so special about this. Well, nothing, I guess, but then it was a cool thing to do.

On this one particular evening we had the float and afterward stopped for a chicken dinner. It just happened that I got a wishbone on my plate. (I suppose you have heard about making a wish and then breaking the wishbone with someone else.) Harley said, "If you hold the wishbone under the table and make your wish, it will come

215

true, regardless of who gets the biggest bone." We tried it his way. He never can remember what he wished for. I do.

We have had so many chats and discussions since we've been together. Believe me, he pops off a dandy now and then. We were sitting watching television a while back. Now, I really wasn't making fun of this lady, but I said, " Isn't she ugly in that color?" Harley said, "She's ugly in any color." I meant the color just wasn't her.

A few nights ago we had finished our dinner and, as usual, Harley was stretched out, leaning his heavy foot on my foot under the table. I said, "Why is your heavy foot on my foot?" He said he thought it was the table leg. I told him I would like to think my foot was a little sexier than a Duncan Phyfe table leg. He probably does, too.

This has been a good year for cucumbers. Sherri and Russ brought me twenty pounds for pickles. As I told you before, Papa and Mama taught us to share, so I thought I'd be nice and take my neighbor some freshly made sweet pickles. A couple of days and a empty jar later, she brought the jar back and said, "Here's your jar." She never said thanks or anything else. Hey, maybe they tasted one and did a Ray Sexton twist and threw them out to someone's hogs. Oh, well, maybe I'll take her something else one of these days, and just maybe I'll get a smile. That will be dandy.

Sherri told me that once she and Gary were staying at Grandma Clark's house and Grandma gave them each five cents to go around the corner and get an ice cream cone. That was quite awhile back to be able to get them for a nickel. I remember when we could get two big dips for five cents. Since then the dips have gotten smaller and the nickels have turned into quarters. The name of the little neighborhood ice cream store was "Clarks." (No, they weren't related to us.) It was just a little store located about a block from Mama's house that sold candy, pop, ice cream, magazines and several other items. I suppose it was what we call a convenience store now, except he sold the hand-dipped ice cream.

Sherri told me also that she and my granddaughter Kristi were at Aunt Margie's house, and auntie asked Kristi if she would like to have an ice cream cone. Kristi said, "Yes, but can I have some ice cream in it?" Cute, huh? I thought they always came with ice cream. I take my ice cream in a cup, because I can't get much in a cone. Besides, there isn't anywhere to pour that chocolate topping. I don't need much of either one.

One time I was getting dressed to go to a friend's wedding. I made a nice dress out of some material I had bought. For this wedding, I had to put on heels, hose, and really get dressed up. I was talking to my sister, Wilma, and I told her, "I don't like to dress up anymore. It's more comfortable in flats and pantsuit. I never feel like I look just right." She said, "You go ahead and get all dressed up, and next to the bride you will be the prettiest one there." (How did she know this? Beats me.) It was a beautiful thought anyway.

While I was still working at the ammunition plant near Parsons, we (I had riders) started to work one day and it was a little icy. I wasn't really driving too fast, but all at once my car started sliding. I was just lucky that we were the only ones on that stretch of highway. I was always told not to hit the brakes at skidding time, so we eased across the highway into the ditch and stopped with my car doing a half a turn headed to the west. The highway ran north and south. It was slicker then the dickens in that ditch, and with no chains on I was helpless. Well, I got out on the shoulder by foot and flagged a motorist. The nice man was going towards Ft. Scott, so he gave me a ride back to town. My son, Gary, got a set of chains and pulled me out to civilization, and off to work we went. You can bet your bottom dollar we (or I) drove very carefully from there on. By the way, we weren't late to work.

Not to long ago I was visiting Sherri when a storm came up. The electricity went off, and it got so dark inside we needed a candle. We were sure a tornado was coming, so we got things ready to go to the basement. Kristi ran upstairs to get her valuables, and she came down with what were the two most important things to her. Rusty's graduation picture and her stuffed horse named Biscuit were what she brought down to take to the basement.

Have you ever driven through and parked in a parking lot and took notice of all the different makes and colors of cars parked around you? This is quite a pastime, huh? I had to run to the supermarket not long ago and just happened to park my little '75 Scamp next to quite an expensive burgundy car. That color took my eye right away. As the gentleman was getting out of his car, I had to mouth off and told him I would almost trade cars with him, but I supposed he would have to have a little to-boot. He told me he would. I ran into him again inside the market. He picked up an item, then put it down over and over again. It seemed as though the food was too expensive. He was sure checking prices. Maybe that was why he could drive that great big expensive automobile, don't you know? You can bet your

This picture is of some of the Clarks I have been telling you about in my book of memories. All of the living Clark "kids" (except Margie) attended a family reunion in 1987 and this picture was taken.
Left to right, back row: Vena, Wilma, Dana, Pansy, Helen, Meryl. Kneeling: Ruby, Gayle.

bottom dollar he wasn't going to trade automobiles with me.

Sometimes I feel like I want to go shopping, not because I need anything, but just to get out of the house, or maybe get a seventy-five cent cup of coffee somewhere. Well, when I go shopping, I usually get a gift for Harley. One time I found him a beautiful red clip-on necktie. He had it about three years when he had to dress up in a suit and tie to go to the funeral of a relative. Before the service started, the family members were standing around the entrance of the funeral home, just talking and crying. One of the male employees walked up to Harley and visited with him a little while and said, "How would you like to trade ties?" Harley kept his red tie and has loved it more every day since then. I think this is cool. This young man was in his early twenties, I guess.

Do you remember in past years when you would go into a department store and the minute you stepped through the door a sales lady was on your heels to wait on you? (She would stay on your bumper just to help you.) Before you could get your gloves off your hands, someone would ask if they could help you find something. Now days you have to look and sometimes wait for assistance. It could be back in the olden days they got paid by how much they sold, like a commission. Now I suppose it is by the hour. Where I do most of my shopping, if you can find someone, they are very nice to help me.

One day I was at the supermarket and I was having a little trouble walking because of a hip problem. I asked an associate where the soda crackers were and told him that I was having trouble getting to the check-out. This young man asked if I wanted salted or unsalted crackers. I told him what I wanted, and he told me to wait right there and that he would get a box for me. Now once in awhile, you can't find anyone to help. When you do, they are nice to help you.

I mentioned before that we ate a lot of gravy at the Clark Usta Place. I can remember stirring the gravy, and when it was ready I wasn't big enough to lift that big old skillet, so Papa would lift it and let me scrape the gravy out. I thought I was just about grown-up after that. He could have easily done the whole thing, but I suppose he was teaching me the tricks of the trade in the gravy department. I guess I do make good gravy now.

I dated a boy once and we were talking about what we liked and didn't like to eat. He didn't like gravy or cooked cabbage. That told me right then we wouldn't get along. I didn't tell him, but that was the best reason I never dated him again. You see, I love cabbage and gravy, any way you serve them.

Not too long ago we were visiting some relatives and something was said about having some cream to churn. Well, I said, "Get the jar ready and I'll churn it for you." I ended up churning two one-half gallon jars of cream. Since we were staying all night, I was really planning on some real butter I had made on some hot toast. Guess what? The butter wasn't put on the table. Can you imagine having something special like homemade butter and not sharing? If I had people staying with me, I would probably have gotten up early and made biscuits.

When my daughter was born in Idaho on January 10, 1950, several babies were born that night and everyone was very busy. It was feeding time, so the babies were brought from the nursery to the moms to be fed. They brought this baby to me, and naturally I knew my own baby. I said, "Nurse, this baby isn't mine. Where is my baby Sherri?" She looked at the bracelet and, sure enough, this baby belonged to someone else. Again I said, "Where is my baby?" She got in gear quickly and found my little girl. The baby she brought me was a little boy. It didn't happen the second time. This nurse must have been new or half-asleep. I didn't want someone else's baby. I wanted mine. I had big plans for her and me. There were four mothers in the ward when I had my daughter, which was a lot for that little hospital.

A short time after we were all released from the hospital, the family of the child that was brought to me in error was involved in a bad car accident. The father, daughter, mother of the baby brought to me and her new baby were all killed. It was so very sad.

All of you who have taken quinine know that it's a bitter medicine. When our Mama had to give it, she would take that thin skin between the onion layers and wrap the medicine in a small ball to make it easier to swallow. You could bet your bottom dollar it would be easier to swallow the way she did it. I'm not particularly fond of taking medicine, and I don't if I can get out of it.

Sherri and I were talking about cute little remarks kids say when they are little. Some are really sweet, and then there are some that need to be thought through. When we lived on the farm, Sherri was small and would hear us talk about the cow's udder. She would call it the cow's "under." She had the position on the cow right anyway.

Sherri and I were also talking about things we remembered from childhood. She asked me if I remembered when we lived out in the country and, of course, did not have air conditioning. That summer of 1953 and 1954 were so terribly hot and almost unbearable. Sherri remembers one time when I stripped her and Gary down to just underwear, wetting sheets with cool water and laying the sheets over them when they took a nap. I would turn the fan on them, and when the sheets got dry I would wet them down again. Sherri would have only been three years old, but she remembers it. The heat was so bad those summers that people actually died because of it. The father of a close friend of mine died of a heat stroke. I don't think I want to go back to those "good old days." I like to be cool.

My lovely sisters and I have talked about being buried in our old family cemetery, located close to the Usta Place. This is the cemetery where our parents and grandparents are buried. I've heard a couple of them say they didn't want to be put there because there are too many sad memories from the Usta Place. Well, we had a lot of precious memories from down there, too. I think it would be a beautiful place to lay all of those memories to rest.

There are too many people who live without working and too many who work without living.

CHAPTER 18

SOMETIME BACK my grandson Rusty and his wife, Stacy, came to visit overnight and we had the nicest time. I think it was midnight when we finally quit talking and went to bed. Stacy is so precious and is as good at listening and she is at talking. We enjoyed having them here very much. As I mentioned earlier in my story, they own the *Star Journal* in Hillsboro. Well, Stacy brought me a clipping she had printed in their newspaper and I just felt like I wanted to add it to all of my precious thoughts. I hope all of you who read this enjoy it as much as I did. Here it is:

"The Reverend's Wife Tells About Her Day"
"The other day I went to a local religious book store, where I saw a bumper sticker with these words on it: 'Honk if You Love Jesus.' I bought it and stuck it on the back bumper of my car and I am really glad I did. What an uplifting experience followed. I was stopped at the light of a busy intersection, just lost in thought about the Lord. I didn't notice the light had changed. That bumper sticker really worked. I found lots of people who love Jesus. Why, the guy behind me started to honk like crazy. He must really love the Lord, because pretty soon he leaned out his window and yelled Jesus Christ, as loud as he could. It was like a football game with him shouting, 'Go,

Jesus Christ, go!' Everyone else started honking, too, so I leaned out my window, waved and smiled to all these loving people."

"There must have been a guy from Florida back there, because I could hear something about a sunny beach. I saw him waving in a funny way, with only his middle finger stuck up in the air. I had recently asked my children what that meant. They kind of squirmed, looked at each other, giggled and told me it was the Hawaiian good luck sign. So I leaned out my window and gave him the good luck sign back. A couple of people were so caught up in the joy of the moment that they got out of their cars and started walking toward me. I bet they wanted to pray, but just then I noticed the light had changed and I stepped on the gas. It's a good thing I did, because I was the only car to get across the intersection. I looked back at them standing there, leaned out my window, gave them a big smile and held up the Hawaiian good luck sign as I drove away. Praise the Lord for such wonderful folks."

When Gary was in high school, he and others in his art class had an opportunity to design a new school crest. Gary's design won the contest, and since there was so much talent and artistic ability it was quite an honor for his design to be chosen. Well, I have to admit the one that was chosen was the best one.

The art class went to Lawrence, Kansas, one fall just to tour the museum and get out of class for a day. They asked for parents to go as chaperones. Well, I called all my salon appointments and booked them for later. I put on my school clothes and went to Kansas University. The bus driver told all the students, "I have your lunch tickets. If you want to eat, you will be at the cafeteria at noon." Guess what? They all showed up. The bus driver and I attended a movie in the afternoon, while the students did their thing. When it came time to come back to Ft. Scott, every last one of them was there to board the bus. I guess they didn't want to walk all the way home. I don't think the driver would have left anyone up there.

Gary has written several poems and recently wrote one and gave it to me. I knew he was a talented artist, but I didn't know he could write poetry. I want to share the poem he wrote for me with you. I was so touched when he read it to me. You can read it later on in the book.

I told you before I love to listen to the birds in the morning. They sound so happy, and it seems like they sing louder during the morning hours. A bobwhite was out here a day or two ago, and I started to whistle his tune right back at him. I did a good job, but he was so much better, don't you know?

A bunch of geese went over this morning and brought back a precious little memory. Gary was little but old enough to hunt with a bow and arrow, so Hubert and Gary went to the lake to go duck hunting. When they got there, Gary saw some ducks on the lake and, being the sportsman that he was and still is, took a shot with his bow and arrow. This was one of his few mistakes. You see, someone had left their decoys anchored in the lake, and Gary thought they were real. You guessed it. His arrow went to the bottom of the lake. I never found out how his father consoled him from that one.

I'd like very much to add this little bit of laughter to my story. Please remember you would have had to be there to appreciate the comedy of that evening! Harley's daughter and son-in-law, some of their friends, Harley and I, of course, were invited to attend a dinner theater in Kansas City a few years ago. It was really quite an experience. The buffet was really nice with good food and everything you would want to eat. We were seated just next to the stage while having our dinner and remained in the same place for the show. I had not been out in a place like this one too often, but except for one or two things, I did what everyone else did. After our table and the food were cleaned up, the play started. I can't remember the name of the play, but it was a comedy and the actors and actresses were top-drawer. Everything was going just great, and about thirty minutes into the play the audience was very quiet. One of the young actors said something in his part that struck me so funny, I forgot I was supposed to be nice and quiet and show my good manners. When he spoke, I laughed. The problem was that I was the only one who laughed out loud. I embarrassed myself so bad I could have crawled under the table. Well, being right up next to the stage, everyone could see me and knew I was suffering embarrassment. Three or four people "cackled," and then the whole audience started laughing and applause came from all over the room. By now, all of the people in the play also got tickled at me, so they started laughing and laughed so hard tears ran down their faces.

After the place quieted down, the play continued, and after a little while it was over. One or two gentlemen came over to our table and shook hands with me, I guess to try to make me feel better. I thought a little bit about going into show business after that evening, but I didn't have time. (Too many other things to do, don't you know?) I made a lot a people laugh that night. I really think to a certain extent I've always like to show off.

I have friends in all the right places, and they haven't let me down so far. Several years ago at Halloween I decided I would dress up like a bum and trick-or-treat a friend of mine. I put on my "bum" suit and mask (yes, I needed a mask) and left my car elsewhere. I knocked on Jackie's door. When she came to the door and held out the candy dish, I walked on by her and into the kitchen. I helped myself to a piece of fresh fruit from a bowl on her table, went to the refrigerator and got a bite or two of something, gave her a "salute" and left. She never knew who I was until a week or so later I released the news, and there was one surprised lady.

Can any of you remember buying mustard for ten cents a quart? A little store where we used to shop sold it for that. Do you suppose that is why there isn't a little store there anymore? I can remember what a lot of items sold for many years ago, and when I'm shopping I find myself thinking about how much difference there is in the price.

I was getting along quite well writing my precious memoirs, and I thought of some more happenings back in the Usta Place days. I'm going to add them here, because I know you will enjoy reading them. I've told you a lot about the Usta Place and all the hard times we had and the luxuries we did without. It was hard for everyone, but Papa and Mama hung in there and kept all of us kids fed, clothed and a roof over our heads.

One thing that would have been a luxury would have been an indoor throne. We had a three-seater, which was a must for a family the size of the Clark clan. In those days, the Sears & Roebuck catalog was a necessity at this outdoor throne. At night the outdoor throne was too far away for us little kids to go. Being the "top-drawer" parents they were, they provided us with a portable galvanized throne with a lid. Now you can bet your bottom dollar that little jewel was ready to be taken to the big outhouse by morning.

The older kids who were really ambitious and brave took turns carrying that bucket out. This portable throne saved a lot of steps for everyone who would have had to march out on cold dark nights.

I have a cute planter in my bathroom that would probably make some of you want to "up-chuck." I took a bedpan (yes, it was new) and filled it full of artificial flowers. Sister number eight, Gayle, bought me a bunch of sweet peas to dangle through the empty-out route. It may surprise you, but it really is cute!

Also, do any of you remember as children not wanting to do the

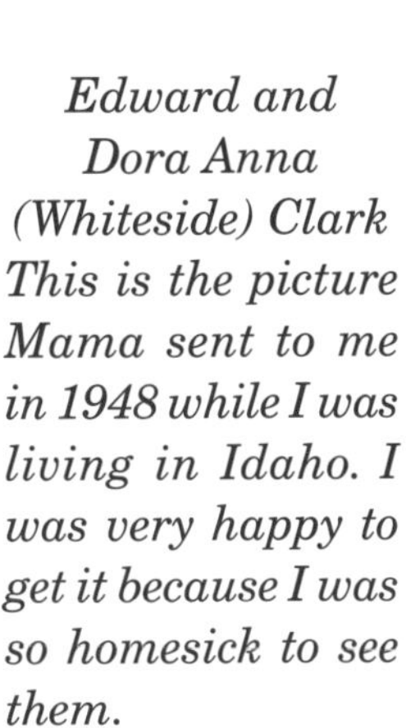

Edward and Dora Anna (Whiteside) Clark This is the picture Mama sent to me in 1948 while I was living in Idaho. I was very happy to get it because I was so homesick to see them.

supper dishes? I can remember it very well. I didn't like to do them any time, but nighttime I was tired. I would ask Mama to let up and let them go until morning. This would not happen. I made up my mind when I got my own kitchen I was not going to do the supper dishes. Guess what? I think dirty dishes are bad enough at breakfast and lunch. The evening dishes, left overnight, are ugly. The only dishwasher I have is ME! I like to do them the minute the meal is finished.

I may have mentioned before, Sherri asked me to make aprons for my granddaughter's wedding reception. She mailed the lace to me, I quickly got them made and mailed them back to her. Sherri let me know the aprons were satisfactory right away. She loved them and told me she was going to tell everyone I had made them. Do you suppose perhaps I will drum up a little business?

This precious memory just came to my mind. Harley and I were invited to a Christmas party several years ago. We could take a guest, so I invited my sister, Margie, and her husband, Bob, to go with us. Well, I wanted to dress formal, so I made a white metallic floor-length gown. I guess I looked pretty good. We planned to meet our guests at a local steak house for dinner, then go on to the party. They were waiting for us when we went inside. Bob looked at me and said, "Helen, you look just beautiful." I thanked him and wanted to ask him what took him so long. When the four of us would go out dancing, he and Margie would sometimes dance to *It Had To Be You.* I would always "cut in," and I don't think Margie liked it too well.

Dana had a lot of space at her home in Nevada, Missouri. Besides a fairly large house, she had a double garage and a small building in the backyard which she used for a beauty shop. She also had a big yard for flowers and a garden. A section of the yard was fenced off for her eight geese. Dana was planning an auction to sell some of her household items and her geese, because she just couldn't care for the geese anymore. About two months before the auction, Dana was in her front yard when a police car drove up. She couldn't imagine what was going on. The officer came up to Dana and said, "Are those your geese down the street?" (He had to have known they were hers; they were the only geese in town.) Dana told him she was sure they were hers and that they weren't supposed to be out of the yard. She looked down the street and, sure enough, they were where they weren't supposed to be. She clapped her hands a couple of times and called to them. "All of you get back up here. You aren't supposed to be out of the yard. Come home right now!" The geese heard her and started squawking, flapping their wings and trying to run at the same time. I guess the officer was stunned to see such a sight. These geese were like children, obeying her better than most children obey their parents. When it came time for that auction, Dana told me she didn't mind selling her belongings, but she cried when they started to sell the geese. Poor Dana, she really loved her birds!

Have you ever had a desire or a feeling like you want to do something and maybe think the idea is too far out? I have several times. A few years ago Dana said, "Do you know what I would really like to do before I die?" I said, "Dana, I don't have a clue. What?" She said, "I'd like to drive an eighteen-wheeler." That would have been my last guess! I told Dana if she ever got behind the wheel of one of those rigs, to be sure and let me know so I would make plans to stay home that day. She would have been cute sitting up there at the wheel. She would look so small with that big piece of truck around her.

I love to talk to people who have the same hobbies I do. I get ideas, share mine and try to learn something every day. I love most all kinds of word puzzles, except crossword. I know a few people who can do them with a pen instead of a pencil. Those people surely know a lot about many topics. Well, I know a little bit about a lot of things, a lot about a few things, but not a lot about a lot of things. Now to do the crossword puzzles, I have to have an eraser. I'm one of those whose eraser wears off before the pencil wears out.

I asked Harley if he learned a lot about punctuation when he was in school. He said, "I knew where to put a comet." He has a vocabulary all his own. It just cracks me up sometimes.

I feel I would like to share this little story with you. First, let me say some of you reading my story might think anything as personal as this next story should be left in the bathroom, but I think anything this sweet should be shared with all my other memories. Now, remember, you would have almost had to be there to appreciate this conversation. Harley and I were undressing and getting ready for bed. I was feeling a tad under the weather and I said, "Hon, I feel just rotten. I ache all over like I'm taking the flu. I think I'll just sit up for awhile." There he was, a seventy-nine-year-old man standing there in his underwear, barefooted, his dentures in a cup in the bathroom. He looked at me and grinned and said, "Just come on and go to bed with me and you'll feel better." I thought to myself, "Do you honestly think something like this could take the place of medicine?" He looked so funny standing there, and we both started laughing. I told him we should have had a tape of this.

I was talking to my cousin some time ago, and she was telling me about visiting with our cousin at Aunt Etta's home. It was very hot that day. Doris, our other cousin and my childhood playmate, was wearing a long-sleeved dress and was getting hot. So Doris would be cooler, Lois got the scissors and did a little trimming. Aunt Blanch probably bought the dress, so I don't suppose she liked that too well. We were all only about five or six years old and too young to be playing with scissors anyway.

FOR MY MOM

Mom, I want to thank you
> For all the things you've done,
For the values you have instilled in me,
> And the gentleness you've shown.

You've done the best that you could do,
> With all that you have had.
To provide a loving home, with food and clothes,
> When times were good and times were bad.

I know it's not been easy,
> For as a child I knew that times were tough.
But through it all, with love and pride,
> We always seemed to have enough.

God gave you the ability to be creative and wise,
> With a talent to sew and a talent to cook.
He placed within you and ability to write,
> Guiding you to be the author of your book.

It seems that God makes certain people extra special,
> Able to rise above the rest.
So He placed within you those special qualities,
> For I know He made you one of the best.

So, Mom, I just want to tell you I love you,
> And thank you for all that you've done.
For being blessed with you as my mother,
> Makes me a special son.

By Gary Allen Rhodes (July 15, 2000)

CHAPTER 19

INSTEAD OF HAVING AN AUCTION after my sister number eight, Gayle, died, her husband, Bob, decided to have a garage sale. He wanted Margie and me to come and take anything we wanted that had belonged to Gayle. When Margie and I were looking through things at the sale, you can't imagine the priceless pretties that were lying there for strangers to finger through.

A little while before Gayle died, we had gone to Kansas City to visit Harley's daughter, Peggy. They took me over to Gladstone to see this darling sister number eight, dropped me off so I could spend the night and then picked me up the next morning. We got up early Sunday morning, and Gayle got her coffee grinder and the coffee beans out. We had freshly ground coffee in a few minutes. We fixed English muffins, scrambled eggs and bacon for breakfast. We took our cups to her backyard and had a very nice talk. (Over the years, we had several good talks out there). We found comfortable chairs, talked for several hours and drank our coffee. We ran out of coffee long before we ran out of conversation.

I'll never forget that last visit we had. The vegetable garden and her yard were so beautiful. I enjoyed it so much. Gayle had diabetes and died a short time later of diabetic complications.

When Bob got ready to sell their house in Gladstone, he told me when people would come to view the home, it was the huge beautiful back yard turned them against buying the place. They would make the comment that the yard would be too much to mow or the yard would be too much trouble to take care of. People are getting so lazy. Just think, you could grow tomatoes, melons, green beans, corn, squash and get a couple of goats to mow the rest of it for you.

Dana had made padded picture albums and wanted to give one to each of the sisters. Gayle and Bob had come this way and were going to spend two or three days. On their way home, they were going by to see Dana to pick out the picture album she wanted. They spent the night with us and we had a great time. I had fixed Chicken Tetrazini. Since Gayle hadn't been feeling well, Bob had been the chief cook and dishwasher. He welcomed the home-made noodles and another Tetrazini casserole I made to send home with them.

The picture album that Dana had given Gayle was at the garage sale. I bought it, of course, along with several other items. As I was digging in boxes, I found a small picture called "The Shepherd's Call." It was waiting for me, I guess. I turned it over, and on the back was written "Merry Christmas to Mama from Vena and Earl." Mama had received it from Vena in 1939 and had sometime given it to Gayle. I grabbed it up right quick. There was a picture like it, only larger, hanging on the wall at Totten School. I also got a picture of Mama taken in 1910. She was so pretty when she was young and still was as she got older.

When we were really little and were lucky to get to ride a merry-go-round, Papa was afraid we would fall off. He got on the merry-go-round and stood between the horses and pretended to hold us on. Even though he wasn't horseback himself, he got a free ride.

I asked Harley if he got to ride the merry-go-round when he was a little boy. He said he did. When I asked if anyone had to hold him on, he told me he didn't get to ride until he was old enough to hold on. He told me that it didn't have a motor and was operated manually. I never knew there was such a thing. Now I've seen several moons, but those manual merry-go-rounds must have been before my time. Whoever had to push that ride wouldn't have to go to the gym four or five times a week or run several miles a day.

It just seems rather strange to me what goes on in the retirement plan. I think it's absolutely hilarious when a man retires. He quits his job, locks the door and throws away the key. When a woman retires, she quits clocking in at her job, but she can't see the door at home for all the coats, shoes, newspapers, fishing tackle, remote controls, candy wrappers, dirty clothes and shoes. Plus there all the "honey-do" jobs that didn't get done before you-know-who retired. All this besides cooking, laundry, grocery shopping, gardening and canning still has to be done. She doesn't have time to look for the door or key. How in the world did we get so mixed up in all of this?

When Harley and I celebrated our twenty-fifth wedding anniversary, May 17, 1995, I invited friends and relatives to help us celebrate our luncheon. As it turned out, sisters Dana and Pansy were supposed to come from Nevada, Missouri, and Pansy was to take pictures of the occasion for us. A tornado went through early that morning, tearing down several trees in Dana's yard and driveway, so they both missed our big day. I told the manager at the restaurant my photographer didn't make it because of the storm and we wouldn't get any pictures. Well, guess what? The manager came back to our table carrying a camera. She just happened to have a camera in her car and had two shots left on the roll. She took the pictures of us. Wasn't that sweet of her to do that for us? I baked our anniversary cake, which was shaped like a piano on legs. No one believed I really baked it, but I did. Baking special cakes like this is one of the many hobbies I love.

Harley and I celebrated our 25th wedding anniversary in 1995. This is the picture the manager took for us since my photographer couldn't come.

My sisters have all been there for me in a lot of ways. Dana took care of all of us when Mama would be busy with chores and, believe me, there was always work for Mama to do. Dana helped me with my homework many times. Wilma also helped take care of me when I was little. Do you remember me mentioning the time Wilma had to dig in her purse to find money to buy me the red comb for my hair? You can bet your bottom dollar I haven't been sorry for any little old thing I've done for any of my sisters, and I will continue as long as I am able.

Today I was telling Harley I believe "bullies" are born bullies. We had a few of them at Totten School. I'm sure I told you one of the big people at school tried to get me in trouble. (Her name was also Helen.) Mr. Whitworth, my first grade teacher, told her to go back outside because he had seen everything.

I think I mentioned before about our neighbor, Joe, giving Marc and Trenton fish and fishing tackle. Well, Joe is a giving man and a good neighbor. He loves to grow vegetables and then share his produce. Joe's wife, Betty, died a few years ago. She was also a sweet and loving person. She told me once that she couldn't understand why Joe worked so hard growing this stuff and then giving it away. It feels good when you can sack it up and take it to a neighbor or shut-in. I've taken plates of candy and cookies and homemade blackberry jelly to loved ones through the years. The smile on their faces is pay enough for me.

One year we had some neighbors who worked on the railroad. They planted spinach behind their house in a little garden spot. I watched it grow. One day there was a knock on the door. There stood one of the men with a sack of spinach he had just harvested from his garden. It sure beats all that canned stuff.

Do you all remember me telling you about Bob taking Harley and me out of the flood in a boat? Now he was definitely one of the good guys. He came to our house two or three times and tilled the ground for my tomato garden. I tried to pay him, but I might as well have tried to fly to the moon with no wings.

Then there is this other man who lived across the street. He took time to build a porch for us. Another neighbor man painted two storage sheds. They did this work because Harley was not feeling too well. We have proof that there are still good guys out there. Take time and look around. They don't all wear white hats!

Years earlier, while we were still going to Mt. Orum Church, a member of our Sunday school class just out of the blue said, "I think a woman's place is in the home." It just happened I was the only lady in the class who was working outside the home. As I mentioned, we had some bad breaks. Bad breaks don't pay the bills, so I went to work. By the way, within eighteen months of this statement, every woman in my class had a job. Now their daughters are working, too.

Years ago Mama gave me a bookmarker with the following quotes on it. Hope you enjoy them:

- "Nobody grows old by merely living a number of years. People grow old only by deserting their ideals."
- "You are as young as your self-confidence, as old as your fears, as young as your hope, as old as your despair."
- "In the central place of every heart, there is a recording chamber; so long as it receives messages of beauty, hope, cheer, and courage, you are young."
- "When the wires are all down and your heart is covered with the snows of pessimism and the ice of cynicism, then, and only then, have you grown old."
- "God grant me the serenity to accept the things I cannot change, courage to change the things I can, and wisdom to know the difference."

Several years after Gary and Sherri grew out of the famous baby buggy, I put it in a garage sale. Now I had that little jewel priced so that most anyone could have bought it. Anyway, I cut the price so this woman could buy it. She paid part of it and promised to pay the balance later. She owed me for a permanent wave, too. I never saw her again. Want to know something? I'd rather she owes me than for me to have cheated her, don't you know?

I want to tell you something real sweet that happened when we were still going to Mt. Orum church. We always had a beautiful program at Christmas time. One year, they needed a Mary, Joseph and baby Jesus. I don't understand why we were chosen, but Hubert and I played the part of Joseph and Mary. Our little "gems" were too old to play baby Jesus, so Mark Hartman played that precious part. We all did well and the program was admired by all. It was an honor to get to play the part. Those were the days, don't you know?

I don't know why we were chosen to do this either, but another couple, Hubert and I were asked to buy and sack the candy to be passed out after the Christmas program one year. We always had a big attendance at Christmas. The Sunday School fund paid for the treats, but it was up to this other lady and me to buy the candy and oranges for the sack of treats. Since I absolutely love peanut clusters, they were the first candy to be weighed and in my basket. Back then, candy was on display in bulk form at the candy counter. You would tell the clerk how much you wanted and she would weigh out the correct amount and put it in a sack for you. Do you remember being able to go in and buy it that way? When it came time to bag the goodies, I had to sample a cluster once in awhile, so I could remember how good they really were. I don't know why no one ever wanted to do this job. It wasn't hard to do and it was a "sweet" thing to do. There were always several people who showed up once a year (at candy time), and you wouldn't see them again until it was time for candy sacks again. We always made sure there was plenty so everyone would get one.

Harley told me when he was a little boy, his dad thought Christmas was just another day. Like all of us at the Usta Place, they didn't get to go anywhere and had to work very hard. He said when Christmas came, they went to church just to get a bag of candy. I believe I mentioned before that his mother died when he was only three months old. It is so very sad he missed out on having a mama to show him the way and have proper teaching like mamas do.

Some time ago, while taking my daily walk, I found five strawberry plants. These weren't wild plants. They had come up from a patch where our friend had lived a few years ago. I gave my friend two of them and brought the other three with me to set them out at my home. I've never planted strawberries before, but these took off like wild fire. If I had tried them before, I could have had a big patch by now.

The day Harley and I were married in 1970, Oscar and my sister, Wilma, came to the reception. I looked up and there came Oscar carrying four of the quart boxes of ripe strawberries. I want to tell you about Oscar, this beautiful man who married my sister.

Oscar loved to play pitch with anyone interested. Where there were four people and a deck of cards, he was ready to play. Before the day or night was over, there would be a game going if he had his way. He would be right there, ready to shuffle. Wilma loved to do arts and crafts exhibits, and Oscar would take produce from his garden and sell it to the public at the summer shows. One year he took grapes to a show. I saw half a bushel sitting there, and I told him I wanted the whole basket. He wanted to give them to me, but I wouldn't let him just give them to me. I paid him for them. Oscar really loved his vineyard and the soil. He is the only man I ever knew who could sit on the riverbank and fish all day. He might catch a fish or two, but maybe not. He didn't care. He had more patience than I ever thought of having.

When this dear man was seventy-five years old, the family had a big celebration for him in Garland, Kansas. I baked a cake for this occasion that stood about two feet tall. Do you want to know what Oscar said when he came in and saw that big bunch of baking talent? I'll tell you. He said, "Who got married?" I guess he thought only brides and grooms have tall, beautiful cakes. On the very top of this cake I put an angel playing a harp. Now Oscar is up there, maybe playing the harp with the angels. You can bet your bottom dollar he is.

Speaking of fishing, Harley had a nephew who loved the river. Gerald lived in Erie, Kansas, but during the summer months he stayed at his small cabin down by the river. We were out driving one time and stopped at his cabin for a chat. It just happened he was cooking a pot of beans. He asked us to stay and eat with him, and as I've mentioned before, I really like beans, so we stayed. (Remember my bean sandwiches?) You can't tell a Sexton no anyway.

We were poured a bowl of beans, and I had taken three or four bites when I found a bone. It was too small for a ham bone, too big for a fish bone. Nothing left to imagine with, so I decided it was a squirrel bone because of the shape.

I lost what appetite I had. Gerald had a heart problem, so there was no salt or seasoning in the beans. I told Gerald it was too soon after breakfast to be hungry. I lied, don't you know, but I was telling the truth somewhat. I told you I had lost my appetite.

Gerald took us out riding in his pick-up to show us around the dikes. There were times I thought we would drive on over the top. The engine died once and it was scary, but fun. I was glad to get home.

I had bought a hundred pounds of cracked pecans from one of Gerald's friends, and he brought them to us one day. Gerald had picked up a hitchhiker on the way here. They came inside and had coffee with us, but were on their way to the bus depot. Later Gerald told us the "thief" had borrowed forty dollars from him and was going to mail him the loan when he got home. I said, "I hope that kiss was a long one, because you will never hear from him again."

Gerald said he thought he would hear from the guy, but he never did get his forty dollars. Do you suppose this thief sleeps well at night?

About eighteen months later, Gerald was on his way to his cabin from Erie, had a heart attack while driving and ran into a freight train. He was killed at the scene. During the funeral service the minister paused in his prayer, and at that very moment a train whistled in the background. I believe it was the same track where Gerald died. They blew the whistle during this silence. It just happened at the right time. It made cold chills run all over me. I'm sure it affected a lot of people the same way.

I saw an ad in the paper once that went like this: "The only thing more powerful than a mother's touch is a mother's touch with Vicks Vapor Rub." All of the Clark Clan wouldn't argue that one.

I made scrapbooks for Gary and Sherri, starting them with the doctor's and hospital receipts from when they were born, a lock of their first haircuts, baby pictures and birth certificates. I put everything I could think of in them and gave the books to them as a Christmas gift. It was a joy for them and me, too. They are lucky kids to have a mom like me.

Let me say right here, I am also so fortunate to have my children. They have never given me any reason to worry. Not only that, but they are respectful, giving, thoughtful, loving and kind. The grandchildren are coming right along in their footsteps. Isn't that just absolutely fabulous?

I got a splinter in my forefinger once, and since I don't often do splinter-picking with my left hand, I needed help. I went to see Dr. Sisk. He numbed it and started in after the splinter. The blood started flowing. He said, "You don't have AIDS, do you? I snapped my finger and said, "Good grief, doctor. I forgot to tell you!" He wasn't expecting me to answer that way. He knew more about my blood than anyone. Our friend, Bob, stopped by and I was telling him about it. He told me I should have told the doctor, yes, Rolaids, Band-Aids, Kool-Aid. That would have been a good answer, too.

This is sort of changing the subject, but I felt like I'd like to jot this memory down for you. Going back a few years, two of Harley's sisters were in the hospital in Kansas City, and we spent quite a lot of time up there. St. Luke's Hospital is a huge place, but his sisters were in the same hospital on the same floor.

While sitting in one of the rooms, I glanced out into the hall and saw three ladies walk by. Well, no one walked like the one lady but my sister, Vena. I told Harley I just saw Vena walking down the hall. He told me it was probably someone who just looked like her. I'd know that walk anywhere, so I had to go check it out.

As it turned out, my brother-in-law was just five rooms down the hall. I hadn't heard he was ill, so naturally it was really a shock to see her walk by. Vena was getting ready to leave for a short time, but I told her I would keep an eye on Earl and see that he got fresh water and anything else he needed. Bless his heart, it was only a short time later that he passed away.

We have a large storage building close to our mailbox. We had to go down to the mailbox today, so Harley drove the truck, and just for the exercise I walked. When we finished, I started back to the house, walking again. Harley slowed down as he drove by and said, "Hello, pretty woman. Would you like a lift?" I asked him if he just drives around trying to pick up pretty women. He told me he did, but none of them would get in. I told him we all know a bargain when we see one. Do you suppose that's why the passenger seat was empty? I may never get asked again, at least not by this one anyway.

When I was at our supermarket, I had my groceries loaded, but walked down the aisle of candy. I picked up a box and could almost taste the maple middles. I was sort of talking out loud to myself, saying, "Helen, put those down. You don't need them because they will only make you fatter." I guess I thought I was the only one in this supermarket. Some male creep following in line behind me said, "It's easier to put on than to take off." I bit my tongue to keep from telling him to put a sock in it! You see, he looked like he hadn't had the willpower to put back the boxes he had picked up several times.

I actually don't believe the person who made up the "it takes all kinds" saying, really realized how much truth there is in it. I know you won't believe me, but I didn't even answer the creep. I figured he had said plenty. I told Harley about what had happened. He said, "He is right, isn't he?" Now that remark certainly helped the situation along. You can bet your bottom dollar I was glad I put the box down, because I didn't need all that chocolate.

Since my only granddaughter, Kristi, is getting married soon, she is planning her wedding. I will fill you in on the details of the wedding a little later in my story. Now I think a lot of her fiancé and I really want her to be happy, but she is so young. However, she is two years older that Sherri, her mother, was when she and Russ were married. I was about Kristi's age when I took the steps to the altar, so I guess she is old enough.

I can remember when she was about three and she would come to granny's house to visit. Kristi loved Grandpa Harley, and when she would see him take a pinch of chewing tobacco she thought it was really cool. He gave Kristi his empty can, and she took her little finger and would go around the bottom of the can pretending she was going to chew. She told me sometime later that one time he gave her a can that still had a little bit of tobacco in it, and she managed to get a pretty good-size pinch and put it in her mouth. She admitted swallowing it, and I guess that was enough. Kristi said it really made her sick. (It's enough to make anyone sick. We won't have to worry about her getting the habit.)

One time when I was visiting Sherri at her home in El Dorado, she and Kristi had to run to the store for something. When they returned, Sherri noticed her car was getting a flat tire. It was pretty low, but not clear down. Russ was away and she wasn't sure what to do. Kristi suggested she go get her Elmer's glue to fix the tire. It was so cute. She, as a little girl, thought you could fix anything with Elmer's glue or silver duct tape.

Our doctor's nurse, Mandy, thought so much of us that she wanted to name her baby after Harley. Well, she had a girl and sort of named her after him, but it's Haley instead of Harley. I call from time to time to see how Haley is doing. The last time I called, Haley was really crying hard. Mandy said they couldn't get her to quit, so I asked if I could talk to her. Haley got on the phone, and I asked her what she was doing. She quieted down and I asked her again what she was doing. The crying quit and she said, "I'm crying!" It was so cute.

Haley's mom and dad bring her to our house for trick-or-treating. Last year she was dressed like a bee. When I asked her if she was a bee, she said, "I'm a honey bee!" She got her basket and started counting the candy bars, suckers and gum. She said, "One for you. One for me. One for you. One for me." She is so pretty and lovable, as are her mommy and daddy.

Harley and I went to a garage sale some time ago and when we first stepped out of the car two little guys asked if we wanted to buy some pop. Now they didn't have the kind we like, but I bought some anyway. The young man who was having the sale was really a nice person. We talked to him quite awhile, since we were the only ones there right then. I asked him if the boys were his. He told me one was his and that he had lost another son to cancer, who would have been sixteen now. He told us that he takes time to do a lot of activities with the children, such as fishing and baseball and that several of the little neighborhood children like to come play with his children because he spends so much time with them. These children are lacking parents who spend time with them. I told Robert that I was writing a story of my life and that I had mentioned in my story about it not taking much to make a child happy, just a little of time from the parents.

Children miss a lot these days with both parents working. In some cases, I suppose it's necessary, but children need a lot of love and someone to hear their problems. They also need a lot of supervision and understanding. I know that even if both parents are working outside the home, they can still find time to spend with their children. I know this because I worked and still spent time with my children. My daughter worked while Rusty and Kristi were in school, but found time to go to baseball games, swim meets and school programs. It's all in where your priorities are.

Back in the olden days, we didn't have any extra time to get into things. There weren't as many temptations as there are now. When I saw those little guys selling pop, it reminded me of Gary and Sherri selling tomatoes. I think children need to learn at an early age the value of that bottom dollar. I also believe that before they get married, they should be out on their own for awhile to find out what it's like to have expenses such as paying rent and utilities, buying food and clothes, and taking care of all the other responsibilities that come along. I bet they wouldn't be so anxious to have these little babies if they knew what it was like to have to make formula, change diapers, bathe and take care of that wee one all day and sometimes through the night.

My son, Gary, called one afternoon and wanted Harley and me to meet them at our favorite chicken restaurant for dinner, which suited me dandy. I was looking for an excuse not to cook. Grandson Marc was celebrating his twentieth birthday. I had talked to Sherri and told her that Gary mentioned going to eat chicken. She said, "I'm not hungry, but I wish I were going with you." Russ had cooked ribs on the grill and they had just eaten barbecued ribs. I could almost taste them. I could understand why she wasn't hungry! I would rather have had ribs, too. They tell me I can cook chicken, but ribs aren't a specialty of mine.

Do you remember me telling you about Uncle Jimmy buying me

a chocolate bunny? I heard him say years ago, "You don't need a knife to cut up the pork in pork and beans." When I used to stay all night with Norma, his daughter, I can remember standing in their living room and listening to him play on the family pump organ and singing *"Flow Gently Sweet Afton,"* just like it was yesterday. He was sitting at that old organ, pumping with both feet and was so relaxed singing his song. I'll never forget.

Rusty, my oldest grandson, grew up to be a respectful, handsome young man and husband. His grandpa Hubert used to take him fishing a lot, and he still enjoys fishing and hunting. Rusty didn't ask me if he could get married, but then I'm glad he did. The precious young lady he married is Stacy and she is a darlin'. He could have done no better.

I must tell you about a puppy we gave Rusty when he was about two years old. One of our neighbors had some they wanted to get rid of, and being a loving Granny, I took one for Rusty. Everything was all right at first, but it seemed like the puppy grew faster and stronger than he did. He was too rough and would push Rusty down. Rusty didn't seem too sad to see the dog leave.

Some time ago my phone rang, and the woman's voice asked for Helen. I told the lady that I was she. She said my name had been drawn for a prize at Wal-Mart Supercenter. I told her to double-check the name, because I never win anything and there surely was a mistake. So double-checking she asked for my address, etc. It was me, and want to know how I won the prize? I'll just tell you. When you push a grocery cart into the store, you could sign your name and telephone number. Every time you went into the store, if you take a cart in from the parking lot, you get to put your name in a drawing. You get to put your name in one time for each cart you bring in, so I would sometimes push two or three and pull one. I couldn't lose, but worked hard! I won a Mr. Coffee Pot. I was tickled pinkish, for I had finally won something.

I took off eighty pounds of cans not long ago. You remember, I mentioned before, I have been picking up empty cans, and the cash from them goes into my car fund. I think it's going to take a lot more cans than I thought. Have you priced cars lately? I don't need a new one, but I do need a newer model than the1975 Scamp that I drive now.

Harley, my husband of twenty-seven years now, has always thought garage sales were a waste of time and money. I suppose it is unless you like to go to them or are looking for something. Guess what? He has gotten hooked on this garage sale kick and can hardly wait to get dressed and get there. He had to go to three or four, and now it is his thing. He had to learn, don't you know?

He loves tools of all kinds, new and antique, the kind he and I can identify with. We love to look through junk and just getting to go. About three weeks ago I saw a sale advertised in our newspaper that had tools! He couldn't wait to get started. When we got there, I noticed he was still wearing his house slippers.

My daughter, Sherri Ann, and I were talking about her Grandpa Ed Clark. She said about all she remembered about him is whenever she would see him he would say, "Hi ya', Bub." She remembers him being tall and he would have to duck down to walk through a door. She was only about four and a half years old when he was killed, so it's not surprising she can't remember a lot about him.

I can remember our Mama making lots of jelly and, of course, teaching us kids how to make it. She never used pectin and tested its doneness by cooking so long and letting it slide off the stirring ladle. She never had a failure, and the jelly was devoured in any condition. When the jelly sort of clung to the ladle and slid off in chunks, it was immediately poured into the jars and when cooled just a tad of melted paraffin wax was poured over the top of the jar to seal it. All of us enjoyed it later.

I recently made blackberry jelly with blackberries that came from Missouri, the "show me state." I can't very well show you, but it certainly was good. Mama teaching me to make jelly has come in handy at jelly-making time.

I mentioned several pages back about wanting a fur coat. (It was when I asked Papa what he thought about me buying one.) When Harley's grandson, Casey Lee, was about four years old, we were going to Joplin to shop one day, and he was sitting between us in the front seat. He thought he was pretty big getting to sit in the front seat. He said, "Grandma, when I get big and get a job, I'm going to buy you a fur coat." I've wondered several times where that came from. He is twenty-four now, and I haven't heard about a fur coat since! Could it be he found another lady's back to hang that fur coat on?

Harley has to be on oxygen part of the time, and every time he turns it on it reminds me of when Mama was visiting Gayle up in Gladstone, Missouri, and suffered a heart seizure. She and Gayle were picking tomatoes in Gayle's vegetable garden when she became ill. Gayle called an ambulance and Mama was admitted to the hospital.

When I heard about it, I closed my beauty salon and went to be with her. When I walked into her hospital room, she said, "Now that you are here, I don't need this." We called the nurse and Mama could breathe all right. You see, I think she was afraid.

I'm changing the subject completely, but I was just thinking that you don't need a long-handled shovel to dig far enough to see a little good in everyone. Now you may not agree or like their ideas or behavior, but be patient; just maybe you will be a better person by listening. You just might learn something by keeping your mouth closed tight and listen.

Mama always made lye soap for laundry and dishes, too, I suppose. Now I want to tell you right here, stirring that iron kettle over an open fire was not a cool job. It definitely was hard work, but all of us had to stir and stir and stir. I can't remember just how they knew when it was ready to set up. It may have been the texture or color. All I remember is that I was glad when it was finished. Mama would take a sharp knife, cut it into bars and store it for later use.

When Dana died in 1995, the family had to find a new home for her cockatiel, Johnny Cake. Now this little darlin' was really a lot of company for Dana. She loved birds and used to raise parakeets, canaries, and cockatiels. Johnny Cake would talk to Dana, but when we would go there, Johnny would clam up and not say a word. I told Dana she could tape Johnny talking to her and play it for him to help keep him company. I guess he talked constantly when it was just Dana with him.

When our precious sister died, Johnny just quit talking, and you could tell he was sad, too. He knew something was wrong and missed her voice. Well, Dana's granddaughter, Maranda, has a bird, so she took Johnny home with her to Aurora, Missouri. He still wouldn't talk. He still missed Dana's voice. Maranda has cats inside her house and plays with them. When it comes time to eat, Maranda yells, "Here, kitty, kitty, kitty, kitty." Johnny Cake has picked up this "kitty call," and it's all he will say. Wouldn't that be precious to hear a bird call to a cat? I have a strange feeling this precious bird would be sorry, don't you know?

When the children had an auction after Dana died, I got three or four bars of soap Dana had made. Let me tell you right here, that lye soap not only cleans, but it's good for a lot of things. I love to smell it.

I want to jot down this little part of my story while it is still in my thoughts, about something that happened at Dana's auction. Dana and I talked often about patterns, proper English and a million other things in general. She had mentioned to me she had a horse quilt block pattern. Every time we talked, she would tell me to come over and we would eat some fried ice cream, then copy a set of patterns off the horses for me. This way, if one set gets lost, there would be still be another set. As it turned out, Dana passed away before this project could be finished. After telling Patty, Dana's daughter, about wanting the pattern, you couldn't guess the number of patterns we looked through trying to find it.

Dana's children decided to have an auction. The day of the auction, through box after box, I kept looking for the pattern. The auction was about halfway through, and I just happened to be walking past a trailer that was piled high with Dana's treasures. All at once, I noticed a cleared area on the trailer, about eighteen inches across. The place was clear of everything except one envelope.

Out of curiosity, I picked it up. On the outside of the envelope, Dana had written "Horse Pattern for Quilt Top." I wish someone could or would explain this one. This one pattern, out of two or three thousand patterns, was lying there in this cleared place on the trailer! I teased the nieces about laying it right there where I would be sure to find it, but they knew nothing about it. This is unreal! Do any of you reading my story believe that a certain person, who knew exactly where this pattern was, could have put it right there in sight so the ninth of the twelve Clark siblings would be sure to get it? I do. I have the blocks all embroidered, ready to set together when I find the right material. The material has to be just the right fabric, don't you know? Dana would be so pleased.

Of course, you all remember me telling you about Papa and Mama teaching us at an early age to share. Well, we all still share, and you can bet your "bucks" we have all learned life is much sweeter when you give and not always be a taker.

Dana, my oldest sister, was truly a giver. Several years ago, she somehow met a lady who was homeless, living wherever she was allowed to park her cart and belongings. This woman was drawing a social security check, amount being not too shabby, but she lived on the outside by choice. I'm not sure how they met, but they developed a friendship that lasted a long time. Sometimes this lady would ask Dana to cash her check and pick up a few items at the store.

I can imagine Dana saw this woman parked somewhere and, being Dana, she was anxious to help her somehow. This lady (certain ones called her the bag lady) had a small one burner kerosene stove that she cooked with and kept warm with when chilly weather hit. She seemed contented and happy living outdoors. I met her one time and visited with her for awhile. She talked intelligently and was very attractive. Although she didn't have jewelry, fur coats or lots of material belongings, she was happy in her own little world. In the extreme cold, I suppose she found better shelter. The last I heard of her, she was living in a car and the city was trying to move her on away from where she was parked. You can bet your bottom dollar Dana enjoyed every minute she helped this dear lady. Dana would sometimes have a casserole for her, a loaf of homemade bread or fresh water.

We were talking of the olden days and making things. I told Harley we used to have a piece of pasteboard to use as a fan and that sometimes we would go to sleep fanning. I asked him if he remembered the little pasteboard fans with wooden handles that were used in church and funerals. Would you believe I still have one of them?

As a little child growing up, I had such an inferiority complex. As I wrote earlier, I don't remember Papa and Mama ever telling me I was pretty or giving us little ones a hug now and then. I didn't feel loved or wanted, but I was. I look back now and in my childhood pictures, I looked unhappy, never smiling. When something would happen, such as something getting broken or lost, I would feel guilty. If anything disappeared or messed up, I felt guilty, even if I hadn't been close to the scene of the incident. I didn't smile much because I thought I had an ugly mouth and teeth. I wonder if any of my siblings felt the same way I did as a child. I won't ask.

That all changed one day, long after I grew up. A person (I can't mention who this person was) at work one day did it for me. One day I smiled before I realized it. He said, "Has anyone ever told you that you have pretty eyes and a beautiful smile?" Would you believe I was completely speechless? I thought to myself, "Well, blow me down!" Why had that taken so long to happen? Just think of all the precious time wasted. What this all boils down to is I did a lot of worrying for nothing. Surely I could have used all that precious time to a happier advantage.

I realize since I grew up, I not only was a cute little girl and a pretty young woman, I have many other characteristics that just won't stop. I can sew, cook, cut and set hair, play the piano and organ, garden, home can vegetables and fruits, make jelly. On top of all of that, I'm a good mother, grandmother, neighbor, sister and aunt. I almost forgot, I'm a good wife, too. My only hang-up is that I may brag and talk a little too much. I'm a good listener to go along with the talking. Papa and Mama always let us talk. We thought we were supposed to.

Parents, hug you child, talk to them, make some time for them. At the same time, teach them the difference between yes and no, from the time they are old enough to understand. You will have no regrets and neither will they. Experience is the best teacher. Someone told me this one time, but by the time I had heard it, I had decided it all by myself. Believe me, it's true.

I was sitting here writing, with all the doors and windows open and everything was exceptionally quiet, except for the birds and maybe a passing car. I was sipping my coffee, you know, the beverage you shouldn't drink because it isn't good for you! I counted about five different birds singing at the same time and a cool breeze was blowing through the windows. When we have our hearing and sight, are able to walk and breathe, we have so very much going for us. That makes us all so very rich. I said, "Thank you, God, for this precious moment!"

Sure, we have a lot of illness and deaths that affect our lives, but He will help us get through this, too. God doesn't lay any more on our shoulders than we can carry, and then He helps us carry it, don't you know?

Out of all of the eleven children of the Clark clan who married, we had only one sister, Dana, whose children could each say they had a sister and brother. Some of the sisters had one boy and girls, some had one of each, some had two boys and one girl. Confusing, isn't it? It isn't to all of us.

My granddaughter is planning her wedding for this summer. We will be seated in the second row from the front. This is a formal affair and, boy, oh boy, do I dread dressing up in those heels! Maybe since I am just the granny, I could get by with wearing flats and a nice pantsuit. We'll see.

Sherri said, "Since I'm the mother-of-the-bride." She stopped and said, "Mom, do you realize this is the only time in my life I'll be able to say I'm the mother-of-the-bride?" She finished and said she had to be dressed formally, but it didn't matter what I wore. I'll have more about this precious event a little later in my story.

One day when I got up, I was feeling a little down. When I went to the kitchen to start breakfast, I opened the carton of eggs, glanced in the top of the carton and read, "This is the day which the Lord has made; let us rejoice and be glad in it." (Psalms 118:24) I said to myself, "Why not!"

While downtown later that day, a pretty young lady beamed with a big smile. "Hi, Helen!" she said. She then hugged me and said, "I'm Susan." She was the same girl who got the much-needed pixie hair cut by me back in the sixties, when she was three years old. I asked her if she remembered the cut and she did. You could hardly forget something like that, even though hers was a one-time thing. (My haircuts lasted until I was twelve years old. I'm referring to Mama's famous bowl cut.)

I asked Susan about her parents and told her I was surprised they didn't sue me after giving her the hair cut. She got a free cut though, and it really was cute. I also asked her if her dad, Leon, ever told them about the mixed-up sandwiches. I told her about the mix-up in the lunch sacks and that I had gotten his bologna sandwich. She said they used to eat a lot of that stuff and that her mom used to fry it for sandwiches. I guess if you are hungry, it's mighty tasty. You can bet your bottom dollar I had to be hungry there at work that day to eat his bologna.

I went shoe shopping recently, and the sales clerk asked my size. It brought back a memory of years ago. We didn't get to go to town to try on a pair of shoes. If we were lucky enough to get new ones, Mama would take a piece of cardboard, trace around our little feet for an outline to get the correct size and mail it into Chicago Mail Order. They would sometimes take the outline into Ashbaugh's in Moundville and they would match the size.

Times have certainly changed. I imagine shoes back then cost two dollars a pair, and they would search for a pair that would last for awhile. These days you have a truckload to choose from, and if you can't make up your mind, you buy more than one pair. I love high heels, but I don't wear them anymore. I have a hard time standing straight in flats. At one time, I never left the house without my spike heels. I dressed up in my heels just to go grocery shopping.

Way back in the olden days, giving a child an allowance at the Usta Place was unheard of. We did our chores and got paid with clothes to wear, food to eat and the other items we needed that our

Papa and Mama could afford.

When my precious children were little, the pattern was set to fit them. If they needed something, they usually had it. They liked to jump on the bus and go to S.H. Kress & Co. to shop. It was much cheaper then.

I want to share a few memories with you that did not happen so long ago, but are still precious to me. You see, I make memories every day, and since I have lived at this same address in Pittsburg, Kansas, since 1968, I have lots of memories here, too. As you read in my story earlier, I shared some stories with you that were not such good ones at this address. (Remember the flood?) Now I want to get to the good memories I have of living here and share with you a little about my life as I live it now. I don't want to leave anything out.

One day a man, probably in his late twenties, and his two young sons moved in across the street. Days went by and I never saw a woman or mother around, so I figured she might have died. Here comes Helen again with some of her homemade cookies. All little boys and girls need a papa and mama and cookies, don't you know? I took them cookies and other goodies from time to time.

Some time later, I stopped at a cafe to have a cup of coffee and ran into this father and his sons, having the special of the day, spaghetti red. I told the father that I hoped he didn't mind me baking for the little guys. He said, "I'm glad someone cares about them." He told me their mom had left the family some time back.

The following Christmas, Dad took the little guys shopping. Little Clint bought me a green candy dish made like a chicken on a nest. They moved away, but about five years later I ran into them downtown. Clint said, "Do you still have my chicken?" Cool! He remembered me and the little gift. By the way, I still have his chicken.

While enjoying a cup of coffee this morning, I heard footstep behind me. I turned and saw Harley standing there buttoning his shirt. He was looking at our wedding picture of twenty-seven and a half years. He turned to me and said, "We sure have changed, haven't we?" I said, "No, I don't think so, not inside anyway." He answered, "Heck, no! That part is getting better every day."

I think he has an eye open for Santa, trying to be good, don't you know? Anyway, it made me feel very good and made my day. Now that I got that little "jump start" on the day, I made biscuits, gravy and sausage for our breakfast. They say we shouldn't eat all this good food. Who knows for sure, and at the age of seventy-two, who cares?

While enjoying our breakfast, I was telling Harley about the little one passenger air ship Clyde O'Bannon had shared with the neighbor kids at the Usta Place. He said when he was a young man he had a good friend who had an air ship similar to Clyde's. One day just the two of them went up. There were gas fumes everywhere. Harley said they got up as high as they were going, and this "friend" struck a match to light a cigarette. If they had run out of fuel, Harley said he wouldn't have been any more scared. I guess he turned down all rides with this guy after that little jaunt.

One time I accidentally put my slacks on backwards when I was getting ready to go to the store. I was telling my dear sister number five, Pansy, about the hasty mistake I made. She came up with one even better. She reminded me of the time she had dressed in a hurry and probably, because we lived two miles from school and it was so early, had dressed in the dark. After she got to school, her teacher told her she had her dress on wrong side out. If she had needed her pockets that day, she would have eventually realized it. She went outside to the outdoor throne and changed. You can bet your bottom dollar she was uncomfortable until she got it turned out right. She is always neat as a pin, don't you know?

When I first get up in the morning, before I start breakfast or do anything else, I like to start the coffee. While the coffee is dripping, I dress and put on my face. The coffee is usually finished dripping before I get my face done. By this time I've gotten the morning paper. I'm then ready to sit down and enjoy my cup or two of decaffeinated coffee and read all the news. I've probably heard all of it the day before, but it's my time of the day to just sit back and enjoy. I like to start on the back page of the first section, which includes the obituaries. If I don't see my name, I take another "sip" and turn the page.

I recently turned to the memorial column and read a "loving memory," written by the mother of a daughter. The last couple of lines read: "God broke our hearts to prove to us He only takes the best." I suppose there isn't a doubt He takes the best, but it made me stop and wonder if we neglect to see the best in the bad. We must remember He takes us when He is ready. We sometimes wonder why our loved ones are taken from us. We can assume it's to end the pain and suffering and shouldn't question it.

I must tell you a story that adds a bundle of spice to my precious memories. Of course, I wasn't here yet, but sister number five, Pansy, and I were reminiscing about Christmas at the Usta Place and how hard it was when Papa and Mama were trying to "do" Christmas gifts for all of us kids during their young years.

Mama dressed Pansy and Ruby alike, and all the personal items they owned were identical. They had talked about what Santa might bring, but didn't think they would get much in their stocking, except maybe a piece of peppermint stick. Mama (Santa) would take a long red-and-white-striped peppermint stick and divide it in enough small pieces so there would be a piece in each stocking. In the olden days, you could buy a long stick for five cents.

This particular Christmas many years ago, the girls awoke and were expecting only candy, since there were so many socks to fill. They were still excited that morning. They ran to the big box where the socks were hung. There wasn't room around the chimney. All at once, each noticed Santa had slipped a little gold ring on their pinky finger. I guess they were two very happy little Clark kids.

I recently noticed in the morning paper our President had pardoned the sixty-pound turkey that was to be served in the middle of the big dining room table at the White House. As this lucky bird will be returned to Virginia from Washington, Mr. President said, "There will be one less turkey in Washington." Now I suppose there will be a replacement of this sixty-pound feathered friend that went back to Virginia. What do you think his name will be? (Charlie, Sam, or maybe "Bill.")

Although former President Truman got the pardoning of these precious white birds started in 1947, from the article I read the first instance of a reprieved turkey happened when former President Lincoln spared the life of a turkey named Jack, eighty- three years earlier.

While I was preparing to make a pie today, it brought back memories of the Usta Place and all of the olden days when it came time to bake. We never heard of a boxed cake mix or frosting. We had to bake those little jewels in a wood-burning oven, without a thermometer. Mama would say, "Walk easy. There is a cake in the oven!" (She also made good gingerbread.)

Now this won't cost you a cent, but I want to throw in a big piece of news for all of you gentlemen learning to bake a nice cake for "her." Before preparing the batter, generously grease and flour the baking pan. Then take a strip of terry cloth or flannel material, about four inches wide and long enough to reach around the pan. Wet the material, fold it in half lengthwise, and stretch it around the outside of the pan. Pin the ends together securely. Bake as usual and about 100% of the time, you will have a nice level cake to show off to the better half and the neighbors. Enjoy!

While cleaning kitchen cabinets, I found a stack of letters and with them was a little note that had been handed, not mailed, to me by a little friend, probably fifteen years ago. Keep in mind, I bake lots of cookies and make candy, so it isn't a big job to make friends with big people and especially the little ones, if their moms don't care. I love to give. This little guy was about five years old. He would come over about every day to talk to Harley and me. He loved to visit, and I always had snacks of some kind. Perhaps that is what drew his attention.

His father got a job far away in another state, so naturally they moved away. This little guy hated to leave so much, he made me a valentine letter. It was so precious. It said, "I love you very much, Helen Sexton. Love, Craig Mitchell Carter." Then he added a picture that he had drawn by himself.

I try to get some exercise every day walking to pick up our mail. It's two blocks one way, I suppose. Once in awhile, I'll have a letter that is marked "postage due." Tom, our postman, leaves it in my box anyway, and then I leave the money in the mailbox for him in an envelope. What other carrier would be so kind?

Do you remember me telling you about the fur coat Hubert wanted to buy for me in Idaho Falls? Papa told me "that would be uphill business." Well, he got to own one once. It was made from a big black bear hide. Papa looked just dandy strutting around. He wore it when he was going to "dress up" to go somewhere. Matter of fact, he looked like a two-legged papa bear. It would have been really cool for Mama to have one and one for one of the little Clarks. They would have looked like the three bears. I don't know where Papa got this coat or what ever happened to it. I do know he never went bear hunting. Maybe he had a good friend who went hunting and got it for him.

Speaking of the three little bears, this reminds me that I didn't get to hear bedtime stories. You would have thought with all those children running around, there would have been someone to read to the little ones, but there was no one free to read to us. We didn't have storybooks at home to read, but we did get to hear them at school.

If it seems like I spend a lot of time in the supermarket, I do.

Every time I go, I see people, young and old, having a hard time making the dollar go further. As a matter of fact, once in awhile I have the same problem of making it go further than the necessities myself. I notice it more with the elderly who are on fixed incomes and too proud to ask for help, like Mama and Papa were. When I see people like this, it makes me want to help them, and then I ask myself, "With what?" My help certainly wouldn't overload a cart.

I'll watch older ladies pick up something and put it back. I suppose she's thinking she can get along without it. It makes me feel so sad when I see they don't have what they need. Yes, it reminds me of the old days, the Usta Place and two or three homes after that, don't you know?

Just recently I was at the supermarket and noticed a handsome young couple, poorly dressed and, as I, were trying to find something for the cart. They would pick up a package of meat and put it down, again and again. Would I have been out of line to offer to buy something to eat with the three loaves of bread they left with? If it happens again, you can bet your bottom dollar, I'm going to buy them a package of meat or cheese. Maybe they had bad luck or maybe illness. Who knows? I sure could have slept better that night if I had done something to help. I felt guilty eating dinner that evening.

Sherri says she and Russ go through the same thing when they are shopping. They almost bought a roast for an elderly man and his wife, after watching them shop around trying to find something they could afford, finally buying nothing. She said if they could have done it anonymously, they would have purchased something for them. That's my little daughter. She grew up too soon.

Gary said awhile back, "Mom" (that's what he calls me), "it just scares the hell out of me to see you and dad getting older and the kid's birthdays coming twice a year." It makes me realize that I'm coming right along there with those birthdays, too. I just don't know where the years have gone. He is a forty-niner now, going on thirty-five.

As usual, before going to bed, I check to the make sure the doors are locked for the night. I was just looking outside into the darkness to see if there were any raindrops or snowflakes falling, not that I could do anything about it if there was.

When I looked out, I saw a yearling deer standing about six yards from my front door. I keep my birdbath full of fresh water, so I suppose he was there for a nightcap. I'm sure the acorns on the ground provided a delicious bedtime snack. Anyway, he watched me a little while and then off into the darkness he ran. There is no doubt he would be back, because there is plenty of water and gobs of acorns. My "deer" came back the next night. He must have been taught to share, too, because he brought two more yearlings and a fawn to feast on the acorn buffet.

Well, you could bet you last "bucks" (no pun intended), they are safe for a little while. The hunting season opens soon. Gary, Russ and all three of my grandsons hunt and usually get their deer. They hunt wild turkey, too.

I know I mentioned before that Harley is on oxygen. He has the concentrator, which makes oxygen. This machine has to be serviced on a monthly basis, so a service man comes to our house to check it. This man was telling Harley and me that he and his wife had taken six foster children into their home. I'm not sure how long they have had these little boys, but they are all teenagers now.

He told me these children have missed out on so many childhood experiences living in the orphanage, and most of them not ever having a father image. These young men are like you and me, but they are growing up without a papa and mama. Their dad died and their mom didn't care about them. In some cases, the mother just walked out and left them alone in the house. I haven't met any of these six boys, but you can bet your bottom dollar they are precious little darlings in God's eyes. He loves each and every one of them.

I know it must be hard for this man to buy food for them, even though foster parents get some financial help. I can remember when my son was a teenager, we would get up from the table and Gary would ask, "When do we eat?" I would tell him at mealtime, but both Gary and Sherri were allowed to eat between meals if they were hungry.

I gave our service technician some mini-fruitcakes for the boys. He told me the boys had never had homemade snacks like fruitcake and maybe not even a store-bought one. They have missed out on a lot, but I believe that now they are in a good home.

Now, this is the story stopper. He told us the oldest of the six boys wanted to stay up all night before Thanksgiving, just so he could watch the turkey cooking. None of these foster children have had all of the fun times like all eleven of us little Clark kids. I don't suppose anyone has. It tears me inside out to see children thrown away. That's what it all boils down to — the hard-ball stage, don't you know?

I had to run to the supermarket recently for a few items, and as I was going in I met a lady and her son coming out. I had met this nice lady at a sale one time. She smiled and said, "This is my car." She had a two-wheeled shopping cart chained to a bicycle, plus a wire basket mounted to the back of the bike. It looked like she had money for food, but it sure was a sad way to take it home. I assume this was her only means of transportation.

Some families have three and four cars. Papa had one, but that was enough for us. There wasn't anywhere to go, except to the mailbox every day. As I've told you before, we walked the two-mile distance.

As I was putting dinner on the table one evening, it reminded me of when Sherri learned to cook a long time ago. She learned to and loved to cook at an earlier age than most girls. She could fix a complete meal at the age of nine. Now, she didn't just cook the meal, she cleaned up the kitchen, too.

She came up with the idea to keep hot dishwater in the sink. As she was preparing her meal, she washed the dishes and utensils as she used them. Then as she dished the food up, she would also wash those cooking utensils as she emptied them. She had the pots and pans done when the meal was finished, and it saved so much time when she did the rest after supper. The counter top would be clean to stack the supper dishes. Oh, my goodness! It was such a good idea and saves so much time and work later. I started doing mine that way also and clean-up in the kitchen can be done in nothing flat.

I really like being punctual. I think I've always tried to be on time anywhere I go. I would rather be twenty minutes early than five minutes late. Tardiness is absolutely not my cup of tea. I had to pick up medication recently at the pharmacy. I always push a cart in from the parking lot, not only to have one once I get inside, but it keeps the lot clean of carts bumping into cars. I was hurrying to get inside to get the medicine, and I noticed a gentleman merging on my left. We almost sideswiped. He let me have the road. I suppose I might have tried to bluff him out, but I told him I was in a hurry. He gave me a great big smile and said, "I can tell!"

I mentioned at the beginning of my story that my great-grandfather founded a little town in northeast Missouri and named it Cainsville. I picked up the newspaper recently and turned to the obituaries. I still don't know why I did it, but I noticed the gentleman's name. It didn't ring a bell to me, but something told me to read on.

This deceased man, who was born in Cainsville, Missouri, on February 27, 1913, had a daughter living here in Pittsburg. I wanted so badly to call her right then, but I waited a few days. At first she thought it was a nasty hoax or trick someone was playing on her.

I gave her my name and telephone number and told her several facts that could verify I was legitimate. We talked for a long while, and it wouldn't surprise me if we get together some time for coffee or lunch. Rita, who has a beautiful name, sounds like a very sweet person.

One day I was looking in my refrigerator at 11:10, getting ready to fix lunch. I noticed the jars in the refrigerator were rattling, so I stood up and watched them for just a few seconds. I had never seen or felt anything like it before, but wondered if it might have been tremors from an earthquake. I called the local police to see if they had calls from anyone else. He told me they had not had any calls nor a report of an earthquake. Well, that evening on the local news, the story was different. A police officer reported they had a few calls from local residents about feeling tremors, so they called the officials to see if there had been one in the vicinity. Sure enough, tremors showed up on the Richter scale at the same time I felt and saw the shaking in my refrigerator. That was the only time I have had an experience like that, and it was enough for me.

I cooked ham, beans and cornbread for dinner recently. Harley and I were watching television and talking during the commercials. Harley said, "I feel like my pants are too tight since I ate dinner. I think I will loosen my belt." I was also feeling a little full and said, "I think I'll unsnap my bra." If we could have had the right music playing, this could have been quite interesting, don't you know? I have this thing of overeating when I make beans and cornbread. You can bet your bottom dollar I didn't throw away the leftovers. They are just as good when warmed the second time.

While shopping recently, Harley and I ran into a friend and her son who moved from next door about five years ago. When they lived here and I would go visit them, their little son, Daniel, would jump up and down and scream with joy, reaching his little arms up for me to pick him up.

I invited them to come see me sometime, and if they would let me know ahead of time, I could make treats. Daniel said, "What kind of cookies will you have?" Next thing you know, this one will be making me valentines and letters, expressing his love for me. It must be something in the sugar that gets to the hearts of these little ones.

Harley's little name-sake, Haley Hope, just three years old, stopped in a few days before Christmas this year with her mom to bring gifts from them. When she opened the musical card Harley and I gave her, Haley said with her eyes open wide, "It sings!" She played with that card all evening.

It seems like some people really are into giving during the holiday season. Others go all out for the season, not the reason. I really praise all of the organizations that participate in projects during Thanksgiving and Christmas to help those who are less fortunate than ourselves. Why not keep the spirit of Christmas all year? Yes, why not?

I try to look and usually find some good in everyone. Once in a while it takes a magnifying glass, but I can usually find something. I believe a person should not look for the bad in people all the time, but try to always look for the good qualities.

I was in the supermarket again, getting baking supplies for Christmas, you see. A young mother, grandma, and a five-week-old baby girl stood in line. The baby, who was getting really fussy and crying, was dressed for outside with two blankets over her. I mentioned to them that she might be too warm. The grandma told me the baby was just spoiled, because every time she wants attention she cries to be picked up. Since the baby kept crying, I told them this little one needs to be picked up and let her burp because she sounded sick in her tummy. I suggested to the mother to pick her up, put her over her shoulder and give her a rest from the car seat. By this time, we were up next to the check-out. Mommy picked her up, and if you hadn't known better, you would have thought you heard a small thunder. The checker and everyone laughed, because I was right. You see, I have raised two children and helped with four grandchildren. I know a baby needing to be burped when I see and hear one. When you get to be big babies, you can take medicine to get relief, but that little baby needed help and attention. I gave her just that.

I stood in this shortest line for fifteen or twenty minutes, but after I got through the line and was loading my groceries into the trunk, I asked myself if I had remembered everything. I thought, oh, my goodness, I have forgotten the ham! I headed back in to get the ham and again looked for a short line. By this time, there was not a short line, but I fell in behind two boys and a girl who all appeared to be in their middle teens.

It was a joy to stand back and listen to them. The girl said she just came out of the store next door and she couldn't believe how rude she was treated. People were shoving and pushing to get in front of her in line. Then one of the boys said he hated Christmas because everyone is rude and out to rip you off. I wanted to tell him he probably disliked the season, not the reason.

I said to the group, "Oh, my goodness. I was ready to ask you nice children if you would mind me going in front of you, since I have only one item." (They had a full cart.) They looked at each other and agreed. The girl said, "Those people just ahead of us have two carts loaded. Why don't you ask if you can fall in ahead of them?" Before I could say anything, she asked them if I could go ahead of them since I just one item. They were happy to do it. I asked them if they would believe me if I told them I didn't like to leave my husband at home for very long, because he is on oxygen. They believed me.

I'll start my candies and fruitcakes in about two or three weeks. I have to start early, because I love to send "goodies" to relatives and friends. Don't you wish you were on my list? If all these people eat this stuff and don't refuse it next time, that's thanks enough for me to do it again next year. I enjoy so much making and taking these goodies.

I had to go to the doctor recently to get results of some X-rays taken. Since I don't always know what he is talking about when my doctor tells me, I told him Harley would want to know what my problem is. He told me to tell Harley that I didn't have any broken bones or pulled ligaments, but what I have is a frozen shoulder. I got a shot and some medicine. They call this horrible pain capsulitis. Now let me say right here, I know I've been accused of giving people a cold shoulder, but I never thought I'd ever have a frozen one. Anyone can have it if they just ask. I'll give willingly, since it's Christmas.

There was one last gift I had to get this evening, so I finished at the doctor's office and zoomed to the Supercenter to look. I had to stop by the company "throne" and figured I would have to wait in line there, too.

It reminded me of the little "three-seater" outdoor throne at the Usta Place. If you were first in line there, you were in luck. If not, you could pass it by a few yards and make your own little private throne. We did that once in awhile. It was sometimes quite a busy place.

I finished all of my candies and have them plated for delivery. I told Harley I wish everyone had a plate of it. I was pretty tired after I got the plates ready, so I sat down for a short rest. While resting, I got to thinking about the taffy that Mama let us make. I was too little to help with it, but I remember the older children pulled that taffy for what seemed like half a day. Maybe I got to be the boss that day. I'm still good at that!

I find each Christmas is rushed a little earlier. This year I saw decorated trees before Halloween. I also saw Christmas candy on the counters at the same time the trick-or-treat candy was on display. It seems like there are a few who want to cash in as soon as possible.

As it gets close to Christmas, once in a while we have a tendency to forget the reason for the season. As Christmas is becoming more and more commercialized, we really need to stop and give some thought to what we are doing and why we are doing it. The children are anxious to sit on Santa's lap and let him know all of the presents they want. I suppose they will get most of them. Back when I was a little girl, we didn't get to see Santa, since he didn't make personal appearances. We just waited anxiously. We took what he left for us and were thankful for it. Since we didn't ask for gifts, we weren't disappointed. Mrs. Santa worked so hard to see that all of the little stockings had something inside!

I never had the opportunity to sit on Santa's lap and give him my order, but then I probably wouldn't have done it anyway. I never liked sitting on anyone's lap. Since I was such a busy little girl making mud pies and robbing birds' nests, I didn't have time.

This is about seventy-three years later. When I see old Santa in the store talking to the little ones, I still do get the urge to run up and tell him what I'd like. But then, I have all I need anyway, don't you know?

As I am writing this, it is Christmas Eve and counting down. I was doing just fantastic with everything. All the pies and cookies were baked, the ham was baked, and all the dinner was ready except the rolls. I put them in to bake and checked them in about twenty minutes. They weren't brown, so I turned the oven up a bit. Well, it was then I found the baking coil had burned out. I got a little panicky, but remembered my little broiler oven. It might work. I heated it up and the first pan came out pretty well. The second pan was cremated, probably because I had never used this oven before. You can bet your bottom dollar I called a serviceman the next day to fix that oven. You know me, I can't be without my oven.

I was so pleased when Sherri managed to be off an extra day from work at Christmas. Mamas and daughters should be together as often as possible. Don't you think so? We thought there would be some after-Christmas sales lying there just waiting for her or me. We were sure there would be treasures we couldn't live without, so we fixed lunch for Harley (he doesn't shop well, so he stayed home), and we headed for the Supercenter for our big day out. We found some good bargains, but since shopping makes you hungry, had to stop shopping to get some chicken, fries and coffee. Believe it or not, this little snack gave us the boost we needed to hunt for more bargains.

We celebrated Christmas on Saturday, so all of Sherri's families could be here. We, of course, all went to Chicken Annie's instead of spending all of our time cooking and doing dishes. We sort of made it the maid's day off, don't you know? (I'm the only maid this house will ever see.) It suited me just fine when someone suggested breakfast out on Sunday morning also.

As I mentioned before, I really get depressed during the holidays. Even though I was feeling a tad low on Monday, I had to run to the pharmacy. If I'd had a set of broad shoulders standing by, I would have given them a workout. By the time I got home, I was teary eyed and really feeling down.

I had been home a little while and, lo and behold, the florist stopped in front of my house. I said to Harley, "They are coming here!" The lady came up the steps and I said, "I bet you are looking for me." Her reply was, "If you are Helen, I am." She delivered a beautiful arrangement of white, red and pink carnations. Carnations are my favorite.

Sherri seems to know when I need flowers the most. I called her and told her how pretty they were and asked her why she had sent them. She said, "I was just thinking about you." Isn't that just absolutely beautiful? Sherri is truly a loving, beautiful, caring, thoughtful daughter. I am so proud of her. She has a birthday right away. I'll get back at her and teach her a thing or two. I love you, Sherri Ann!

I have read a poem about someone wanting their flowers and a friendly smile while they are living instead of tears and flowers at their funeral or on their grave. I agree with the person who wrote that poem and feel the same way.

Trenton Rhodes
and
Marcus Rhodes

These photos of my four grandchildren were taken when they were just little. All four are grown now, but are still very precious to "granny."

Rusty Stenseng
and Kristi Stenseng

CHAPTER 20

WELL, IT FINALLY CAME TIME to get ready for the wedding of the year. Earlier in my story, I promised to tell you about my granddaughter's wedding. Gary asked if we could come to Ft. Scott and travel with Marcus and Trenton from there. This way, if one of us had trouble, there would be a set of wheels to go for help if necessary. The boys were waiting for us when we got there at 9 a.m.

I had planned on stopping at a restaurant and buying their breakfast. We pulled in and told them to order anything they wanted. They told me they had been eating chips and drinking pop since they left home and weren't hungry. Harley and I had a cup of coffee and pie and then continued our drive to El Dorado. When we arrived at the house, Sherri, mother of the bride, had left a note saying she was at the church decorating. We put some perishables in the refrigerator, checked into our motel, then headed for the church to help decorate. Since Marc and Trenton were going to be ushers, they went to the tux shop to get a final fitting of their tuxedos.

Sherri had most of the decorating finished, and the reception room was looking so pretty. Kristi had chosen purple, lavender and ivory for her colors, which really made for an elegant wedding.

We had an early dinner Friday evening and after the wedding rehearsal turned in early. We knew Saturday was going to be a big day, and we wanted to be rested and ready to help Sherri with last-minute plans that needed to be done.

There were plenty of last-minute things to be done on Saturday morning. There were balloons to blow up and some to fill, table-cloths to measure and cut, punch to be picked up and flowers to be set out. Sherri had us fill with helium the purple, cream and lavender balloons that had Ted and Kristi's name on them, with helium and tie a string with a small bell on the end of it. The bell was just enough weight to keep the balloons floating right at the floor. It made it look like they were coming up like a garden. They were so pretty and it went over big-time with the children. Howard and Winnie Rholl, Russ' sister and brother-in-law, helped with the balloons, and we all helped finish up the table decorations. Sherri had made all of the table decorations herself and even included purple and lavender candy in dishes on all of the tables for the guests.

I was so afraid to wear a pantsuit and flats because I would stand out like a sore thumb, but I don't think anyone noticed. Everyone had their eyes on the beautiful bride. Sherri and Kristi both had told me it didn't matter. I think they were right.

The wedding started. Of course, Kristi came down the aisle on the arm of her daddy, like Sherri did on her daddy's arm, and like I did on my Papa's arm. Just as Russ and Kristi got to where he was going to give her away, the room was really quiet. A recording of the song, *"Daddy's Little Girl,"* was played. After about four or five lines of that song were sung, I wasn't too sure that daddy was going to make it. Kristi had kept it a surprise for her daddy. He had no idea Kristi had planned on having that song played for him. She said she felt it just fit her and him. It was a touching song for this special occasion. I doubt there was a dry eye in the house. One aunt said she didn't cry. Maybe she wasn't listening to the words.

Anyway, they made it to the altar. The vows were exchanged, and it came time for the rings. Everything was going pretty well. It was time for the best man to hand the ring to Ted to put on Kristi's finger. Ted opened the box. There was no ring in it! You see, the best man played a trick on Ted and he had it in his pocket all the time. He finally handed it to Ted. The minister said, "Now that we have a gold ring, will you, Kristi, take thee, Ted," etc. I don't believe I've ever seen that done in a ceremony before and probably never will again.

We got them married and started through the receiving line. This is what Kristi said to me. She said, "Granny, do you remember when I stayed with you one time and you took me to the emergency room when I got sick? The doctor gave me a chalk board?" I remembered it all right. She was about three or four years old.

The groom's mother baked the cake. Some layers were chocolate and some were white. It had stairs, two flights to the top with a lavender waterfall. It was so beautiful. She had also made the decoration for the top of the cake, with the bride and groom dressed like Kristi and Ted, including the bouquet.

My eighty-four-year old sister, Wilma, was able to come to the wedding. Paul, her son, had driven her out to El Dorado so she could see her great-niece get married. We were all surprised and pleased she and Paul were able to make the trip.

We were all standing around visiting after the wedding. A young man, I think someone in the wedding party, came up and talked to Grandpa Harley for awhile. This young man looked down at Harley's new shoes and told him they were sure good-looking shoes he had on. He didn't mention Harley's tie, probably because he wasn't wearing one. You see, he also went to the wedding casually dressed.

Russ, the daddy of this little girl who had grown up too fast, was holding several silver heart-shaped, helium-filled balloons that were used in the wedding. After the mini-bags of birdseed were opened and thrown at Ted and Kristi, they started to pull away in their car, decorated with shaving cream, aluminum cans and bows. Russ released the balloons into a blue sky, creating such a beautiful scene. It sort of signified that his daughter was "flying away."

My daughter, Sherri, certainly knew how to get everything done and on time. As a matter of fact, I believe she could make it a profession. Just give her a pad, pencil, a pair of scissors, and let her get started. She was so organized for it to be the first wedding she had planned. Since Kristi is the only daughter, it is the only one she'll get to do.

After all the guests had left, some friends and family jumped in and helped get the gifts and everything else loaded up, so the reception hall and church could be cleaned for church the next day. So that the gifts would be there when they got back from their honeymoon, we delivered them to Kristi and Ted's house. It didn't take long with so many helping. Sherri had done so much to prepare such a beautiful wedding, it was a little sad that it was over so quickly.

By then, Harley and I were getting pretty tired so we decided to return to our motel room for a little rest before it was time for dinner. We made a wrong turn and got lost for a little while, but finally found our way back to the street where our motel was. Guess who we saw headed west out of town in a car covered with purple bows, shaving cream, a string of cans and a police car following them? I'm not sure how long the officer followed them, but they were still going west lickety-split the last we saw of them. Kristi turned around, saw us and waved. I bet they thought we were following them, too.

Later in the evening several of the family members got together for dinner at a restaurant in El Dorado. My son, Gary, and grandsons, Marcus and Trenton, had to leave after clean-up was done and head back to Ft. Scott, but the rest of us had a nice visit after dinner. It certainly was a busy weekend, and we were all ready for a good night's sleep.

Harley and I left the motel early Sunday morning and naturally stopped by Russ and Sherri's house to let her know we were heading home. I wanted to tell her again how pretty she was at the wedding and that it was the most beautiful wedding I had ever attended.

A few days after Kristi got married, Sherri and I were discussing the subject of cooking. Sherri told me Kristi wasn't too excited about cooking, but I think she will like it better as time goes by. Sherri told me Kristi had made Ted a casserole for dinner one evening and he told her it was "awesome." I guess that meant it was delicious. Kristi certainly had a good teacher. As I wrote before, Sherri could cook a nice meal when she was only ten years old.

How many of you women reading my story agree that husbands make better sweethearts that husbands? When you are courting, there are more flowers, candy, and dinners out than after you get married. You never see a two or three-dollar tip under the coffee cup after you tie the knot. Perhaps we should give this some thought.

I always thought you would see more robins in the spring. As I was sitting here writing this morning, I saw three of those little rascals taking a shower in the birdbath. One was sitting on the edge of the tub. I counted twenty-five sitting and eating. I don't know what is here in this yard, but there were more flying in and out. I have never seen so many in one landing. I wonder what it means.

It seems like when I do something or go somewhere, it reminds me of another memory. I suppose I could keep writing from now till the cows come home and still think of more happenings at the Usta Place and other chapters in my life. You know, I really don't know if that old saying is correct. Maybe it should be "till the cows *go* home."

(I bet after what Oprah has been through recently, she would agree it should be "go home!")

Ft. Scott has their Fall Festival the first weekend in October. I dearly love to attend this event. The exhibitors cater to old relics and some demonstrate making cornmeal, molasses, firewood and shelling corn. Oh, yes! I watched them make molasses. It looked easier than back in the twenties. Now they have a machine to render the juice, which was drained into a large bucket. This sweet "stuff" was poured into the vat and cooked for a long time. It finally was done and ready to eat. Samples were given. Naturally, I bought some. I had some on a hot biscuit this morning.

When we were all little Clarks at the Usta Place and a big job had to be done, we all took part and shared the work. I was talking to one of the older sisters recently about this. She said she could remember one of the younger sisters hiding out so she wouldn't have to carry in heating wood and kindling. I wonder why I didn't notice that. I just imagine I was too busy doing her part of all the jobs.

A few days before the festival in Ft. Scott, my grandson, Trenton, was scrambling eggs and accidentally splashed hot grease on his right hand. He ended up with first and second-degree burns and was in a lot of pain for several days. He did come to the festival with his hand all bandaged and was walking around. Some smart aleck asked him if he had been holding hands with some "ugly" girl and she broke it. Trenton is pretty sharp, so he came back with, "Yes, I think it was your daughter!" He came back to Gary's booth and told him what he said to the stranger. I never saw Gary laugh as hard as he did that day. Now you could expect me to have an answer like that, but not Trenton.

When I was setting my hair this morning, it brought back a memory I would rather forget, but I do want to share it with you. Years ago, sister #7, Margie, and I were living in an apartment together. Everyone was away from the house at the time, so I decided to do my laundry while the machine was idle. (Everyone living in the building shared the machine.) This was when I was sixteen years old.

Now this machine was just dandy, but it didn't spin the clothes dry. You had to push a lever forward and start the clothes through a wringer. If you wanted to reverse the wringer, you pulled the lever backward. I know some of you will remember those old wringer washers. Right? Well, I was busy doing my laundry and reached down to pick up an article of clothing to start through the wringer. All at once, I felt pulling pressure on the upper right side of my head. It got tighter and tighter. My first thought was to "jerk" my head back, but since I didn't want to be bald in that spot, I quickly reached for the lever and stopped that wringing. I reversed the lever and eased my hair clear.

At the time I was wearing my hair much longer than I ever have since! After all, my hair wasn't wet and it sure didn't need to go through a wringer. We had hair dryers for that. I got through that little episode all right, but I cut my long beautiful hair after that and have never worn it long again. I've heard that experience is the best teacher. They got that right!

When I first went to town to work, Papa said, "You lads keep all those doors locked and keep them shades pulled at night!" He didn't say anything about me keeping my long hair away from the washing machine wringers. How was a kid like me supposed to know those little things? After all, I hadn't been around them before. Having just moved to town, there were lots of new experiences for me.

It must have been hard for Papa to see me move to town at such a young age, but I did okay. I was used to getting about four dollars and fifty cents a week working for people in their homes. Now that I was living in town and working, I was bringing home sixteen dollars a week! I was excited about that.

CHAPTER 21

I ALWAYS THOUGHT it would be nice to be remembered for something good or special that I've done for someone in my lifetime. Now I've worked hard, please don't misunderstand, but it boggles my mind that nothing stands out that I've done. I can't think of anything I've accomplished in my lifetime that might have made a lasting memory. Perhaps a friend or an acquaintance will think of something. Put on your thinking cap and maybe, when and if you write your story, you could and would find a small space between the lines and jot down a memory of me. I'm not asking for very much space, just a line or two, so I'll know when I'm gone, I'll be remembered for something. Deal?

It has been a lot of fun writing my story for you. Someone asked if I had trouble remembering. I said, "No, it isn't like things happened just yesterday, but maybe in the last twenty-five or thirty years." The main thing that puzzles me is, where have my seventy-two years gone? I suppose when you are busy all the time, like me, making eighteen eggs into noodles, time just passes quicker. When Sherri reads this, she will say, "That's my mom." I just like to stay busy doing something. I believe it is important to keep our minds and bodies busy, getting the most out of and making the best use of every minute God has given us. I do just that.

It has always been my idea to live the very best I know how and be very thankful for everything I have. Most of all, I thank God for every breath I can take with or without help. I am so thankful for good health, good eyes and to be able to swallow, all of those blessings so many just take for granted.

By now, I bet you are wondering what became of the priceless piece of furniture we pumped in the front room of our old home place. I haven't mentioned it in my story for awhile, so I thought you might be curious about what happened to it.

You'd better get a handkerchief. After all of us Clark kids grew up and moved away from home, I suppose Mama didn't want to see it sitting there with no one sitting in the chair at the keyboard. I suppose she felt sad and missed all of us after we moved away from home, don't you know? Well, Mama loved to build things. Do you remember me telling you about the purple cupboard she made for my little dishes? Do you remember the boxes she made for our personal things? She was pretty good with a saw, hammer and nails. Well, you guessed it. She didn't take it to the sawmill, but she "decked" it herself. She took the saw, hammer and nails to it and made a beautiful storage box. Now she had a place to keep her valuables, the nice things she treasured, her scrapbooks and pictures.

When our precious Mama died, the children came and took what they wanted before the auction sale. I found a scrapbook that had a mercury dime taped on a page where she had printed, "Ed gave me this a long time ago."

Now all of these wonderful people, places, occasions and happenings I've told you about in the previous pages you've read have been a big part of my life. They have been an important part of my life, important enough for me to remember them all these years. How could I have gotten through the hard times and the good times without all of you in my fulfilled life?

Every now and then I read articles where people, men and women, die and leave so much in so many ways to loved ones, charities, churches, and yes, relatives also. I have loved ones who have left me with so much more than materials things, but I would like to do something in my lifetime for which I would be remembered. Now being the kind of lady I am, I'm not wanting this so I could brag, but just to know that when I'm gone, my name will be remembered and referred to as "someone special." It could be just some little old something that would stand out in the precious minds of my children, grandchildren, and maybe if I live long enough, my great-grandchildren. I suppose you could refer to this as my legacy.

Oh, my goodness! I've done just that. I just finished writing my story for you. Even though I've probably missed a memory or two, the Usta Place and stories of my life can now be remembered, and the generations to come can know about their ancestors. I know you will treasure this and will want to read it over and over again. I'll bet my last dollar you'll enjoy it more and more each time you read it.

Thank you, my precious children, for all you have given me through the years — love, kindness and respect.